*Arms
for the Third World*

Arms
for the Third World

SOVIET MILITARY
AID DIPLOMACY

WYNFRED JOSHUA AND STEPHEN P. GIBERT

THE JOHNS HOPKINS PRESS
BALTIMORE AND LONDON

CONTENTS

LIST OF TABLES

PREFACE

Since peaceful coexistence between the Soviet Union and the western nations has gained prominence, the USSR has sought ways to compete for influence in the Third World. Military assistance to the developing nations has emerged as a key element in Soviet-American rivalry.

Soviet foreign policy has been extensively studied, including efforts to penetrate the Third World through economic aid. Scant attention, however, has been paid to military aid as a major component of Soviet foreign policy. This study, therefore, attempts to round out further our understanding of the instruments of peaceful coexistence and Soviet policy in the Third World.

This book grew out of research we originally undertook between 1964 and 1968 for the Georgetown Research Project of the Atlantic Research Corporation under contract with the Air Force Office of Scientific Research. We are grateful to the Atlantic Research Corporation and the Air Force Office of Scientific Research for permission to use some of this material as the basis for further research and analysis.

We are indebted to our former colleagues at the Georgetown Research Project—and particularly to Hans W. Weigert, the Director—for their many helpful suggestions and generous advice. Paul E. Armstrong ably assisted us in numerous ways and his contributions to Chapter 5 were especially valuable. Colonel F. Br. Nihart gave us throughout the study the benefit of his military expertise and knowledge of Soviet weapons.

We wish to express our appreciation for the several important improvements suggested by Herbert S. Dinerstein of the School of Advanced International Studies, The Johns Hopkins University. Charles T. Stewart, Jr., Professor of Economics, George Washington University, contributed several valuable ideas for Chapter 6. We are grateful to William C. Johnstone, Professor of Asian Studies, School of Advanced

International Studies, The Johns Hopkins University, who encouraged the publication of our study.

Our thanks go to Riley Hughes, Professor of English, Georgetown University, who served as editorial critic. Cynthia Livingstone Gibert also assisted us, especially in Chapters 6, 7, and 8. It is a pleasure to acknowledge our indebtedness to John Gallman and Kenneth Arnold of The Johns Hopkins Press.

An earlier version of Chapter 6 appeared as an article in the Fall 1966 issue of *Orbis*. We wish to thank Robert C. Herber, Managing Editor of *Orbis*, for allowing us to use this material.

Wynfred Joshua assumed primary responsibility for the four regional chapters (2 through 5) and the final chapter; Stephen P. Gibert assumed primary responsibility for the first chapter and the three functional chapters (6 through 8). This book, however, is a joint endeavor in the fullest sense of the word. We both reviewed all the presentations and findings of the entire book.

We alone are responsible for the accuracy of facts and interpretations. The views expressed in this book are our own and do not reflect the opinions of the institutions with which we have been or are now affiliated, nor of those who have so generously given us their assistance and counsel.

WYNFRED JOSHUA
Stanford Research Institute, Washington

STEPHEN P. GIBERT
Georgetown University

Washington, D.C.

Arms
for the Third World

1

SOVIET MILITARY AID
IN INTERNATIONAL POLITICS

SINCE ITS revolutionary inception in 1917 the Soviet polity has pursued with extraordinary persistence, if not always consistency, the goals of maintaining its power at home and extending its power abroad. While teleological explanations of Soviet internal and external policies may overemphasize the degree to which Soviet actions have been purposeful, revision of the non-Marxist international system has been a guiding principle of Soviet leaders in conducting their foreign policy. This principle appears to have been acted upon wherever and whenever such a policy could be expected to further Marxist-Leninist metaphysical images of world politics. Abroad, pursuit of these goals occasionally took military, more often ideological, but seldom economic form. Autarky was the hallmark of Soviet policy in the Stalinist era. The granting of economic and military aid to less-developed, non-communist nations would have been regarded by Stalinists as ideologically unsound and counterrevolutionary. But since Stalin's death economic instruments for revising the international status quo have gradually achieved maturity. The Soviet Union today appears fully committed to employing the resources and technology of its economy to influence the less-developed, non-aligned nations of the Middle East, Asia, and Africa.

A prominent role in the Soviet drive into the so-called Third World seems to have been assigned to military aid diplomacy. Since 1955 the Soviet Union has poured some $6 billion in arms into twenty-five developing nations around the world. In the Middle East this massive arms flow contributed to the outbreak of the third Arab-Israeli war of June 1967. In Asia $1 billion in Soviet weapons strengthened Indonesia in its confrontation with the Netherlands and Malaysia. On the

1

subcontinent, the world was given a concrete example of Soviet-Chinese estrangement when Soviet-equipped Indian forces faced Chinese communist troops along the Himalayan frontier. Nor has Africa been neglected. In the north, Algeria possesses a fighting force almost exclusively armed with Soviet weapons, while in the Horn the irredentist ambitions of Somalia are encouraged by Soviet military aid. In Latin America, Cuba so far remains the only Soviet arms recipient, but in no area has Soviet arms diplomacy run greater risks. Russian missiles in Cuba brought the world to the brink of nuclear war in October 1962, with the dramatic confrontation between the United States and the Soviet Union.

After the defeat of the Arab armies in June 1967, the Soviet government demonstrated its continuing resolve to utilize military aid to gain influence in the Third World—even if such policies involve considerable risk of war—by moving quickly to replace Soviet weapons destroyed or captured by the Israelis. Soviet arms diplomacy can no longer be regarded as a passing phenomenon; it appears to have a central if not paramount place in Soviet ambitions to replace western with communist influence among the developing nations. It is with the analysis of this important policy instrument, from its inception in 1955, that this study is concerned. An attempt is made throughout to place Soviet military aid in the context of Soviet foreign policy. This approach first provides insights into the military program itself. Second, it serves to indicate the broad directions of Soviet policy toward the less-developed world. Finally, it points up the implications of arms diplomacy for American-Soviet competitive coexistence in the dangerous decades to come.

CHANGING SOVIET IMAGES OF INTERNATIONAL POLITICS

When the first Soviet bloc arms aid agreement was signed with a member state of the non-aligned world in 1955, it was not realized, perhaps not even by Soviet leaders themselves, that it marked the beginning of a new era in Soviet diplomacy. In the perspective gained since that decision, it is clear that the Soviet government renounced the rigidities which had characterized previous relationships with the so-called neutralist countries. Soviet leaders belatedly accepted the possibility that the world contained not only communists and "western imperialists" but also millions of persons uncommitted to either side in the cold war. Reality had finally succeeded in modifying ideological precepts out of harmony with a new international scene characterized by the presence of dozens of newly emerging nations. Soviet recognition of the existence of the Third World had profound implications for international relations in general and for the role of the Soviet Union in world politics in particular.

Under Stalin's regime Soviet attitudes toward the less-developed countries reflected either a cautious indifference, or a lack of understanding of the situation in which nationalist and communist movements found themselves in the period immediately following World War II. Preoccupied with the communization of Eastern Europe, the problem of Germany, and Russian relations in the Turkish-Iranian area, Soviet leaders paid only cursory attention to most of the developing world. Consistent with the so-called Zhdanov doctrine, revolutionary leaders in the still-dependent areas, such as Nehru of India, Sukarno of Indonesia, and U Nu of Burma, were dismissed as imperialist lackeys.

Even before Stalin's death, however, there were indications that some of his associates had begun to recognize that viewing the world as divided into imperialist and communist camps was a serious distortion of reality, which unnecessarily limited opportunities to exploit weaknesses in the capitalist-colonialist alliance. Stalin himself in his last theoretical writing, *Economic Problems of Socialism,* returned to the Leninist position, which emphasized the contradictions within the capitalist world. According to Stalin, the liquidation of capitalist empires had increased the likelihood that the next year would be a struggle among the imperialists for a larger share of the diminishing regions available for colonialist exploitation. Conflict between the imperialist and the socialist camps was viewed as less likely. This thesis was also expounded by Malenkov at the Nineteenth Communist Party Congress in Moscow in 1952, when he urged a stronger role for non-communist nationalist leaders in the less-developed world and stressed the contributions which their opposition to the western powers made to the overall position of the Soviet Union. Malenkov cited the situations in Vietnam, Burma, Malaya, the Philippines, Indonesia, and India in Asia, and in Egypt and Iran in the Middle East.

Hints of a return to the pre-1928 rightest approach did not result in new policies until Khrushchev emerged as the dominant figure in the Soviet collective leadership. The Soviet government began to emphasize peaceful coexistence and the idea that through economic, social, and ideological competition with the western world, the Soviet Union would emerge as the supreme world power. The Nasser regime in Egypt, with its anti-western posture, fitted well into this new strategy. The first Soviet bloc military aid agreement with a developing country, announced in September 1955 between Czechoslovakia and Egypt, was a manifestation of the post-Stalin flexibility in Soviet foreign policy. In December 1955, Khrushchev, accompanied by Bulganin, toured Asia where he praised the leaders of the neutralist countries and pledged Soviet support for their aspirations. This support took concrete form in Afghanistan with an offer of Soviet military assistance. When this pledge was redeemed in 1956, Afghanistan became the second recipient of Soviet bloc arms aid. Other military aid agreements quickly followed. In 1956 Syria and Yemen were added; in 1957–58 Indonesia and Iraq received Soviet bloc military aid; Guinea, Mali, and Ghana became the first aid recipients in black Africa. In 1960, after Castro's relations with the United States began to deteriorate, Cuba became the first Latin American state to receive Soviet military aid. These actions presented a serious challenge to American preeminence in military aid diplomacy. Despite some setbacks, notably the 1965 coup in Indonesia, military assistance continues to be a major instrument of Soviet foreign policy in the competition for influence in the less-developed world.

The importance the Soviet government attaches to its military aid diplomacy undoubtedly reflects an adjustment to the exigencies of the nuclear age. As the realization that nuclear conflict was unacceptable impressed itself on Soviet leaders, they were faced with the problem of competing with the western powers in ways that limited the risk of general war. Providing military assistance to the developing countries became one of the new policy instruments designed to enhance the influence, prestige, and power of the Soviet Union. It also appeared to provide a means by which the USSR could break out of the western "containment" arrangements developed since 1949, and especially after 1953. At the same time, the Soviet leadership recognized—particularly after the Cuban missile crisis in 1962—that military aid carried serious risks of escalating a crisis into general and strategic war. Military assistance, more than such instruments as "peace offensives" and economic aid, is fraught with danger. Only if the Soviet Union should come to believe that military aid might bring on the nuclear conflict it wishes to avoid is it likely that Soviet military assistance will cease to be an important foreign policy instrument. Accordingly, the USSR has had to weigh carefully its military aid decisions. Nevertheless, to date, the anticipated gains from military aid diplomacy appear to warrant limited risks. It is on this assumption that this study has been undertaken.

APPROACHES AND SCOPE OF THIS BOOK

The Soviet military assistance program can only be understood as an integral part of contemporary Soviet global foreign policy. While not neglecting its paramount interest in maintaining preeminence in Eastern Europe, the Soviet Union since the death of Stalin has accorded a much higher priority to extending its influence into the less-developed regions of the world. This objective is pursued by a variety of instruments, a key one of which is the furnishing of military aid to selected countries in the Middle East, Asia, Africa, and Latin America. Dependent upon individual circumstances, aid includes weapons, spare parts, military training, and the construction of military and para-military operational facilities. The program appears designed to promote the image of the Soviet Union as the champion of anti-colonialism and to support those objectives of aid-recipient nations consistent with Soviet foreign policies. Further, Soviet leaders hope to forge or strengthen links between the armed forces of the recipients and the Soviet Union, and to foster diplomatic and military dependency on the USSR. Soviet decision-makers apparently anticipate that accomplishing these aims will strengthen the international position of the Soviet Union at the expense of the United States. It also will prevent Communist China from establishing itself as the champion of and model for the developing countries.

Soviet military aid policy appears to operate within the parameters of two constraints: the necessity not to take actions in furnishing military aid that will bring on nuclear confrontation with the United States; and the requirement that aid programs be consistent with the level of development of the recipients, as well as with the conditions imposed by the nations themselves. Throughout the book an attempt has been made to assess the impact of these constraints on Soviet military aid decisions. For this reason, although the study focuses on Soviet military aid diplomacy, the conditions in the recipient countries and their objectives in requesting military assistance have been discussed where relevant. This approach permits an emphasis upon the international security implications of Soviet arms diplomacy and avoids a mere accounting sheet of weapons transfers. Stated differently, this study analyzes the impact of Soviet military aid to the developing countries on the international diplomatic scene in general, and on the great powers' struggle for influence in the Third World in particular.

The study starts with an analysis of Soviet military aid to the major regions of the developing world. The regional approach has been selected because the impact of Soviet arms deliveries is seldom limited to the particular recipient country. More often, it affects as well the politico-military strategy of the major world powers and lesser states adjacent to or near the recipient. Within each world region the key nations receiving aid, such as Egypt in the Middle East, India and Indonesia in Asia, Somalia in Africa, and Cuba in Latin America, have received special attention.

Subsequently, certain functional topics important to an understanding of Soviet military aid diplomacy are considered. These include the alternatives open to the Soviet Union in pursuing military aid policies, arms aid used to support wars of liberation, and the competitive aspects of Soviet and American military aid programs.

This analysis is concerned only with Soviet military aid diplomacy in the so-called non-aligned or Third World countries of the Middle East, Asia, Africa, and Latin America. No consideration, accordingly, has been given Soviet aid to East European countries or to other communist countries such as China, North Korea, Mongolia, and North Vietnam. This restriction was necessary because the objective of the book is to assess Soviet arms diplomacy as an instrument of competition for influence among non-European and non-committed nations rather than to consider relationships among communist countries themselves. Also, it is difficult if not impossible to secure reliable estimates of weapons flows among the communist countries. This limitation, however, has been modified to allow the inclusion of Cuba, since its position in international affairs is quite distinct from that of other communist states and because reliable data on Soviet military aid to Cuba is available.

Throughout the study value estimates of Soviet military aid have been given in U.S. dollars. The choice of dollar estimates was arrived at since dollar figures are usually cited in the press. Although the terms of an agreement frequently specify that Soviet arms aid has to be repaid in raw materials or commodities, the use of dollar values permits a ready comparison of the magnitudes of the various arms aid programs.

While Soviet arms diplomacy is referred to throughout the study as "military aid" or "military assistance," in fact the more technically accurate term in most cases would be "military loans." While much American aid has been in grants, almost all Soviet military aid has been in the form of long-term, low-interest loans. Since this is a marked difference between the Soviet and American programs, the technical distinction between loans and grants has been discussed separately, as have the relationships among military aid, trade, and economic aid.

The terms "Soviet aid" and "Soviet bloc aid" are used interchangeably except where noted otherwise. Nearly all Soviet bloc aid has in fact been aid from the USSR itself. Only Czechoslovakia among the Soviet bloc countries has contributed a measurable amount of military aid. "Soviet bloc" refers to the USSR and the members of the Warsaw Pact. The use of the term "Soviet bloc" is merely a shorthand expression and does not imply monolithic unity among the Warsaw Pact countries. Military aid by Communist China is not included in computing Soviet bloc aid totals.

The history of Soviet military aid is now sufficiently developed to permit an assessment of the program's current usefulness to the Soviet Union and its utility in the foreseeable future. Since present indications are that military aid diplomacy will assume an even greater role in Soviet foreign policy in years to come, an understanding of its impact on the security of nations has become of vital importance.

2

THE MIDDLE EAST

M ORE THAN two and one-half centuries ago Peter the Great dreamed of extending his empire's influence into the Middle East. His successors tried from time to time to realize that vision. During much of the nineteenth century the Russians competed with the major European powers in the Middle East, but by the turn of the century Britain had emerged as the most powerful external influence in the region and retained that position until the end of World War II.

The postwar period witnessed renewed Soviet efforts to penetrate the Middle East. The Soviet rival became primarily the United States, while the impact of the British and French presence gradually grew weaker. In the contest between the Soviet Union and the United States, military assistance and economic aid became increasingly important elements in the Middle East. Between 1955 and 1968 the Soviet Union channeled about $3 billion in arms aid to the Middle East, or almost fifty percent of its total military assistance to the developing world.[1] In Soviet economic aid to the developing regions, the Middle East ranked second. The volatile region bordering the southern and eastern Mediterranean and stretching from Turkey and Iran to Aden remained an area of vital interest to the Soviet Union.[2]

THE MIDDLE EAST IN SOVIET FOREIGN POLICY

Soviet interests and objectives in the Middle East have been conditioned by some basic geopolitical factors, which have influenced Russian policy since the days of the Tsars. The contiguous Middle East countries have served both as a buffer protecting Russia's southern borders

[1] See Table 8-1.
[2] For the purpose of this study the Middle East includes Morocco, Algeria, Tunisia, Libya, Egypt, Cyprus, Turkey, Syria, Iraq, Lebanon, Israel, Jordan, Iran, and the Arabian peninsula.

7

and, for its adversaries, as a barrier preventing Russia's expansion southwards. The Turkish straits limited the accessibility of Black Sea ports. Penetration of the Middle East and access to warm water ports on an open sea have traditionally been Russian objectives.

The advent of U.S. power in the Middle East and Mediterranean during and after World War II constituted a challenge to these age-old Russian ambitions. The erosion and ultimate withdrawal of U.S. power therefore became Soviet aims. The achievement of these goals would establish the Soviet Union as the most powerful nation in the region.

Soviet interests derived further from the region's importance to the western powers. The Middle East includes part of and guards the rest of NATO's southern flank. It lies across the shortest route between Europe and the Far East. The region provides almost eighty percent of Western Europe's oil and contains more than three-fifths of the proven oil reserves in the world. Soviet access to forward bases in the Middle East, or the permission to use such bases, would enable the USSR to threaten western interests in and near the area. The establishment of Soviet naval and air base rights in the Mediterranean and Red Sea littoral would be a first step toward inhibiting the use of the Mediterranean and toward disrupting military and oil transit between Europe and the Persian Gulf or the Far East. Landing and refueling rights in North African states would facilitate Soviet access to Africa.

On the other hand, a number of developments have reduced the significance of the Middle East for the United States and to a lesser extent for Western Europe. The development of long-range and sea-based missiles eliminated the U.S. need for land bases at the Soviet periphery in the Middle East. The use of giant tankers has reduced the cost of taking the longer route around the Cape from Europe to the Far East and has thereby limited the value of the Suez Canal. The discovery of oil fields outside the Middle East has made the west less dependent on Middle Eastern oil. The gradual erosion of the strategic, transit, and economic value of the Middle East to the western powers could conceivably lead to a decline of Soviet concern with the area. The proximity of the region to Russian borders, however, remains a paramount factor in Soviet geopolitics. Domination of the region by an adversary of Moscow is a threat which Soviet leaders can ill entertain and one to which they are bound to respond.

Soviet Arms Aid Relations with the Arab Nations

In 1955 Egypt became the first country with which the Soviet Union established a military aid relationship. Through the years Cairo has remained a major target of Moscow's arms aid efforts. Of all military aid recipients Egypt received the largest dollar value of Soviet and Eastern European equipment, estimated at the outbreak of the Arab-Israeli war in June 1967 at approximately $1.5 billion.[3]

The same factors that prompted the first Soviet venture in arms aid diplomacy set the pattern for subsequent military aid agreements with Egypt and other Arab states. The impairment of the western, and particularly U.S., presence in the Middle East, and the breakup of any alignment of countries that was or could be pro-west—such as the Baghdad Pact of 1955, the CENTO Pact of 1959, or the more loosely grouped Islamic alliance of 1966—remained the major objectives of Soviet arms aid policies. Appeal to Arab nationalism and exploitation of Arab-Israeli hostility emerged as Soviet techniques that helped to drive the Arabs toward the Soviet bloc in their search for weapons.

The First Arms Aid Recipients: 1955–59. After Stalin's death in 1953, it became increasingly evident that the Russians were in the process of reassessing some of the principal tenets of communist doctrine. The evolving new theory of peaceful coexistence—officially confirmed at the Twentieth Communist Party Congress in 1956—modified the rigid division of the world into a capitalist and a socialist camp by introducing the existence of a third group of uncommitted nations, led by the "nationalist bourgeoisie." Recognizing the nationalist and neutralist aspirations of the leaders of the emerging nations, the Soviet Union would henceforth attempt to cooperate with them in order to facilitate their eventual entry into the communist camp.

The revolutionary slogans against imperialism and colonialism of the Egyptian government of Gamal Abdul Nasser fitted into this new Soviet concept of the nationalist bourgeoisie. Equally important, Egyptian and Soviet leaders shared the basic objective of eliminating western influence in the Middle East.

One of Nasser's principal aims was the unification of the Arab nations under Egyptian leadership, with all the personal and national prestige attached to such leadership. Believing that the tide of popular feeling in Egypt, and in the Middle East in general, favored a show of independence from western influence, Nasser was opposed to any alliance between Arab and western nations. At the Afro-Asian Conference in April 1955, Nasser became a self-appointed spokesman of the neutralist world.

During the same period, 1954–55, the United States was engaged in building a system of mutual security pacts in the Middle East and Far East in an effort to contain Soviet expansionism. Members of these mutual security pacts could expect U.S. arms assistance to help build

[3] Walter Laquer, "The Hand of Russia," *Reporter,* June 29, 1967, p. 18.

their military establishments. The efforts to forge a defense alliance among the northern tier countries along the Soviet southern border met with a major success in January 1955, when Nuri al-Said of Iraq signed the Iraqi-Turkish treaty, the forerunner of the Baghdad Pact. This treaty undermined Nasser's policy of non-alignment and challenged his claim to supremacy in the Arab world. That Nuri al-Said was Nasser's main rival for leadership of the Arab nations accentuated Nasser's need to offset the impact of Iraq's move.

From a Russian standpoint, these events intensified the need for a strong response to counter the emergence of an anti-Soviet bloc in the Middle East. In an effort to dissuade other Arab states from joining the western-sponsored alliance, Moscow began to demonstrate its support for Arab nationalism by establishing close ties with Cairo. To win the confidence of Arab leaders, the USSR started to support their side in the Arab-Israeli dispute, even though it had been one of the first to endorse the establishment of the state of Israel in 1948. The Gaza clash between Egyptian and Israeli troops in February 1955 provided Soviet policy-makers with the chance to strengthen their relations with Nasser. The Arab-Israeli problem, the most persistent source of conflict in the Middle East since the founding of Israel in 1948, would offer Moscow in later years frequent opportunities for cementing Soviet-Arab ties.

Hostility to the Jewish state was the single important issue upon which the otherwise feuding Arab countries could unite. No Arab ruler who aspired to a position of lasting power at home and in the Arab world could afford to compromise on his opposition to Israel. When the Egyptian army suffered its crushing defeat at Gaza, Nasser came under mounting pressures from his officers to acquire weapons that would match Israeli equipment. His dependence on the support of the officer corps thus became an additional motivation for an intensified search for arms. Britain offered only token support; France refused support until Egypt stopped assisting the Algerian nationalists. The United States made substantial military aid conditional upon Egypt's agreement to join a mutual security pact, or was only prepared to deliver a limited supply for cash in dollars. Nasser, feeling that he could not accept any of these conditions without sacrificing part of his domestic following, turned to the Soviet Union.

In September 1955 the arms aid agreement with the Soviet bloc was announced. This first accord was signed by Czechoslovakia rather than by the USSR; it covered some $250 million in arms aid credits to Egypt.[4] Although the terms of this particular agreement were not pub-

---

[4] U.S. Congress, Subcommittee on Foreign Economic Policy of the Joint Economic Committee, *New Directions in the Soviet Economy*, 89th Cong., 2d sess. (Washington, 1966), p. 965.

licized, they were probably similar to those of most subsequent Soviet bloc weapons deals. The Soviet Union generally offered its military aid for repayments in commodities or local currency over a period of ten or twelve years at two to two-and-a-half percent interest. Communist-made weaponry which reached Egypt as a result of the September 1955 negotiations included MiG–15 fighters, Il–28 bombers, two destroyers, tanks, heavy artillery, and light infantry weapons.[5] Egyptian personnel went to Eastern Europe to learn how to handle the new equipment, while a group of Soviet and Czech military advisers and technicians arrived in Egypt to provide instruction. The Russians hoped that Soviet-Egyptian military cooperation would meet with widespread approval throughout the Arab world and tend to keep other Arab nations from joining the Baghdad Pact. Military assistance would thus help to reduce and eventually to exclude western influence, increase Soviet prestige and influence, and give Moscow a foothold adjacent to the vital Mediterranean waterways.

Once Egypt had assumed the role of the bellwether country in Soviet Middle East policies, the Russians provided massive military aid to Egypt as the leader of the Arab world. Moscow consistently portrayed Washington and its allies as the enemies of Arab nationalism. Exploiting the existing Arab hatred of Israel, the Soviet Union after 1955 pictured Israel as the instrument by which western imperialism sought to divide the Arab world and against which the Arabs should defend themselves.

The arms deal between Egypt and the Soviet bloc was greeted with vociferous approval by militant Arab nationalists throughout the Middle East, particularly in Damascus. For long the focus of extreme Arab nationalism, Syria became more bitterly anti-west following its defeat in the 1948 Arab-Israeli war. Like other militant Arabs, Syrian leaders deeply resented the creation of Israel, which they regarded as a tool of western imperialism. The formation of the Baghdad Pact in 1955 intensified their desire to express their independence of western influence. Relatively weak, Syria was also the target of the more powerful Arab countries, Egypt and Iraq, which had traditionally competed for influence over Syria as a means of enhancing their own positions. In early 1955 pro-western Iraq and Turkey tried to force Syria into joining the Baghdad Pact, while Egypt applied counter pressures. Lacking the power to resist these moves, Syria approached the Soviet Union. In early 1956 Syria accepted military aid from the Soviet bloc and became

[5] *Al-Akhbar*, June 12, 1956; *New York Times*, March 25, 1956; *ibid.*, June 21, 1956.

thereby the first country to emulate Egypt's example. Shortly afterwards, shipments of T–34 tanks, artillery, anti-aircraft guns, and small arms started to arrive in Syria.[6]

The Soviet Union's well-timed diplomatic backing, implemented with military assistance, bolstered Syria's opposition to the western powers and Israel and enabled Syria to resist pressures from its neighbors. The arms accord prevented the further expansion of the Baghdad Pact within the Arab world. The Russians were also able to exploit the propaganda line that without their aid the Syrians would have been forced into an alliance with the western imperialists. The willingness of the Soviet bloc to accept a barter arrangement made the arms aid particularly attractive to Damascus, which throughout the fifties had experienced increasing difficulties in selling its surplus grains and cotton on western markets.

The sharp disapproval of the Egyptian arms deal in London and other western capitals was not lost on Yemen's royalist government. Yemen's major foreign policy objective was to regain Aden and the Protectorate of South Arabia from Britain, and its traditional policy was to develop close ties with any rival of Britain. In early 1956, shortly after the dramatic Egyptian arms deal with the Soviet bloc, Yemen applied to the same communist donor for military assistance. Although the Soviet Union displayed a certain ambiguity in its attitude toward Yemen's virulently anti-colonial but nevertheless feudal regime, it decided to support the Imamate as a means of impairing the British position in the Arabian peninsula. Between 1956 and the overthrow of the Imam in 1962, Yemen received some $30 million in Soviet bloc aid, which included Il–10 bombers, Czech and Russian T–34 tanks, anti-aircraft guns, personnel carriers, and a variety of infantry weapons and equipment.[7] As in Egypt and Syria, Czech and Russian military advisers were stationed in Yemen to instruct troops in the use of the new arms.

Egypt, Syria, and Yemen signed their initial arms aid agreements with Czechoslovakia, which acted as intermediary for the Soviet Union. Moscow's use of Prague as a cover for its early military aid accords was substantiated by the stationing of Soviet as well as Czech military experts in the recipient countries and by the shipments of both Russian and Czech weapons to them. The Suez crisis of November 1956 brought the Soviet Union directly into the Middle East as an arms provider. In the political arena the Russians espoused the Arab position against Israel

[6] *Al-Ahram,* February 19, 1956; *New York Times,* March 19, 1956; *ibid.,* December 16, 1956.

[7] *New York Times,* August 9, 1957; *ibid.,* August 10, 1957; *Wall Street Journal,* May 8, 1958. Between 1956 and 1962 Yemen apparently signed only one arms aid accord with the Soviet bloc; this was the 1956 agreement with Czechoslovakia.

and the western allies. As tangible evidence of Soviet support, Moscow extended new arms credits to Cairo to replace the weapons destroyed by the French, British, and Israeli forces in the Suez fighting. Similarly, credits were granted to build up Syria's military capability. As a result of the new Russian arms credits, Egypt in the first half of 1957 obtained submarines, MiG–17 jets, tanks, and other unspecified equipment.[8] Materiel Syria received included MiG–15 and MiG–17 fighters, motor torpedo boats, armored troop carriers, and artillery.[9]

Despite the Egyptian military defeat, the Suez war provided the Soviet Union with one of its most illustrious cold war victories. This episode, together with other instances of western military alliance diplomacy—notably the Eisenhower doctrine and the U.S. intervention in Lebanon—contributed to proving to the Arab world that all of the major western powers were equally guilty of neo-colonialism and beholden to Israeli interests. As a result, Moscow's position as the principal source of arms for Cairo and other militant Arab capitals was firmly established.

This fact was illustrated in Iraq, where the pro-western monarchy was overthrown in July 1958 and replaced by the militant government of General Abdul Karim Kassem, who denounced the Baghdad Pact and in November negotiated an arms aid agreement in Moscow. Within a month tanks and light and heavy arms arrived at Basra, shortly followed by MiG–17 fighters, anti-aircraft guns, howitzers, rockets, and other unspecified artillery. Some two hundred Soviet instructors began to train indigenous air force personnel in Iraq.[10]

The Soviet Union's political and military support of Iraq, however, soon created strains in its relationship with Egypt. Although General Kassem shared Nasser's anti-monarchist bias and revolutionary outlook, he did not seek a rapprochement with Nasser, but resumed his predecessor's traditional rivalry with the Egyptian leader for hegemony in the Arab world. Aware of Soviet efforts to court Kassem, Nasser became concerned that the Russians were trying to groom Kassem as an alternative to him as the leader of the Arab world, and his relations with the Russians deteriorated. Soviet-Egyptian tensions were further aggravated by Nasser's suppression of local communists in Egypt. Another contentious point in Soviet-Egyptian relations was Moscow's practice of

[8] *Al-Ahram*, June 18, 1957; *New York Times,* July 24, 1957. By September 1957 an Egyptian spokesman could claim that the strength of the Egyptian air force had doubled since the Suez war (*Middle East Journal* [Autumn 1957], p. 418).

[9] *New York Times*, January 16, 1957; *ibid.,* February 3, 1957; *ibid.,* February 8, 1957; *ibid.,* August 27, 1957.

[10] *New York Times,* December 4, 1958; *Christian Science Monitor,* August 1, 1959.

selling abroad the Egyptian cotton which it received in payment for aid. This practice helped to lower the world price for cotton and excluded some Egyptian cotton from its customary markets. In May 1959 Cairo showed its dissatisfaction with Soviet policies by limiting cotton exports to the Soviet Union. Moscow apparently retaliated with a delay in weapons deliveries. Partly because Nasser promptly indicated a renewed interest in better relations with the west and accepted American economic aid, Soviet leaders attempted to settle the differences between Moscow and Cairo. In November 1959 Premier Khrushchev announced that the Soviet Union was prepared to continue its aid to Egypt.[11] Shortly afterwards Cairo received nine more Soviet-built submarines.[12]

The Entrenchment of the Soviet Union as Supplier of Arms Aid. After 1959–60 Soviet military commitments to Egypt were made with marked consistency. On a smaller scale and with some variations the Soviet-Egyptian pattern continued for other Middle East recipients. Russian relations with the recipients were not always cordial, nor were American relations with the same recipients always distant, but on the whole, Egypt and the other recipients continued to move closer to the Soviet Union. While there were at times interruptions in Soviet arms aid programs—owing to a change in government in the recipient country, or simply the expiration of a program before a new agreement was concluded—in the main Soviet military assistance in the Middle East became more and more entrenched. Weapons requirements of the Arabs increased rather than waned. The continuing Arab-Israeli dispute was the principal reason for the maintenance of a high armament level in Egypt, Syria, and Iraq. The protracted civil war in Yemen, where a republican regime ousted the Imam in 1962, increased the arms requirements in that state.

New states were added to the roster of Soviet arms recipients in the Middle East. After a limited experience of supplying arms to Morocco during 1960–62, the Soviet Union began to concentrate on building Algeria's military capability. The Cyprus crisis of 1964 presented Moscow with the opportunity to establish military assistance ties with the Makarios government. January 1967 witnessed the successful completion of Soviet-Iranian arms aid negotiations.

Among the new arms beneficiaries of the period after 1960, Algeria proved to be the most important addition for the Soviet Union. The substantial arms aid which Russian decision-makers poured into Algeria after 1963 reflected not only Soviet appreciation of Ben Bella's potential

[11] *Middle East Journal* (Winter 1960), p. 85.
[12] *Ibid.* (Spring 1960), p. 198.

to become another Nasser, but also Soviet efforts to counteract Chinese communist influence in that country.

Largely through the use of third countries, Soviet leaders had already provided a limited supply of weapons to Algerian nationalists in late 1960, during the French-Algerian war. In formulating its policy toward the Algerian insurgents Moscow had labored under conflicting pressures. Communist China was bitterly attacking the Soviet Union for failing to support the Algerian national liberation movement. Soviet aid to the Algerian rebels, however, threatened to jeopardize French-Russian relations. Certain features of General de Gaulle's foreign policy, such as his efforts to balance German power on the continent and to reassert France's independence from the United States, were clearly useful to the Soviet Union. In its support of the rebels, therefore, Moscow had tried to avoid a serious rupture in its relations with Paris. Accordingly, Soviet military assistance to the Algerian insurgents had not started until the end of 1960, in virtually the last stages of the French-Algerian war.

After Algeria gained independence in July 1962 and until the Algerian-Moroccan border fighting broke out in October 1963, Russian military aid remained largely limited to the supply of some MiG–15 jets and training. Soviet willingness to reassess its policy toward Algeria grew, however, as Ben Bella's criticism of the western powers and his opposition to moderate African governments intensified. Algeria, moreover, became increasingly an object of Sino-Soviet rivalry for influence in the developing world. The major Soviet arms aid commitments to Algeria were made in October 1963 and May 1965, during periods of intense competition in which the Russians and the Chinese tried to outbid each other in providing aid to Algeria. The May 1965 accord, in particular, occurred at a time when the Soviet Union sought to persuade the Algerians to sponsor its attendance at the forthcoming Afro-Asian conference in Algiers.

Colonel Houari Boumedienne's ouster of Ben Bella, a few weeks after the Russians had signed the May 1965 arms aid deal, was greeted initially with silence in Moscow. Partly to divert domestic attention from the array of socio-economic problems at home, partly to enhance Algeria's revolutionary image abroad, and partly to satisfy his own aspirations, Ben Bella had tried to capture the leadership of the Afro-Asian world. He had, therefore, adopted an extremely militant and pro-communist position on international issues and had attempted to subvert those governments which he considered colonial or neo-colonial—that is, pro-west. The Russians lost in Ben Bella a collaborator who had been paving the way for the spread of Soviet influence in Africa. Nevertheless, Algeria's position at the western entrance to the Mediterranean, its oil wealth, and its potential for threatening its western-supported neighbors made it important for Moscow to retain close ties with the new Algerian regime. Once Boumedienne and his associates made clear that in spite of anti-communist measures at home they would maintain their anti-western and militant stance in foreign affairs, the Russians resumed their courtship of the Algerians, and in December 1965 they officially reassured the Algerians that military aid would continue.[13]

From Moscow's point of view, moreover, closer relations with the Algerian leaders and their revolutionary counterparts elsewhere in the Middle East began to assume growing importance at the end of 1965. The split between the moderate and militant Arab states had emerged again. Under the guise of an Islamic Alliance, Saudi Arabia was trying to rally the moderate Middle Eastern states against Egypt and other militant Arab states.[14] Concerned that a pro-western coalition might reappear in the Middle East, the Soviet Union bitterly denounced the Islamic Alliance as a "new imperialist plot"[15] and encouraged the militant Arabs to step up their opposition to Saudi Arabia's scheme. Iraq was granted substantial Soviet arms aid credits in April 1966. Syria, where in February 1966 the extreme left wing of the Baath Party seized power, also received new military and economic aid commitments from the Soviet Union. Egypt and Algeria were permitted to draw extensively on past arms credits.

Like the Arab-Israeli controversy, the endemic rivalry within the Arab world thus became a major issue which stimulated the flow of Soviet arms into the Middle East. The heavy military buildup continued until the Middle East war of June 1967. The eruption of the Arab-Israeli crisis served at the same time to galvanize the factious Arabs into a show of unity.

[13] *New York Times*, December 15, 1965.

[14] King Faisal of Saudi Arabia, like other traditionalist Arab leaders, was concerned that Arab radicalism would spill over into his country. His concern was intensified by Egypt's refusal to withdraw from the Yemeni civil war in which Nasser backed the republican forces and Faisal the royalist troops. In January 1966 the King called for an all Islamic summit meeting. His call was addressed to Arab and non-Arab Moslem states and the stated aim was cooperation among Islamic countries. In fact, however, the objective was a coalition against Nasser and revolutionary Arabs. Syria countered Faisal's efforts by calling for a meeting of the revolutionary Arab states of Egypt, Iraq, Algeria, and Syria.

[15] *New York Times*, April 24, 1966. For a more detailed discussion of Soviet policy toward the Islamic Alliance, see Benjamin Shwadran, "The Soviet Union in the Middle East," *Current History,* vol. 52, no. 306 (February 1967), pp. 76ff.

PATTERNS AND MAGNITUDE OF SOVIET ARMS AID

Between the start of Soviet arms aid in 1955 and the present, sufficient time has elapsed to permit drawing a distinction between the more enduring and the more ephemeral factors and patterns in Soviet arms aid diplomacy. In providing military assistance, Moscow plainly attaches importance to some factors and is willing to overlook others. Most arms aid candidates have to meet certain qualifications, although since 1964–65 the Soviet Union has apparently been prepared to dilute some of the requirements for becoming an aid recipient.

As a rule, the USSR displays little concern for the domestic political orientation of the recipient states. Egypt, like most other Arab recipients, continues to enjoy Soviet military assistance in spite of its measures outlawing or restricting internal communist activities. In only one instance in the history of Soviet arms diplomacy in the Middle East did the Soviet Union halt its aid program to register its protest against the recipient's anti-communist policy at home. This case involved the Baath regime of Iraq, which had ousted General Kassem in February 1963. The Baath leaders, members of a militant Arab nationalist and strongly anti-communist movement, embarked on a violent purge of indigenous communists. Moscow's intense disapproval of Baghdad's domestic course was expressed in a warning that Iraq's persecution of local communists prejudiced the future of Soviet economic and other aid.[16] Exacerbating Soviet-Iraqi tensions was Iraq's armed offensive against the Kurds, who had started a guerrilla war to win autonomy. The Soviet Union, which sympathized with the Kurds' demands for autonomy, threatened to terminate its aid to Iraq if Baghdad continued its military operations against them.[17] When the Baath leaders refused to stop their actions against Iraqi communists and Kurdish insurgents, the Soviet Union in the summer of 1963 halted its military supplies and training programs for Iraq.[18] A thaw in Soviet-Iraqi relations did not occur until the most extreme Baathist ministers were dismissed in November 1963 and a new government began to relax the repressive measures against domestic communists. In May 1964 Iraq obtained new military aid credits.[19] Although the offensive against the Kurds was resumed with full force a year later, Soviet arms supplies continued to reach Iraq without interruption.

[16] *Pravda*, February 20, 1963.
[17] *Ibid.*, June 20, 1963.
[18] U.S. Department of State, *World Strength of the Communist Party Organizations*, 18th Annual Report (Washington, 1966), p. 101.
[19] *Daily Telegraph* (London), May 24, 1964.

Except for Iraq, the Soviet Union did not use its arms aid instrument to try to effect a change in the recipient's policies toward domestic communism, nor did Russian arms aid imply approval or disapproval of these policies. Military aid transactions reflect Soviet recognition of the value of tolerating the personal attitudes and preferences of leaders who have a national, if not also a regional, following. This explains Soviet forbearance of Nasser's frequently arrogant and scornful attitude toward Soviet ideology and at times even toward the leadership. Similarly, the Russians lionized Ben Bella, notwithstanding his repression of the Algerian Communist Party.

Moreover Nasser and later Ben Bella, because of their anti-western bias and their relentless commitment to wars of liberation, promoted Soviet interests by transferring some of their Russian-made weapons to other militant regimes and to insurgent movements in white-dominated and so-called neo-colonial African states. While Moscow may not have originally intended to supply arms for re-export purposes, the Russian arms carried by the Egyptian army into Yemen served to effectuate Soviet hostility toward Saudi Arabia. The Soviet weapons Egypt and Algeria shipped to the Congolese rebels who fought the Tshombe government in 1964–65, helped to enhance Soviet prestige in militant Afro-Arab circles. This tactic of supporting wars of liberation by proxy partly offset Chinese charges that the Soviet Union had betrayed the wars-of-liberation commitment. The re-export device also helped to protect the Russians against risks of escalating a local conflict into a confrontation with the western powers.

Another key factor in the framing of Soviet military aid policy was the importance of the military elites in the Middle East. Soviet military aid strategy could succeed only with the support of the military, which plays a crucial role in the political life of Middle Eastern countries. On the military devolved a large institutional responsibility for sustaining national efforts toward modernization. In several Middle Eastern countries, notably Egypt, Iraq, Syria, Jordan, Yemen, Algeria, and Turkey, the military establishment provides either the national leaders or the most vital organizational support of the government. In the long run, this ascendancy of the military may appear in Soviet eyes as a negative force in the building of socialism. But in establishing a foothold in the Middle East, the Soviet Union has not hesitated to exploit the military elites' ready perception of the advantage of arms aid, both for the nation and for their own political role.

The Aggressive Pattern. During the first five or six years of Soviet arms diplomacy in the Middle East, there emerged certain basic criteria that had to be met before a country could qualify for Russian arms aid.

The recipient was expected to uphold an anti-western variant of neutralism and to pursue an aggressive policy toward its regional opponents, especially toward a pro-western opponent. Egypt, Syria, Yemen, and Kassem's Iraq had these credentials to a high degree. Even Morocco, at the time it joined the group of Soviet arms aid recipients in 1960, showed some promise of meeting these requirements.[20] It was no accident that King Hassan was dropped from the list of aid recipients in 1962 when his preference for the west was clearly re-established, while his principal opponent President Ahmed Ben Bella of Algeria increasingly displayed desirable attributes.

This aggressive pattern in Soviet military aid diplomacy was essentially an outgrowth of bipolar rivalry in the early years of the cold war. The United States had been the first to use military and economic aid as instruments. In the Middle East the Truman doctrine, the SAC and other U.S. air bases in Morocco, Libya, and Saudi Arabia, the Baghdad and CENTO Pacts, and the attendant military aid programs were developed in reaction to the overall Soviet challenge. A major U.S. objective in the Middle East was to protect western interests against the Soviet Union; and while this was not synonymous with the maintenance of peace and order, it automatically brought the United States into the Middle East as the guardian of stability. The response of the Soviet Union was to exploit intra-regional rivalries. Massive Russian arms supplies fanned the local arms races between Arab and Israeli, between revolutionary and moderate Arab, and between Algeria and Morocco, thereby undermining American efforts. In framing their policies, however, Soviet decision-makers observed one basic restraint: they tried to avoid the risk of a direct armed confrontation with the United States. During the 1956 Suez crisis, for example, Moscow raised the spectre of nuclear retaliation against London and Paris only after Washington had made clear that it did not support the French-British-Israeli action. Similarly, the Soviet Union did not invoke the threat of sending volunteers to the Middle East until the cease-fire had been accepted and Khrushchev and his advisers knew that they did not have to act upon their threat. The goals of Soviet arms aid diplomacy were to sustain a

---

[20] Morocco accepted in November 1960 a Soviet offer for military aid. The Soviet gift, which consisted of twelve MiG–17 fighters and two MiG–15 trainers, arrived in February 1961. Morocco's acceptance of Soviet arms aid was partly designed to appease the domestic left wing opposition which criticized previous arms aid from the United States and clamored for independence from western influence. Morocco also hoped to put pressure on the western powers and to obtain support from the Soviet Union and militant Afro-Asian states in the United Nations for its claims on Mauritania. The announcement of the MiG deal came shortly before the Soviet Union cast its veto against Mauritania's U.N. membership.

high level of tension, eliminate western and especially American influence, draw the recipients more closely into the Soviet orbit, and outflank the northern tier and NATO.

The recipients themselves facilitated the establishment of this aggressive pattern. More concerned with regional problems and rivalries than with cold war issues, they exploited major power competition and precipitated thereby the entry of the Soviet Union into the Middle East as an arms supplier. Egypt, Syria, and Yemen first tried to obtain western arms aid, more specifically U.S. aid, before they accepted the Soviet alternative. Morocco, Jordan, and Iran used the threat of accepting Soviet military aid to pressure the United States into supporting their objectives.

The Pattern of Intrusion. Another significant pattern gradually emerged in Russian arms diplomacy. This pattern reflected Soviet realization that the importance of the Middle East to the west was gradually diminishing as a result of the changing strategic world context. Intercontinental ballistic missiles in the United States and the perfection of submarine-based Polaris missiles obviated the necessity for the United States to deploy intermediate range missiles in countries near the Soviet periphery. Washington was thus able to remove its missiles from Turkey and did not need to establish missiles on Iranian soil.[21] The threat these countries represented to the Soviet Union declined, and the Soviet Union was enabled to adopt a more flexible position toward countries closely aligned with the United States. In consequence, these states felt that the Soviet menace was receding. On the other hand, the credibility of U.S. commitments to defend these nations against the Soviet Union also declined, which made the northern tier countries even more susceptible to Soviet overtures.

Under these circumstances the Soviet Union in 1963–64 launched a policy of intrusion into pro-western countries in order to undermine the links of the western defense alliances along its southern border. At the same time, in the more relaxed world climate that followed the Cuban missile crisis, Moscow sought to promote a more general détente with the nations along its border. Soviet economic and military aid were major instruments in this effort. Moscow's policy in this pattern of aid relations was characterized by a conciliatory rather than an aggressive approach. It tolerated continued ties between the recipient and the United States, but it still tried to wean the recipient away from the west toward a more neutral position by gradually increasing Soviet influence.

[21] In fact, partly under pressure of the Soviet Union, the Iranian government announced in 1962 that it would not allow the establishment of foreign missiles on its territory.

Iran, with its oil wealth and desirable location along the Persian Gulf, became a major target in this intrusion endeavor. A relatively modest $38 million in economic credits to Iran in 1963 was increased to a $290 million economic aid loan in 1965. This amounted to forty-four percent of the total Soviet economic aid commitment in 1965 to the developing non-communist world.[22] When it became clear during 1966 that Iran was growing dissatisfied with U.S. arms aid policies,[23] the Soviet Union sensed another opportunity for intrusion into Iran. In January 1967 Soviet leaders signed an agreement to supply Iran with $100 million in equipment, primarily anti-aircraft guns, trucks, and armored personnel carriers.[24] To make the loan particularly attractive, the Soviet Union offered to accept most repayments in natural gas, which Iran had not fully exploited and which was therefore essentially a wasted economic asset for Iran. Nevertheless, Moscow moved cautiously in its first arms deal with Teheran. Soviet policy-makers refused to sell surface-to-air missiles that the Iranians wanted for the defense of the Persian Gulf against a potential Egyptian threat. The anti-aircraft guns which Moscow agreed to deliver were considerably less effective than the SA-missiles against Cairo's supersonic Soviet fighters and bombers.

Soviet intrusion efforts into Turkey influenced Moscow's policy in the Cyprus crisis of 1964 and affected its arms aid to the Makarios government. At that time the Soviet Union was trying to effect a rapprochement with Turkey and to dissuade the Turks from endorsing the American plan for the creation of a multilateral force (MLF) in NATO.

The 1964 phase of the chronic Cyprus crisis arose out of President Makarios' efforts to eliminate the special constitutional privileges of the Turkish Cypriot minority. The most serious clash occurred in August 1964, when a Greek Cypriot attack on Turkish Cypriots invited

[22] U.S. Department of State, *Communist Governments and Developing Nations: Aid and Trade in 1965*, Research Memorandum RSB-50 (Washington, June 17, 1966), p. 2

[23] By 1966 Iran felt that it faced more immediate threats from its regional opponents in the Middle East, the revolutionary Arab states, than from the Soviet Union. Iranian alarms intensified with the prospect of British withdrawal from Aden and South Arabia, which, should Egypt succeed in filling the vacuum, would leave Iran face to face with its major Arab foe. Although the Shah expressed his preference for meeting his defense requirements in the United States, other political and economic considerations led him to accept the Soviet offer. The experience of the brief Indo-Pakistani war in 1965, in which the United States adopted a neutral position and froze U.S. arms aid to Pakistan in spite of the fact that Washington and Rawalpindi were military allies, reinforced the Shah's conviction that Iran should try to reduce its dependence on U.S. military supplies. Washington, moreover, had in recent years shifted its aid terms from grants to sales of arms to Iran, while Moscow was prepared to accept a barter arrangement.

[24] *New York Times*, February 8, 1967.

Turkish reprisals by air. In reaction to the Turkish air strikes Archbishop Makarios appealed to the Russians for military aid.

The Soviet Union was interested in perpetuating the crisis, since the Cyprus issue divided two NATO allies, Greece and Turkey, and weakened NATO's southeastern flank. On the other hand, Moscow did not wish to alienate Ankara. On August 10 the Soviet Union responded with a vaguely worded offer to start negotiations with Cyprus without committing itself fully to the Archbishop. At the end of September, however, Cyprus obtained a pledge for $28 million in Soviet arms and equipment.[25] Makarios wanted to obtain planes and submarines that would give Cyprus a limited offensive capability,[26] but the Russians provided the type of weapons that primarily served the defensive needs of the island. SA–2 Guideline missiles, some artillery pieces, thirty-two T–34 tanks, transportation equipment, and six Komar class motor torpedo boats were eventually shipped to Cyprus.[27]

In additional efforts to alleviate Turkish resentment of its aid to Cyprus, Moscow probably gave Ankara some form of assurance that the arms supplied to Cyprus would not be used in an offensive against Turkey. Although the Turkish foreign minister denied reports to this effect after the Russian-Cypriot arms deal was announced, he nevertheless hinted that some understanding had been reached between Ankara and Moscow.

In the autumn of 1966 the Archbishop called again for Soviet arms assistance. Moscow apparently did not wish to jeopardize fragile Soviet-Turkish relations but permitted Prague to supply a limited quantity of arms to Nicosia.

The Soviet Union's policy of intrusion was further reflected in its relations with Morocco, which also became a target of the new diplomacy. A notable example of this conciliatory approach in Soviet foreign policy can be seen in 1967, when the USSR was instrumental in effecting a Moroccan purchase of Czech tanks and field artillery.[28]

Weapons Flow. The pattern of intrusion in Soviet arms aid diplomacy did not replace the earlier aggressive policy toward the militant Arab states. These patterns continued simultaneously, with the aggressive pattern most distinct in all aspects of Soviet arms aid to the Middle East. In fact, after the initial five years the aggressive pattern became more and more discernible, for by 1961–62 Moscow began to intensify its

[25] *The Times* (London), October 18, 1965.
[26] *Observer* (London), August 23, 1964.
[27] *The Times* (London), October 18, 1965; *New York Times,* March 30, 1965.
[28] *New York Times,* July 16, 1968.

Table 2-1. Estimated Soviet Bloc Arms Aid to the Middle East: 1955 to June 1967 (In Millions of U.S. Dollars)[1]

UAR		$1,500
Syria	at least	300
Yemen		100
Iraq	at least	500
Morocco		20
Algeria		200
Cyprus		28
Iran		100
	Estimated Total:	$2,748

[1] These figures do not fully convey the true costs of the arms aid. As far as the Russians are concerned, much of the early materiel was obsolete and had lost much of its value for them. As far as the recipients are concerned, occasionally they obtained Soviet arms at a discount rate. The figures, moreover, do not reflect what it would have meant to the recipients had they been required to make repayments in hard currency. Nor can these figures be compared with figures for U.S. arms aid to the Middle East, since the United States made most of its aid available as grants. The problems in assessing the dollar value of Soviet military aid are discussed in Chapter 6. Data presented for the UAR, Cyprus, and Iran are derived from sources documented in previous pages. For the figure for Algeria, see Joseph Palmer II, Assistant Secretary of State for African Affairs, Address, *U.S. Department of State Press Release No. 109* (May 9, 1967), p. 7. The figures for Syria, Yemen, Iraq, and Morocco are based on reports on the successive military assistance accords in daily newspapers and journals.

efforts to penetrate the Middle East through its military assistance program. Whereas the earlier shipments largely consisted of weaponry which was obsolete or obsolescent by Russian yardsticks, after 1961 the Russians provided more modern and sophisticated equipment, much of it in standard use with their own armed forces. A substantial part of Egypt's Soviet arsenal was offensive rather than defensive.

The first MiG–21 fighters reached Egypt in 1962 in compliance with Nasser's request to match Israel's acquisition of advanced aircraft from France.[29] The same year MiG–21 jets appeared in Iraq; they were in Syria and Algeria in 1964 and 1965, respectively. Between 1960 and 1962 both Egypt and Iraq received their first Tu–16 bombers. In 1963 SA–2 Guideline missiles were placed in Egypt. These and other missiles went to several recipients. Komar class patrol boats armed with surface-to-surface Styx missiles arrived in Egypt in 1962 and in Syria shortly afterwards. The larger Osa class guided missile patrol boat reached Egypt some time after 1964. Algeria obtained both types, probably as a result of the May 1965 agreement.

By the eve of the June 1967 war, Soviet arms deliveries had reached impressive totals. The dollar value of cumulative totals of Soviet arms aid indicates the monetary dimension of the Russian military assistance effort.

[29] *Al Ahram,* July 1, 1962.

The magnitude of the military value of Soviet arms aid is perhaps better reflected in summarizing the types of equipment the major recipients obtained.[30] The Egyptian air force boasted more than 160 MiG–21 jets, some of which were equipped with air-to-air Atoll missiles; at least forty MiG–19s and more than one hundred of the earlier MiG fighters; fifty-five Su–7 fighter-bombers, twenty-five to thirty Tu–16 bombers; various types of cargo aircraft, including the An–12; trainers; and helicopters.[31] Egypt's anti-aircraft command was equipped with a radar network, guns, and SA–2 Guideline missiles. Its army of 180,000 men was furnished on a lavish scale with Soviet and Czech weapons, including some sixty heavy Js–3 tanks, light and medium tanks, and surface-to-surface anti-tank Snapper missiles. Four Skory class destroyers, fifteen submarines, submarine chasers, Komar and Osa class patrol boats armed with surface-to-surface Styx missiles, motor torpedo boats, landing craft, and other vessels contributed to Egypt's naval strength.

By June 1967 the Syrian air force possessed, in addition to MiG–15 craft, about fifty MiG–17 jets, and at least a squadron of MiG–21 fighters. Syria had, further, some SA–2 Guideline missiles, a small number of Il–28 bombers, Mi–1 and Mi–4 helicopters, transport planes, and an unspecified number of Soviet and Czech trainers. The Syrian navy had received two mine sweepers, at least four Komar class patrol boats with surface-to-surface Styx missiles, and a dozen or more motor torpedo boats.

The Iraqi air force had obtained before the June 1967 war ten Tu–16 medium bombers, a squadron of Il–28 light bombers, and about one hundred Soviet MiG fighters, approximately half of which were the more advanced MiG–21 and MiG–19 jets. Military transport craft included the large An–12 models. The 70,000-man army of Iraq was mostly equipped with Soviet armor and was supported by some four hundred T–34 and T–54 tanks. Twelve Pt–6 motor torpedo boats and three SO–1 submarine chasers had been delivered to the navy.

[30] The discussion of arms aid to the various recipients does not necessarily imply a comparison of the aid to the recipients. Different countries have different absorption levels with respect to arms aid. Yemen, a smaller and less advanced country, for example, can not only absorb smaller quantities of weapons, but can also absorb less sophisticated weapons than Egypt.

[31] Data for the Egyptian, Syrian, and Iraqi armed forces are derived from newspaper reports and Institute for Strategic Studies, *The Military Balance: 1967–1968* (London, 1967), pp. 39-42; Michael Howard and Robert Hunter, *Israel and the Arab World: The Crisis of 1967* (London: Institute for Strategic Studies, 1967), pp. 50-51; David Wood, *The Middle East and the Arab World: The Military Context* (London: Institute for Strategic Studies, 1965), pp. 14, 17-20; Raymond V. B. Blackman, ed., *Jane's Fighting Ships: 1967–68* (Great Missenden, Bucks., England: Sampson Low, Marston & Co., Ltd., 1968), pp. 74-76, 145, 259.

Soviet shipments for the Algerian air force totalled some 180 planes, including approximately thirty MiG–21 jets and thirty Il–28 bombers, in addition to almost fifty helicopters.[32] The army had sufficient equipment for a motorized infantry division, four to five tank battalions, about fifteen artillery battalions, and several anti-aircraft batteries, as well as SA–2 missile batteries.[33] Soviet equipment for the fledgling Algerian navy consisted of eight Pt–6 class motor torpedo boats, Komar class patrol boats, three SO-class submarine chasers, a torpedo retriever, and an electronic intelligence trawler.[34]

On paper the arms buildup of the militant Arab states was thus considerable and outranked that of Israel. But the Arab-Israeli war of June 1967 showed that superiority in quantities of weapons could not compensate for inferiority in quality of leadership, training, morale, and tactical competence. Within a week much of the Arabs' Soviet armor had been destroyed or captured.

THE AFTERMATH OF THE JUNE 1967 WAR

Soviet Response to the Arab Defeat. Through its vast military aid, substantial economic assistance, and consistent political support for the militant Arab states against Israel and the western powers, the Soviet Union has kept tensions in the Middle East at a high level. Moscow's policy nurtured in particular Cairo's expansionist ambitions and eventually encouraged Nasser to embark on his collision course with Israel in the summer of 1967. The June war revealed that in essence the aggressive pattern in Moscow's arms aid policy had changed little since its courtship of the Arabs began in 1954–55. The Six-Day War further showed that the major effective restraint on Soviet arms aid policy remained the need to prevent an armed encounter between the two superpowers. Moscow's refusal to take up Arab allegations of Anglo-American aircover for Israeli forces and its eventual reluctant endorsement of a U.N. call for a cease-fire without an Israeli withdrawal indicated that Soviet leaders were not prepared to intervene militarily on behalf of Arab nationalism and risk thereby a response by the United States.

The failure of the Soviet Union to intervene undoubtedly disillusioned many Arabs. The hostility which the militant Arabs harbored against the Anglo-American powers went much deeper, however. Nasser's charges of Anglo-American support to Israel inflamed the anti-western passions in Egypt and in other Arab states. Compounding these sentiments was the realization that in the diplomatic arena only the Soviet

---

[32] *Le Monde*, December 30, 1966; *The Times* (London), June 24, 1966.
[33] *La Revue de Défense Nationale*, January 1967, pp. 154-55.
[34] *Le Monde*, March 30, 1967.

Union could defend the Arab cause with any hope of success. Only the Soviet Union had both the means and the will to rebuild the crippled Arab armies. Thus the militant Arabs felt forced to rely increasingly on Moscow for political and military support.

Although the defeat of the Arabs initially proved embarrassing to Moscow, it also presented an unprecedented opportunity for strengthening the Soviet position in the Middle East. As the champion of the Arabs in the political phase of the conflict, Moscow regained much of its lost prestige and partly offset Chinese accusations that the Russians had forsaken the Arab cause. Moscow's prompt and vigorous new military aid was designed to regain the political ground it had lost in the Six-Day War and to compensate the Arabs for the bitter humiliation they had suffered. In both the Russians succeeded.

Immediately after the Arab defeat the Soviet Union began shoring up the shattered Arab military machines. As early as June 10, the western press reported that an airlift of Russian arms to Egypt was underway.[35] As a result of the major increases in arms deliveries, Moscow replaced eighty percent of Cairo's losses within a few months after the June debacle.[36] The new arms shipments may even have rendered the Egyptian military forces better equipped than they were before the war since some of the destroyed older type of aircraft and tanks were replaced by more recent models. The Soviet Union largely replaced equipment Syria lost in the June war. Iraq's participation in the fighting had only been of marginal importance.[37] Its relatively modest losses, including about a dozen planes, were soon replaced. Iraq received in addition some new MiG–21 fighters and Su–7 bombers.[38] Algeria, which had dispatched MiG fighters to Egypt to participate in the war, also obtained new military hardware.

Moscow further demonstrated its identification with the Arab cause by dispatching units of its Mediterranean fleet to the Egyptian ports of Alexandria and Port Said and the Syrian port of Latakia. After Egypt in October 1967 had sunk the Israeli destroyer *Elath,* and Israel had retaliated by bombing Egyptian oil refineries, Russian ships that had just left the Egyptian ports promptly steamed back into the harbors. Russian warships began to make regular calls at Algerian ports, an action which, in view of Algeria's sharp criticism of Soviet policy in the June war, reflected Algeria's deepening dependence on Russian aid.

[35] *New York Times,* June 10, 1967.

[36] *Ibid.,* October 12, 1957.

[37] The Iraqi expeditionary force was supposed to participate under Jordanian command. Israeli troops, however, intercepted and defeated the Iraqi force before any coordination with the Jordanians was possible.

[38] *Washington Post,* December 21, 1967.

The Soviet Union recognized that costly new equipment for the Arab armed forces would not overcome more basic weaknesses in military leadership, discipline, competence, and élan. Moscow was in a position, however, to lay down conditions for its aid, particularly to Nasser, whose stature was badly tarnished and who was more dependent than ever on Soviet good will and aid. Articles in the Soviet press criticizing the Egyptian military performance and recommending the reorganization of the Egyptian command structure and socialization of the Egyptian officer corps were indicative of the nature of Soviet pressure on Nasser.[39] Partly in response to Soviet insistence on reforms in the officer corps, partly to forestall a conspiracy against him, and partly in reaction to student pressures, Nasser purged or arrested a substantial number of officers. The Soviet military advisory group, which counted some five hundred before the June war, was expanded and its level of competence upgraded. Estimates of the number of Russian military advisers and technicians in Egypt by the end of 1967 ranged from two thousand to three thousand.[40] The number of Soviet military advisers in Iraq and Syria also increased.

Egypt's defeat, moreover, forced Nasser to curtail his military engagements abroad and to withdraw his troops from Yemen. As the Egyptian forces departed from Yemen, the civil war between the Yemeni royalists and republicans intensified. Under these circumstances Moscow was able to step up its direct military assistance to the republican regime of Yemen and replace the Egyptian and Russian aid that had come through Cairo. The Soviet Union in November flew some twenty-four MiG–19s and forty to fifty Soviet aviation technicians into Sana airport.[41] Soviet emergency support amounted more to open intervention than to military aid, since the shooting down of a MiG fighter by the royalists revealed that the plane had been flown by a Russian pilot.[42] While the Russian pilots were reportedly soon replaced by Syrians,[43] the Yemeni war provided the only known incident in which the Soviet Union supplied combat support to a non-aligned state.

Continuity in Soviet Arms Aid Diplomacy. The persistence of the basic trends in Soviet military aid policy in the Middle East was reflected in the aftermath of the Arab-Israeli war. Soviet efforts to shore up Egypt's position after the war suggested that Egypt remained the main target of Soviet foreign policy in the Middle East. The Russians

[39] *Pravda,* July 9, 1967; J. Balayev and Y. Primakov in *Za-Rubizhom,* June 30, 1967. See also *Washington Post,* June 25, 1967; *ibid.,* July 17, 1967.

[40] *Washington Post,* December 21, 1967; *New York Times,* January 7, 1968.

[41] *New York Times,* November 27, 1967.

[42] *Ibid.,* December 13, 1967.

[43] *Washington Post,* February 22, 1968.

recognized that Egypt retained the leadership of the militant Arab world, that it offered easy Soviet access into Africa, and, last but not least, that it controlled the Suez Canal, the major route for Soviet ships to the Indian Ocean. As long as Nasser and other Arab leaders appeared to command popular acclaim and mass following, Soviet policymakers were prepared to support them. Ideological considerations assumed at best a secondary role in Soviet arms aid diplomacy, as repeated Russian offers of military assistance to King Hussein of Jordan indicated.

The rearmament campaign permitted Moscow to deepen its penetration of the military establishments of militant Arab states and of Egypt's armed forces in particular. Soviet participation in retraining and reorganizing the defeated Egyptian army and air force provided the Russians with more effective access to Egyptian military elites and with greater opportunities for influencing Egyptian military policies.

Moscow's arms diplomacy and aggressive penetration goals had undergone no change. In fact, the aggressive pattern in Soviet policy evolved more distinctly than ever. Soviet leaders did try to exclude the risk of a direct armed encounter with the United States. At the same time, however, they proceeded to restore the distribution of military power in favor of the militant Arabs, undermining thereby western interests in the preservation of order and stability in the Middle East. The USSR reinforced its military aid presence at the eastern flank of the Middle East along the Red Sea coast in Yemen, in the center of the region in Egypt, Syria, and Iraq, and at the western gate of the Mediterranean in Algeria.

The growth of the Soviet Union's military presence in the Middle East was further demonstrated by the buildup of its surface task force in the Mediterranean, where only token Russian naval forces had previously operated. By 1968 between forty and fifty Soviet warships were deployed in the Mediterranean.[44] The Soviet fleet received permission to utilize Syrian, Egyptian, and Algerian ports. France's decision of October 1967 to return to Algeria the large naval base at Mers-el-Kebir in early 1968—ten years ahead of schedule—raised the possibility that a base across from Gibraltar would become available to the Soviet fleet in the near future.

Soviet naval presence in the Middle East did not necessarily imply an intention to acquire formal base rights, which would involve sensitive political issues. It is important to distinguish between base acquisition and base utilization. Rather, the Soviet Union appeared to be developing

---

[44] *New York Times*, December 31, 1967; *Washington Post*, December 29, 1967.

a capability similar to that of the United States in being able to project its naval power beyond immediate coastal waters without the benefit of fixed overseas bases with fuel, supplies, and repair facilities. The Russians accomplished this by means of a supporting fleet train consisting of oilers, store ships, tenders, and repair ships which could anchor in a harbor or other shallow, sheltered waters. Compliant Arab countries were the likely candidates to supply such harbors and anchorages, especially since the outcome of the June war had driven the militant Arabs closer to the Soviet camp.

The Six-Day War reflected the impact of the nuclear balance of power between the Soviet Union and the United States and emphasized thereby the growing importance of the military aid instrument. Because the nuclear balance has dictated a tacit understanding between the two superpowers to try to avoid an armed confrontation between them on behalf of a third party, the Soviet Union did not intervene during the fighting. In fact, both the Soviet Union and the United States deliberately limited their actions once the war had broken out; both were eager to halt the shooting. In the end, they had no choice but to accept the *fait accompli* of Israel's victory. Moscow's unwillingness to come to the aid of the Arabs threatened to result in a serious political setback for the Russians. The one option left to the Soviet Union after the defeat of the Arab states was to resupply them with substantial military aid. This was the only effective response the Russians could take to retrieve their losses in the Middle East, and although undoubtedly expensive, it proved to be a highly successful course.

On the whole, Moscow emerged from the June 1967 crisis with its position in the Middle East greatly enhanced. To the extent that Arab dependence on Soviet military and other support deepened, Moscow's leverage in the Arab world did increase substantially. This does not mean that the Soviet Union achieved full control over Arab leaders, but it is reasonable to conclude that the latter are now unlikely to pursue a policy that would antagonize their principal backer, and certainly not as long as they need Moscow's arms. For the near future, therefore, it is justifiable to assume that the Soviet Union succeeded in turning the Arab catastrophe of the Six-Day War into a major Soviet victory.

In terms of the more distant future, however, it is possible that the large-scale Soviet arms shipments after the June war may put the Soviet Union in the role of the sorcerer's apprentice. While the chances of a fourth Arab-Israeli war may be presently remote, Nasser or another Arab leader may feel forced to resume hostilities against Israel in order to protect his position at home. Indications are that the Russians did not want the 1967 crisis to escalate into a full-fledged war. It must be remembered, however, that in spite of extensive arms aid, the Soviet Union was unable to prevent Nasser from taking the provocative actions that led to the June fighting. Although after the June war Soviet control over the militant Arabs increased, Moscow may again be unable to restrain its Arab protégés from launching another war against Israel at some future date, thereby drawing the Russians deeper into the Middle East quagmire.

3

SUB-SAHARAN AFRICA

AFRICA IN SOVIET FOREIGN POLICY

SOVIET MILITARY aid diplomacy in sub-Saharan Africa is closely linked to Soviet foreign policy toward the recently independent countries of that area and forms part of that policy. Before 1950 Western European predominance in Africa severely limited opportunities for indigenous communists and for significant contacts with the Soviet Union. By 1955, however, when nationalist movements in North Africa seemed destined to produce independent states and sub-Saharan nationalists showed signs of imitation, Soviet planners saw the need to formulate a more specific policy toward the independence movements in Africa. Soviet involvement in Africa[1] since then has consisted essentially of an effort "to keep ideology in step with policy, and policy in step with the aspirations of the new states."[2]

This statement of Soviet aims epitomizes the pragmatic nature of Soviet bloc aid policies and operations in Africa. On no occasion has communist doctrine greatly interfered with Soviet economic or military aid policy. The Russians particularly exhibited in the former area considerable ideological flexibility, as their sizeable economic aid to a conservative monarchy such as Ethiopia[3] suggests. Soviet arms aid to the

[1] Since North African countries are customarily included in the context of the Middle East, the term "Africa," as used in this chapter, refers to the countries south of the five Mediterranean African countries.

[2] David Morison, *The USSR and Africa* (London: Oxford University Press, 1964), p. 128.

[3] The Ethiopian credit of $102 million was the largest Soviet aid credit to sub-Saharan Africa as of June 1966. U.S. Department of State, *Communist Governments and Developing Nations: Aid and Trade in 1966*, Research Memorandum RSB-80 (Washington, July 21, 1967), p. 2.

generally pro-western government of Nigeria indicates a similar lack of ideological restraints.

Compared to other developing regions, sub-Saharan Africa commands a relatively low priority in Soviet foreign policy. Moscow has no vital strategic interests in the region, although it would naturally be concerned with the implications of hostile control over the countries adjoining the waterways that connect the Mediterranean Sea with the Indian Ocean. These countries are also important because they offer air fields for entry into Africa. With the exception of the Horn of Africa, therefore, there is no particular area of direct interest to the Soviet Union.

A more general Soviet concern in Africa derives from Moscow's aim to neutralize the paramount influence of the western powers. Moscow's overall interest is further reflected in its efforts to be identified with African aspirations for independence and neutralism and to strengthen thereby the Soviet image as the champion of anti-colonialism in the eyes of the developing world.[4]

The Soviet Union has, in addition, certain specific interests in the region, such as the need for landing and overflight privileges, scientific tracking stations for future space activities, and possible base rights for naval vessels in the south Atlantic or Indian Ocean. On at least two occasions the Russians have sought overflight and landing rights. In 1962, during the Cuban missile crisis, the Soviet Union requested permission for landing rights at Conakry, Guinea, for Havana-bound aircraft.[5] The request, however, was rejected. At the end of 1964, the Russians flew into the Sudan with military supplies for Congolese rebel forces in the northeastern part of the Congo.[6]

The Soviet interest in the right to use naval bases and ports-of-call around the world has been heightened by Britain's hasty withdrawal from areas east of Suez. Since the Russians have not yet fully developed the sophisticated technique of refueling and replenishing their ships underway, the right to use bases will greatly facilitate the establishment of a Soviet naval presence in the Indian Ocean. East African countries are considered particularly important in this respect and are being assiduously courted.

With the emergence of the Sino-Soviet split, the preclusion of Chinese influence became an additional factor in Soviet policies in sub-Saharan Africa. Although during the 1950s Soviet and Chinese activities in Africa were relatively non-competitive and even complementary, an

---

[4] The success with which the Soviet Union has identified itself with anti-colonial issues in world politics is discussed in Chapter 8.

[5] Marshall I. Goldman, *Soviet Foreign Aid* (New York: Praeger, 1967), p. 172.

[6] *New York Times*, December 7, 1964.

active rivalry had developed by the time of the Third Afro-Asian Solidarity Conference at Moshi, Tanganyika, in February 1963. The Chinese supported those groups which seemed to have the best potential for political violence. The Russians pledged moral and economic support to national leaders without regard for their revolutionary credentials and aspirations.

This rivalry reached its most intense level in Tanzania, where Russians and East Germans competed with Chinese not only in the provision of arms and military training, but also in the development of trade and the cultivation of Tanganyikan and Zanzibari leaders.[7] Sino-Soviet competition exists in varying degrees in several African states. The USSR, however, has become considerably more circumspect in its activities, reflecting its efforts to maintain correct relations with incumbent African governments. The Chinese, on the other hand, appear to be more willing to support dissidents and armed insurgents, in keeping with their general commitment to revolutionary tactics.

SOVIET ARMS AID TO SUB-SAHARAN AFRICA

Soviet military assistance programs developed somewhat fortuitously. Because most newly independent African governments retained close relations with their former metropolitan powers, they generally obtained their military hardware from British, French, or other western sources. In fact, only in Guinea were the Russians able to establish a military aid program by the end of 1960. The aid agreements with Ghana and Mali which followed in 1961 appeared to establish a pattern of Soviet aid to similarly oriented governments. All three countries had a leadership which had strong Marxist tendencies in domestic policies and adopted a radical pan-African and anti-western posture in foreign affairs. Each belonged to the so-called militant group of African states. These states were not necessarily pro-communist on cold war issues, but rather anti-west insofar as they identified western nations with colonialism. The more moderate African states, on the other hand, were generally prepared to cooperate with western nations. They did not regard, as the militant states tended to, economic and military aid ties with the west as the re-establishment of colonial dependency.

It is unlikely, however, that the Soviet Union sought out Guinea, Ghana, and Mali for a military aid program on the basis of their political orientations. Rather, Moscow responded to developments

---

[7] This aspect is discussed in detail in the somewhat journalistic, but generally accurate account of John K. Cooley, *East Wind Over Africa* (New York: Walker and Company, 1966), pp. 47-57.

which seemed to offer political gains for Soviet arms diplomacy. Actually, Guinea[8]—and for that matter the Congolese government of Patrice Lumumba in July 1960[9]—took the initiative in the establishment of arms aid relationships with the USSR. The Soviet Union's favorable response to these overtures and its own initiatives in Ghana and Mali were part of a general offensive to undermine the western positions in Africa whenever the possibility appeared.

The Early Recipients of the 1959–61 Period. Guinea was the first black African country that presented the Soviet Union and its allies with an opportunity for military and economic penetration. In late 1958 France had cut its military and economic ties with Guinea and had withdrawn its technicians in retaliation for Guinea's refusal to join the French Community. The infant republic therefore had to look elsewhere for assistance in developing its military capability. After failing to obtain arms aid from the United States, President Sékou Touré accepted a Czech offer for weapons. The arms shipments, which began to arrive in March 1959—allegedly as gifts rather than sales—consisted of a few light tanks, armored cars, artillery pieces, anti-aircraft guns, anti-tank guns, and small weaponry.[10] A Czech military mission of eighteen men was stationed in Guinea. They were joined the next year by a group of Russian advisers and technicians.[11]

In March 1960 Guinea negotiated a Russian loan for military supplies. Reports suggested a figure of some $3 million,[12] but in view of the relatively large amounts of weapons and equipment Guinea received, it can be assumed that the actual sum was at least twice this amount. As a result, the two-thousand-man Guinean army was well supplied with Russian and Czech arms by 1961. Guinean military personnel underwent training in Soviet bloc countries.

To many outside observers, the Soviet bloc arms accords transformed Guinea's newly won independence into Soviet dependence.[13] To militant Africans, however, Touré's solicitation of Soviet aid represented a

[8] U.S. Congress, Senate Committee on Foreign Relations, *Mutual Security Act of 1960*, 86th Cong., 2d Sess. (1960), p. 381.

[9] Ernest W. Lefever and Wynfred Joshua, *United Nations Peacekeeping in the Congo: 1960-1964*, vol. 2 (Washington: The Brookings Institution, 1966), pp. 141, 159.

[10] *Washington Post*, March 25, 1959; *Christian Science Monitor*, April 22, 1959; *New York Times*, April 4, 1959.

[11] *New York Times,* December 8, 1960.

[12] See M. J. V. Bell, *Military Assistance to Independent African States* (London: Institute for Strategic Studies, 1964), p. 11; Goldman, *Soviet Foreign Aid*, p. 169.

[13] Articles subtitled to imply that Guinea was "Swinging to Reds" (*Washington Post*, September 9, 1960), or "Past Point of No Return on Way to Communism" (*New York Times*, February 5, 1961), were typical.

move toward neutralism and away from economic dependency on the west, which they regarded as a form of neo-colonialism. Touré's defiance of the west, particularly in such a sensitive area as military assistance, had a psychological appeal which transcended the military utility of the armaments involved.

Ghana became the next major recipient of Soviet military aid. As the main exponent of a pan-Africanism which called for eliminating western influence in Africa, Nkrumah felt he could ill afford to maintain British officers in the top military positions in Ghana.[14] Following Touré's example, Nkrumah was determined to "Africanize" his army and wean it away from its dependence on Britain.

In September 1961 Nkrumah accepted an invitation to send one hundred Ghanaians to the Soviet Union for military training.[15] The first arms aid accord was signed the same year and it was followed by a number of additional agreements for Soviet bloc arms aid in later years.

The number of Ghanaian cadets training in the Soviet Union remained limited, largely because of the strong resistance from Ghanaian military leaders to having their officers schooled in communist countries. But the group of Russian advisers in Ghana expanded over the years. By the time of Nkrumah's ouster in 1966 they numbered approximately one thousand.[16] Some of them were assigned to Nkrumah's Ideological Institute at Winneba and to other centers where exiled opposition members from African countries were instructed in subversion and guerrilla warfare. Others were engaged to train Nkrumah's special services and his presidential guard, which had been organized as a counterweight to the regular army and police. A portion of Soviet weapons deliveries were allotted to this private army.[17] Soviet officers remained attached to the presidential guard and were apparently in command positions. In the February 1966 army coup that ousted Nkrumah, a number of Russian officers—according to newspaper reports, a total of eleven[18]—were killed during the attack on Nkrumah's official residence.

After Nkrumah's downfall, the subsequent military regime disbanded the presidential guard, closed the Institute at Winneba and other centers,

---

[14] Cf. the memoirs of Ghana's former Chief of Defense Staff, Major General H. T. Alexander, *African Tightrope: My Two Years as Nkrumah's Chief of Staff* (New York: Praeger, 1965), pp. 93-94.

[15] George Weeks, "The Armies of Africa," *Africa Report*, vol. 9, no. 1 (January 1964), p. 9.

[16] *New York Times*, March 3, 1968.

[17] In 1965, for example, among the Soviet arms the presidential guard received were twenty-four pieces of light artillery, twenty-one medium infantry mortars, fifteen anti-aircraft machine guns, twenty heavy and sixty light machine guns, twenty-five hundred submachine guns, and more than two million rounds of ammunition. See Cooley, *East Wind*, p. 161.

[18] *Washington Post*, March 1, 1966.

and requested the Soviet Union to reduce drastically its huge embassy staff in Accra. No new military aid accord has been reported since Nkrumah's disappearance from the political scene. His ouster resulted in a severe curtailment of Soviet and other communist penetration in Ghana and marked at the same time the end of Ghana's role as a center for communist subversion in Africa.

The establishment of Soviet military aid ties with Mali followed a pattern somewhat similar to the one in Guinea, except that aid was on a much smaller scale. Although Mali's break with Paris in September 1960 was not as brusque as Guinea's, Moscow quickly tried to exploit the situation. The attitude of Mali's leaders indicated a receptivity to Soviet overtures, as President Modibo Keita's public endorsement of Sékou Touré's actions had suggested.[19]

In March 1961 the Soviet Union offered Mali a $44 million economic loan as well as military assistance and equipment, presumably worth as much as $3 million.[20] The initial arms aid was largely in the form of artillery pieces, personnel carriers, jeeps, and small arms.[21] As with Guinea and Ghana, Mali accepted a Soviet training mission and sent an unspecified number of military cadets to the Soviet Union for training.

Russian military aid to Congo-Leopoldville, now Congo-Kinshasa, was of a different character, but it can be cited as an example of a Soviet response to a request for assistance after an appeal to the United States had been rejected and assistance from the United Nations had not produced the desired results. The Soviet arms aid venture in the former Belgian Congo also resulted in a resounding setback for Moscow; it is therefore worth discussing in some detail.

The Congo mutinies in July 1960, which followed in the wake of the independence celebrations, caught the new indigenous government of Patrice Lumumba completely by surprise. Initially prepared to enlist aid from any side, the Congolese heeded the advice of the United States and turned to the United Nations on July 10.[22] But Katanga, where the majority of Belgian mining interests were concentrated, seceded from the central Congolese government shortly thereafter. Prime Minister Lumumba and his associates blamed Katanga's secession on Belgian imperialism and western aggression. Accordingly, the Congolese government sent its

---

[19] *New York Times*, January 20, 1961.

[20] Weeks, "Armies of Africa," p. 13.

[21] Goldman, *Soviet Foreign Aid*, p. 177; David Wood, *The Armed Forces of African States* (London: Institute for Strategic Studies, 1966), p. 10.

[22] Lefever and Joshua, *United Nations*, p. 141.

first request for help to the Soviet Union on July 14,[23] the same day that the Security Council authorized the dispatch of a U.N. military mission.

Consonant with its overall foreign policy, Moscow wanted to eliminate Belgian influence from the Congo. The Congo represented for the Russians the classical example of a colony exploited by western imperialism and ripe for a nationalist revolution. To propitiate the leaders of the Congo, the Soviet Union had to identify itself with Congolese nationalism. Moscow also sought to encourage a regime in the Congo compatible with major Soviet policies in Africa. Lumumba, who had been cultivated by the communists, seemed the best candidate to lead such a regime.

To prevent direct western intervention, but aware of its own limited capabilities to intervene militarily in the heart of Africa, the Soviet Union endorsed the introduction of U.N. military power into the Congo instead of acting upon the Congo's request for direct Soviet aid. With this request on file, however, Moscow left itself the option of responding on a bilateral basis if it became desirable.

To demonstrate its cooperation with the U.N. decision, the Soviet Union reported on July 23 that it had authorized the use of five Il–18 planes, assigned to the Ghana government, to fly Ghanaian troops and equipment to the Congo. Moscow further announced that it would ship one hundred trucks, a repair shop, and supporting technicians to the Congo. The Russian airlift of Ghanaian troops and supplies, which amounted, according to Moscow's own testimony, to $1.5 million, was performed under the U.N. aegis.[24] During August 1960, however, Soviet materiel and personnel arrived with additional equipment, interpreters, medical teams and supplies, and some arms, as well as ten twin-engined Il–14 transport planes.[25] On August 15 Lumumba had, in fact, requested transport planes and crews, weapons, and other equipment from the Russians.[26] By that time Lumumba had turned against U.N. authorities because of their refusal to comply with his demands that U.N. troops immediately be used to end Katanga's secession. He intended, therefore, to attack Katanga on his own and use Soviet planes to ferry his troops to Kasai, from where the offensive was to start.

[23] W. J. Ganshof van der Meersch, *Fin de la Souveraineté Belge au Congo* (Brussels: Institut Royal des Relations Internationales, 1963), p. 447.

[24] Lefever and Joshua, *United Nations*, p. 174.

[25] U.S. Department of State, *U. S. Participation in the United Nations: Report by the President to the Congress for the Year 1960* (Washington, 1962), p. 50; Pierre Houart, *La pénétration communiste au Congo* (Brussels: Centre de documentation internationale, 1960), p. 64; Lefever and Joshua, *United Nations*, p. 161.

[26] A reproduction of Lumumba's letter requesting Soviet aid can be found in Houart, *Pénétration communiste,* appendix VI.

The U.N. Secretary General charged that Soviet delivery of planes and other equipment to Lumumba constituted unilateral assistance and was contrary to the U.N. resolutions of July 22 and August 9, which had requested that all states refrain from any action that might impede the restoration of law and order, and had called upon all states to cooperate with the United Nations in carrying out this task. In response to the Secretary General's complaints, Moscow asserted that the U.N. resolutions did not prevent other states from providing direct aid to the Congolese government. Confronted with mounting disorder and the threat of civil war, U.N. authorities closed the major Congolese airports to all except U.N. aircraft on September 5. The effect of this U.N. move was to prevent any further Soviet support for Lumumba's independent military action. When the more moderate Mobutu-Kasavubu faction managed to oust Lumumba, the new Congolese leadership expelled all Russians on September 14 and broke diplomatic relations with the Soviet Union. All Soviet planes were flown out of the Congo by the end of the month.

The Russians not only experienced a setback in the Congo, but they suffered a severe reversal in the Afro-Asian world as well. The majority of the Afro-Asians, although disturbed over Lumumba's ouster, was more interested in U.N. action to insure effective decolonization in the Congo and to insulate the Congo from cold war politics. The Afro-Asian resolution, which the General Assembly adopted in September 1960, prohibited all military aid to the Congo except through the United Nations. This resolution implied a censure of Soviet actions and registered Moscow's political defeat.[27]

By the time the U.N. troops withdrew from the Congo in mid-1964, a number of radical dissident movements had started new revolts. For the militant African states, the issue in the Congo crisis had changed. Their leaders believed that the use of the United Nations as an instrument to effect decolonization was no longer relevant. African militants were, moreover, bitterly opposed to the Tshombe regime, which had come to power in July 1964.[28] The various rebel factions received covert military aid from African and Chinese sources. They succeeded in gaining control of the northeastern part of the Congo and established in August 1964 a rebel government in Stanleyville. The Belgian-American rescue mission in November 1964, however, not only liberated white hostages

---

[27] The resolution was adopted by a vote of seventy to zero with eleven abstentions, including the Soviet Union (*New York Times,* September 21, 1960). For the first time the Soviet Union was forced to split openly with the Afro-Asians on the Congo question.

[28] African militants resented Moise Tshombe, former president of Katanga, because they identified him with Belgian imperialism and because he used white mercenaries.

held by the rebels, but also facilitated the recapture of Stanleyville by Congolese government troops.

Several militant African states reacted to these developments by openly supporting the rebel groups. The Soviet Union promised to finance part of the weapons airlift from Egypt, Algeria, and Ghana to the Congo via the Sudan. Some Soviet arms were also flown directly from Black Sea bases to the Sudan.[29] Soviet and African arms aid activities, however, did not last long. Partly because the rebel movement fell more and more into disarray and partly because in early 1965 the Sudan and other neighboring states[30] closed their borders to arms traffic to the Congo, Soviet and other foreign support to the rebels gradually stopped.

Today, no vestiges of Soviet military assistance either to Lumumba in 1960 or to the rebels four years later remain in Congo-Kinshasa. In contrast, the first three recipients, Guinea, Mali, and Ghana, still show evidence of Soviet bloc aid in their armed forces. The Guinean army was by 1967 equipped with Soviet bloc materiel, including 105mm and 122m artillery pieces, tanks, armored personnel carriers, and anti-aircraft guns. The Guinean air force had acquired a limited number of older type MiGs, An transport craft, and trainers. Soviet aid to Ghana had yielded, in addition to army equipment and weapons, four patrol boats, transport craft, and Mi-4 helicopters for Ghana's incipient navy and air force. Mali had received artillery pieces, carriers, jeeps, some tanks, several transport craft, and more recently in 1966, three MiG-17s to form the nucleus of an air force.[31]

The Soviet Union had further assisted each recipient in establishing and operating a national air line. Guinea had obtained six Czech Il-14 and three Russian Il-18 planes; Ghana had bought eight Il-18 planes for its civil air line; and Mali had acquired five Czech aero-transports, three Il-14s, three Il-18s, and one An-2 plane.[32] For both Guinea and Ghana, however, the Ilyushins proved to be too expensive to operate, and each eventually returned some of their civil transport craft.[33]

[29] *New York Times*, December 7, 1964.

[30] Arms for Congolese rebels also came through Tanzania, Uganda, and Kenya. Some of these arms came from Communist China; other arms, including some Soviet arms, were sent by militant African states.

[31] Data derived from Wood, *African States, passim; Africa Research Bulletin, Political, Social and Cultural Series*, vol. 3, no. 3 (March 1-31), 1966, p. 495B; Goldman, *Soviet Foreign Aid*, p. 177; *West Africa*, November 2, 1966; and daily newspaper reports.

[32] George Weeks, "Wings of Change: A Report on the Progress of Civil Aviation in Africa," *Africa Report*, vol. 10, no. 2 (February 1965), p. 32.

[33] Ghana returned four Il-18s to the Soviet Union in 1963 (*New York Times*, August 25, 1963), and Guinea sent some back in 1965 and replaced them with American DC-4s (*ibid.*, July 4, 1965).

Reappraisal and Continuation, 1961–66. The period between the summer of 1961 and the summer of 1963 seems to have been a time of reflection for African states insofar as Soviet military aid was concerned. No new arms aid agreements were made between the USSR and African governments. Developments which contributed to a more cautious African attitude were Soviet activities concerning the Congo crisis—both in the Congo and the United Nations—and the experience in Guinea, where Soviet subversive efforts had led to the expulsion of the Russian ambassador in December 1961.[34] In addition, Moscow's unfamiliarity with African conditions resulted in various technical and economic difficulties in its military and economic aid programs. Accordingly, the recipients were frequently dissatisfied with Soviet assistance.

The growing hesitance on the part of African governments to link themselves closely with the USSR was not matched by a decline in Soviet willingness to spread its influence in Africa. In keeping with its pragmatic approach to the region, the Soviet Union remained prepared to respond to new developments. The next opportunity for Soviet military aid inroads came in late 1963, when Somalia rejected a joint $15 million arms aid proposal by a group of western nations and accepted instead a much larger Russian offer of $35 million.[35] In contrast to the western plan, the Russian offer was made without restrictive conditions.[36] Soviet credits were made available on easy terms, presumably payable over as much as twenty years.[37] Compared with Soviet arms aid to other black African states, and in light of Somalia's $3.9 million defense budget for 1964, the Russian offer was substantial.

The Soviet Union started its program by stressing the training aspects, which may have been partly dictated by the extremely low educational level of the Somalis. More than ninety Somali officers flew to Moscow for training a month after the original agreement had been signed. By 1966 about six hundred Somali cadets were attending military schools in the Soviet Union, while a military mission of at least 250 Russians had been established in Somalia.[38] The supply of Soviet hardware ar-

[34] Touré had become progressively disenchanted with the activities of Soviet technicians and diplomats in his country. In September 1961, eighteen Soviet technicians were arrested in connection with diamond smuggling. In December Touré claimed to have evidence that bloc diplomats were encouraging subversive opposition groups. See Alexander Dallin, "The Soviet Union: Political Activity," in *Africa and the Communist World*, ed. Zbigniew Brzezinski, pp. 33-35.

[35] Bell, *Military Assistance*, p. 14; *New York Times*, March 8, 1967.

[36] According to Somali spokesmen, the western offer was too late, too small, and unacceptable because of the condition that Somalia was not to procure arms from other sources. *New York Times*, December 17, 1963.

[37] Bell, *Military Assistance*, p. 14.

[38] *New York Times*, March 13, 1966.

rived more slowly than expected. Most of the Soviet armor reached Somalia as late as 1965 and 1966. But in 1967 the Somali air force had a small transport capability and three MiG–15 and seven MiG–17 jets. Somalia's fledgling navy was equipped with six motor gun boats and its 8,000-man army with eighty-two T–34 tanks, vehicles, some artillery, anti-aircraft guns, and infantry weapons.[39] About one-third of the tanks, however, were either defective or not combat-ready.

After the 1963 agreement with Somalia, the next opening for Russian military aid arose in Zanzibar, where the Arab nationalist government was overthrown in January 1964. Both Cuba and Communist China were known to have supported the Zanzibari rebels with military training and some financial backing. While London and Washington withheld recognition of the new regime, Moscow and Peking extended recognition within one week. When the new president Abeid Karume received no sign of support from either Britain or the United States, he decided to bolster his strength with military assistance from communist sources. In March the first Russian technicians and arms, including trucks, mortars, and artillery, landed in Zanzibar.[40] A Chinese shipment of submachine guns and automatic weapons reached Zanzibar shortly after the Soviet delivery.[41] Thus began a minor Sino-Soviet arms race. Chinese instructors organized a military training camp near Mtoni on the island, while Russian and East German advisers established their military training base at Chukwani.[42]

The merger of Tanganyika and Zanzibar, which Tanganyikan President Julius Nyerere engineered in April 1964 partly to counter growing communist influence in Zanzibar, did not stop communist activity on the island. In fact, Sino-Soviet rivalry for arms aid made itself felt on the mainland as well.[43]

A Chinese military mission began to conduct a six-month training program for one of Tanganyika's three army battalions.[44] A similar arrangement was presumably made with the Russians for training a second battalion. The first Chinese rifles and small arms were unloaded

---

[39] Data derived from Wood, *African States*, p. 22; *East Africa Standard*, January 1, 1967; *Washington Post*, March 7, 1967; *New York Times*, March 12, 1967.

[40] *New York Times*, April 1, 1964.

[41] *Ibid.*, June 15, 1964.

[42] *Washington Post*, November 10, 1964.

[43] After helping to effect the merger with Zanzibar, Nyerere became head of a union government that was already receiving aid from the Soviet bloc, Communist China, and western powers. By accepting communist aid for the mainland, Nyerere tried to create a balance among these three forces in order to prevent a single one from gaining too much influence through its aid program. At the same time, Nyerere wanted to extract as much economic and military aid as possible from each of the competing groups.

[44] *New York Times*, August 30, 1964.

in September at Dar es Salaam,[45] while Russian anti-aircraft weapons, field guns, and light arms followed in November.[46] Throughout the next three years substantial amounts of Soviet and Chinese military equipment and arms arrived at Dar es Salaam.

By the standards of Soviet arms aid to other countries in Africa, the total Russian program in Tanzania remained modest; in dollar amounts it probably came to a sum of between $5 million and $10 million. But given the late start of the program and the low absorption level and small size of Tanzania's armed forces—less than two thousand on the mainland and some eight hundred on the island—Soviet arms aid was an important factor in Tanzania's military buildup.

In addition to the establishment of Soviet aid programs in Somalia and Tanzania, there were indications that Soviet military assistance had been offered to at least three other sub-Saharan countries in 1964 and 1965: Kenya, Uganda, and Congo-Brazzaville. In the instance of Kenya, however, the arms aid was destined for sources other than the national government.

Soviet arms shipments into Kenya were first noted in late November 1964.[47] The weapons were presumably en route to Congolese rebels; similar shipments were sent through the Sudan and Uganda at that time. Subsequent reports indicated that some of these arms ended up without President Kenyatta's knowledge in the hands of supporters of Vice President Oginga Odinga, Kenyatta's opponent.[48] On April 15, 1965, Kenyan troops were dispatched to Mombasa, ostensibly to supervise the delivery of a gift of Russian arms. The weapons were rejected as obsolete, and the seventeen-man Soviet team which had arrived to provide instruction in the use of the arms was sent home.[49]

Uganda has been the recipient of aid from both the USSR and Communist China. Ugandan Prime Minister Milton Obote admitted in May 1965 that his government had purchased arms from Communist China.[50] In July 1965 Obote visited Moscow, Peking, and Belgrade, where he signed various aid and cultural agreements. That an arms aid deal may have been made in Moscow can be suspected because of the unusually strong parliamentary criticism of the visit and the alleged cultural

[45] *Neue Zürcher Zeitung* (Zurich), September 5, 1964.
[46] *Washington Post*, November 9, 1964.
[47] *Daily Express* (London), November 30, 1964.
[48] Cooley, *East Wind*, p. 65.
[49] *Africa Report*, vol. 10, no. 6 (June 1965), pp. 23-24.
[50] *Africa Research Bulletin, Political, Social and Cultural Series*, vol. 2, no. 5 (May 1-31, 1965), p. 292.

agreement which resulted.[51] Details of the agreement were not made public, but the small Ugandan air force is reported to have an undetermined number of MiGs on order.[52]

Soviet bloc military aid to Congo-Brazzaville is even more obscure, and while an occasional reference is made to it in the press,[53] the impact of the small amount of Russian arms aid is overshadowed by Chinese and Cuban military assistance activity. The Cubans organized, in fact, the presidential guard which protected the government in the army revolt of June 1966.[54] In the aftermath, a new People's National Army was created, with the mission to "carry out political tasks of the revolution,"[55] in addition to the defense of the country. Whatever influence the Russians may have had through their military assistance program is unlikely to have continued within the newer, more politicized military establishment.

The 1967 Transactions. The 1967 examples of Soviet arms aid diplomacy continue to illustrate the pragmatic nature of Soviet military aid policy. In the Sudan and Nigeria, countries where similar political and sociological conditions obtain, Russian military assistance to the national government is not fully consistent with Soviet doctrine. Both the Sudan and Nigeria are deeply divided between a traditional Moslem north and a Christian and pagan south, with the north in control of the government. Each country faces an insurgent separatist movement, which ideologically would seem more likely to attract communist sympathies.[56] The Soviet Union's military aid offer to the Sudan and Nigeria in the summer of 1967, however, was related to its objectives in the Middle East. Immediately after the Arab-Israeli war, Moscow mounted an intensive political campaign, accompanied with offers of economic and military aid to the Moslem Arabs, designed to restore Arab confidence in the USSR as their most important ally.

In August 1967 Sudanese officials announced the completion of arms aid negotiations with the Soviet Union and Czechoslovakia. The agreements were expected to be made final later in the year. While the

---

[51] *Uganda Argus* (Kampala), August 9, 1965; *Africa Report*, vol. 10, no. 9 (October 1965), p. 57.

[52] "Uganda Army: Nexus of Power," *Africa Report*, vol. 11, no. 9 (December 1966), p. 38.

[53] *New York Times,* September 5, 1967, p. 24; *ibid.,* November 22, 1967.

[54] *Ibid.,* June 19, 1966; *ibid.,* June 30, 1966.

[55] *El Moudjahid* (Algiers), July 9, 1966, as cited in *Africa Research Bulletin, Political, Social and Cultural Series,* vol. 3, no. 7 (July 1-31, 1966), p. 576A.

[56] For a detailed discussion of the tribal cleavages in the Sudan and Nigeria, see Georgetown Research Project, *Africa and U.S. National Security* (Washington, 1966), Chapter 3.

Sudanese did not specify the amount and type of arms involved, British sources reported that the Soviet deal covered the older type of MiGs, some tanks, an aerial defense system, and military training.[57] The Czechs would probably provide army supplies and some weapons.[58]

The Russian arms shipment to Nigeria meant, in effect, Soviet support for the feudal Moslem north against the more progressive, partly Christian and partly pagan secessionist Ibo movement in the southeastern part of the country. In June 1967 civil war had broken out in Nigeria, after the secessionist Ibos had established the independent Republic of Biafra. The breakup of the original federal army left both sides underequipped, and Biafrans as well as Nigerians began a search for arms. Both parties initially turned to the British. London, concerned about its oil interests in areas controlled by the secessionists, granted limited supplies of arms to the federal government, but held up export licenses for larger amounts and planes. A Nigerian request to buy U.S. weapons and planes was turned down.[59] The central government, alarmed by Ibo superiority in the air,[60] felt forced to switch to communist sources. In August 1967 Czechoslovakia landed in Lagos six L–29 jet trainers equipped for bombing and strafing missions. The Russians flew in ten to fifteen MiG–17s. Some fifty Soviet instructors remained in Nigeria to service the MiGs and to teach Nigerians how to fly them.[61] The Russian sale of weapons included some ground equipment, arms, bombs, and ammunition which arrived at about the same time, and three patrol boats which were delivered later in the year.[62] A Nigerian federal government official disclosed that all arms were purchased on a commercial and cash basis. Calculated on the basis of comparable U.S. equipment and assumed to include support items, the Soviet-Czech arms deliveries can be estimated at a value of between $10 and $15 million.

At a time when Biafran troops were making prominent headway, the Soviet Union scored immediate political gains in Nigeria by selling the

[57] *Financial Times* (London), October 13, 1967. It should be noted that the Sudan had actually been an earlier recipient of Soviet arms aid. In November 1960 it had received five armored troop carriers as a gift, and it had subsequently bought a limited number of military vehicles. The transaction, however, amounted to less than $1 million and had little military significance for the recipient. Catherine McArdle, *The Role of Military Assistance in the Problem of Arms Control* (Cambridge, Mass.: M.I.T. Press, 1964), p. 84.

[58] *New York Times*, August 10, 1967.

[59] *Ibid.*, August 15, 1967.

[60] The Ibo forces had acquired from European sources two elderly B–26 bombers, which contributed to their initial successes in July and August.

[61] *New York Times*, August 22, 1967; *Africa Report*, vol. 12, no. 7 (October 1967), pp. 54-55.

[62] *Africa Research Bulletin, Political, Social and Cultural Series*, vol. 4, no. 11 (November 1-30, 1967), p. 917C.

federal government arms—the United States had refused to do so and Britain had equivocated. Moscow's action won approval from Arab states as well as from the various African governments facing potential secessionist threats in their own countries. Significantly, the Soviet Union compared Biafra's secession to the secession of Katanga from the Congo,[63] an analogy which was bound to strike a responsive cord in African thinking.

COMMON FACTORS IN SOVIET ARMS AID DIPLOMACY

The Limitations. In terms of dollar value, Soviet military aid to sub-Saharan African states reflected the region's secondary role in Soviet policy toward the developing world. Cumulative arms aid to Africa still totalled under $100 million by 1967, and with the exception of the credits to Somalia, the various programs were relatively small, as Table 3-1 illustrates.

Table 3-1. Estimated Soviet Bloc Arms Aid to Sub-Saharan Africa: 1959 through 1967 (In Millions of U.S. Dollars)

Congo-Brazzaville	$1
Congo-Kinshasa	1.5
Ghana	10 to 15
Guinea	at least 6
Mali	at least 3
Nigeria	10 to 15
Somalia	35
Sudan	N.A.
Tanzania	5 to 10
Uganda	N.A.
Estimated Total:	$86.5

Sources: Data presented are derived from sources documented in previous pages, except for Ghana, Nigeria, and Tanzania, where cost of equipment reported in the open press has been listed. Costs were calculated on the basis of approximate costs of comparable U.S. equipment and assumed to include such additional items as support equipment for aircraft, tools, spare parts, and other concomitant equipment.

The monetary value of Russian arms assistance programs in Africa, however, should be assessed against the recipients' capability to absorb the aid. In nine of the ten recipients the armed forces numbered fewer than twenty thousand men and in five of these they totalled below ten thousand.[64] More important, the general low level of education and training in the indigenous armed forces precluded the provision of

---

[63] L. Laptev, "From Katanga to Biafra," *New Times* (Moscow), December 27, 1967, pp. 17-18.

[64] In Congo-Kinshasa the armed forces numbered 32,000. In other recipients the armed forces totalled: Congo-Brazzaville, 1,800; Ghana, 17,000; Guinea, 5,000; Mali, 3,000; Somalia, 9,500; Sudan, 18,500; Tanzania, 2,600; Uganda, 5,960. The total number of Nigerian troops before the breakup of the federation was 11,500. Data are for 1966. Wood, *African States, passim.*

sophisticated, expensive arms. None of the African recipients received any missiles or supersonic MiG fighters. The most recent model MiG sent to Africa was the MiG–17. Even so, only Mali, Somalia, and Nigeria acquired these; they remained nevertheless dependent on Soviet and other outside assistance for service, maintenance, and pilots. Similarly, in part because of the maintenance difficulties, Ghana and Guinea could not afford to keep the Il–18 transport planes.

The slow dispatch of military hardware to African recipients, including the Somali Republic, indicated some Russian recognition that Africans were unprepared to cope with a rapid and sizeable influx of weapons. The emphasis on training and on the supply of small and relatively easy-to-handle arms suggested Soviet awareness that Africans were not yet ready to absorb complex equipment. The requests of the African governments tended to be modest, which perhaps indicated their concurrence with Russian appraisals.

If these factors kept Soviet arms aid limited in terms of absolute dollar figures, Soviet aid in terms of African force levels and military development was nevertheless substantial and at times excessive. The first Soviet bloc shipment of arms to Mali in 1959, which included some eight thousand rifles, several thousand pistols, machine guns, and armored cars, was considered by most observers to be in excess of the needs of Mali's small 2,000 man army.[65] The Russian tanks in Guinea, Mali, and the Somali Republic were largely showpieces rather than an effective contribution to local defense needs. From a Soviet point of view, however, Moscow could hope to win important political gains with relatively little effort and expenditure by complying with African requests. This may help to explain the opportunistic nature of Soviet arms aid diplomacy in Africa.

Nevertheless, the achievements of Russian arms aid policies in Africa were very uneven. In general, the Soviet Union garnered prestige rather than influence in the recipient's domestic or foreign policy decision-making process. The Soviet Union's prompt response to the Nigerian appeal for arms won Moscow the good will of usually pro-western Lagos and other anti-secession tribal factions. But there is nothing yet to suggest that the Russians made decisive inroads. Significantly, the appearance of Russian weapons caused Britain to reappraise its restrictions on export licenses and to accelerate its arms deliveries to Nigeria.

In Guinea, Soviet influence as a result of the arms aid program neither prevented the expulsion of the Soviet ambassador in December 1961, nor helped to secure landing rights for Soviet aircraft during the Cuban missile crisis a year later. In fact, Soviet-Guinean relations distinctly

[65] *New York Times*, April 4, 1959; *Christian Science Monitor,* April 22, 1959.

cooled after the December 1961 incident and did not begin to improve until 1965, when the Russians promised to participate again in new development projects. The Russians also granted some new military assistance when a Guinean defense delegation visited Moscow at that time.[66] Soviet inroads, however, have been partly offset by Cuba's training of Touré's people's militia, the instrument primarily responsible for the country's security.[67]

In the former Belgian Congo, and ultimately in Ghana, the overthrow of Lumumba and Nkrumah resulted in the almost complete failure of Soviet policies. The Ghanaian leader was so closely identified with Soviet and other communist support that popular discontent singled out the Russians for attack: "No more Nkrumah! No more Russians!" crowds shouted after the coup.[68] In view of popular sentiment against communist penetration, Ghana's current military government is unlikely to encourage new Soviet arms aid and ties. The experience of the present leaders in having to fight Russian officers loyal to Nkrumah[69] further argues against a resumption of Soviet arms aid in the near future.

Aid by Proxy. If Soviet arms did not yield increased leverage for Moscow with every recipient, it did provide the Soviet Union with an opportunity to support indirectly subversive groups aimed at overthrowing moderate and pro-western African governments and the white regimes in southern Africa. Guinea, Ghana, Mali, and Tanzania transmitted some of their Soviet bloc equipment to exiled dissident groups enjoying base sanctuaries in their territories. Soviet arms were also re-exported by these countries, as well as by Ben Bella's Algeria and by Egypt. Benefiting from these operations were insurgent groups in moderate African states, including those in the former Belgian Congo and the Cameroon, and the national liberation movements in white-controlled areas. Soviet planes flew Russian military supplies from Ghana and Algeria to Congolese rebels who tried to oust the Tshombe government in the 1964–65 rebellion. Russian instructors were attached to Nkrumah's training centers for subversion.

Soviet efforts to support African insurgents by proxy suffered a serious blow with the political demise of Nkrumah and Ben Bella. The increasing opposition of moderate African governments to subversive activities

[66] In early 1966 the Soviet Union presented Guinea with a gift of two An transport craft. *Africa Research Bulletin, Political, Social and Cultural Series*, vol. 3, no. 3 (March 1-31, 1966), p. 495B.

[67] Touré used the army mainly for civic-action type projects and turned the country's security functions over to the Cuban-trained people's militia.

[68] *Washington Post*, February 26, 1966.

[69] *Ibid.*, March 1, 1966.

abetted and supported by militant Africans and communist agents[70] further prompted the Soviet Union to curtail its subversive operations against independent African states and to limit its support to the national liberation movements, most of which were based in Tanzania. Soviet aid to the freedom fighters remained limited, partly because of the logistic problems, and partly because the liberation movements themselves were divided and had little prospect of success.

Sino-Soviet Rivalry. A factor which argued for continued Soviet support of the liberation movements was the need to counter Chinese influence. Various factions of the freedom fighters in Tanzania had Chinese instructors to teach them guerrilla warfare techniques. These groups received Chinese supplies that came through Dar es Salaam. A key reason for direct and indirect Soviet aid to the Congolese rebels was to block the Chinese from extending their support to the rebels and to show Africans Moscow's support for wars of liberation. The Soviet Union sought thereby to enhance its position in the ideological dispute with Communist China.

The Sino-Soviet rift was also an important element in Soviet arms aid to independent African governments. At the same time that Moscow became involved with aid to Mali, Peking started to court the young republic. Chinese economic aid projects turned out to be quite successful, and Peking evidently reaped much more good will than Moscow. In international affairs Mali increasingly supported Chinese rather than Soviet policies. Growing Chinese influence and a new Chinese economic and technical aid agreement in September 1965 precipitated the Soviet decision to grant Mali additional arms aid a month later.[71]

Soviet military aid efforts in Ghana were similarly designed to offset Chinese influence. Sino-Ghanaian cooperation on economic matters began in 1960 and was soon expanded to include intelligence and subversive activities. The Russians succeeded in excluding the Chinese from working with Nkrumah's presidential guard, but Chinese advisers

[70] The opposition to inter-African subversion was evident at the Addis Ababa Conference in May 1963, when after much debate the Organization of African Unity went on record in its charter as eschewing intervention in the internal affairs of member states. This resentment was even more pronounced at the Nouakchott Conference in February 1965, where fourteen French-speaking states established the Organisation Commune Africaine et Malgache partly in order to oppose African subversion collectively. See Georgetown Research Project, *National Security,* pp. 139ff.

[71] Although there was no official news release, there were strong indications that the Russians made a new arms aid commitment to Mali when President Modibo Keita visited Moscow in October 1965. The next year some new Soviet arms shipments reached Mali via Algeria (*The Times* [London], June 3, 1966). Subsequently the Russians presented Mali with three MiG–17s (*West Africa,* November 2, 1966).

were connected with Nkrumah's subversive operations.[72] Russian arms diplomacy in the Somali Republic was partly aimed at countering the Chinese who had started an offensive of their own in the Horn. The two communist protagonists clearly competed for influence in Zanzibar and later in Tanzania. The Russians trained one Tanzanian battalion and the Chinese another. The existence of two completely separate training camps on Zanzibar—one Russian and one Chinese—led one observer to compare Zanzibar's troops to two separate armies.[73]

Areas of Priority. Chinese efforts in Africa have shifted in recent years from countries on the west coast to east African states. This has triggered a more active Soviet role in the area and may cause Moscow to channel its aid resources more to east Africa. The continued geopolitical importance of the east Africa coast was another factor which brought about an increase in Soviet concern. To consolidate the Soviet position in the eastern Mediterranean, a Soviet bid for a naval presence in the Indian Ocean is highly probable. The projected abandonment of Britain's role east of Suez has drawn Soviet attention to the Indian Ocean and surrounding areas. The port at Berbera in Somalia may have been built by the Russians for possible use by Soviet ships. A Soviet advance into the Indian Ocean is likely to be accompanied by efforts to obtain landing and refueling rights for the Soviet air force. Such facilities are already available in Hodeida and Sana in Yemen.[74] A possible step in this direction is the permission Russia's national airline, Aeroflot, recently obtained to open a service between Moscow and Cairo, Hodeida, and Dar es Salaam.[75]

The availability to the Soviet Union of east African bases would facilitate Russian aid to the national liberation movements that operate out of Tanzania. Soviet assistance to aid the freedom fighters in launching a more sophisticated type of guerrilla war against white-controlled Africa would raise Soviet stock with militant African governments. Particularly if Peking were to step up its activities among the liberation groups, Moscow could be forced into intensifying its support.

[72] In September 1964 Accra negotiated a secret agreement with Peking for the dispatch of Chinese military experts to Ghana to train Africans in the use of Chinese weapons and equipment. The agreement was ratified in August 1965 but came into effect in September 1964. There is some indication that these experts left in late 1965 before their two-year tour was over as a result of Soviet pressure on the Ghanaian government; see Cooley, *East Wind,* pp. 157-60. (The text of the Sino-Ghanaian agreement is also printed in Cooley, Appendix G, 260-61.)

[73] *New York Times,* June 5, 1967.

[74] Soviet air force planes were using the bases at Hodeida and Sana for flying in support for the Yemeni republican forces. See, for example, reports in *New York Times,* January 16, 1968.

[75] *Ibid.,* January 15, 1968.

THE BALANCE SHEET OF SOVIET ARMS AID TO AFRICA

A crucial element in Soviet arms diplomacy in Africa continues to be the objective of eliminating western and especially American influence. At times Soviet action was a specific response to U.S. military aid policies. The $35 million Russian arms deal with the Somali Republic, aimed at countering U.S. influence in neighboring Ethiopia, derived at least in part from the $72.6 million U.S. military assistance program there.[76] Russian involvement in the 1964–65 Congo rebellion was to some extent a reaction to U.S. military assistance to the Congolese government. But the existence of a U.S. arms aid program was not a necessary condition for the Soviet Union to act. Guinea and Nigeria were specifically turned down by the United States for arms aid before the Soviet Union moved in with military assistance, and American military aid to other west African countries was insignificant. As a rule, Soviet military aid policies were formulated with broader goals in mind than offsetting a nearby U.S. arms aid presence. They were designed to erode in general the western position in Africa. Whenever the climate suggested receptivity to Soviet overtures, Moscow proved ready to offer arms assistance to African governments. In consequence, no ideological restrictions inhibited Moscow in its arms aid ventures.

This flexibility and pragmatism was facilitated by the relatively modest allocation in Soviet resources required to support arms aid to Africans. No African state could be expected to use great quantities of weapons or highly sophisticated arms. Even the operation of standard weapons required training. Thus a relatively small investment could yield substantial political benefits for Moscow. The training programs, furthermore, provided the USSR with an opportunity to attempt to influence African military elites. In light of the growing number of military *coups d'état,* the good will, if not support, of the military could be essential to the success of Soviet policies in Africa. For all these reasons arms aid will remain a vital instrument in Moscow's African policies.

Soviet direct and indirect military assistance to African insurgent groups has shifted in emphasis. Initially supporting dissident factions in both independent black and in white-controlled states, the Russians later rendered aid primarily to the national liberation movements, which wanted to overthrow the white regimes. This aid remained more noted for its political effects than its contribution to the military capability of the freedom fighters. By their support of the freedom fighters, Soviet leaders sought to appeal to militant Africans throughout the continent

[76] The $72.6 million represents cumulative U.S. military assistance to Ethiopia through FY 1964. U.S. Department of Defense, *Military Assistance Facts* (Washington, May 1966), p. 14.

and to respond to Chinese charges of betraying the national liberation movements.

Efforts to offset Chinese influence were reflected not only in Soviet activities with dissident groups, but also in Russian aid to African governments. To be sure, the prospects of Chinese inroads and the significance of Chinese competition should not be overrated. China's logistic problems and limited support capabilities place Peking at a great disadvantage with respect to Moscow. Nevertheless, rivalry with China is likely to remain an influential motive in Russian arms diplomacy and could trigger Soviet pre-emptive action to provide arms aid. Chinese operations in east Africa helped to focus Soviet attention more closely on this area.

The evolving power vacuum in the Indian Ocean region, owing to the accelerated British withdrawal from the area east of Suez, further portends increased Soviet efforts to penetrate eastern Africa. Within sub-Saharan Africa the Indian Ocean littoral appears to command priority in future Soviet arms diplomacy.

In retrospect, the Soviet Union has not realized any dramatic results from its military aid programs in Africa. In fact, in Ghana and the two Congos Russian arms aid met with failure. These setbacks have not deterred the Russians from embarking upon new military assistance activities, as recent agreements with Nigeria and the Sudan might suggest. Moscow's arms diplomacy in Africa is an integral part of its overall policy of undermining western influence. By 1967 more than one-fourth of the military establishments in sub-Saharan Africa had received Soviet military assistance, whereas ten years earlier external military influence came solely from western sources. Although Soviet arms aid diplomacy has created neither African satellites nor substantial dependency on the USSR, the Russians are now active competitors for influence over the destinies of African states.

4

SOUTH AND SOUTHEAST ASIA

A REVIEW OF Soviet policies in the South and Southeast Asia region[1] during the last two decades indicates some of the basic changes that have occurred in Soviet political strategy toward the developing world. In the early years after World War II Moscow denounced the Asian leaders and looked hopefully toward the outbreak of revolutions in the newly independent Asian states. At the end of 1954 Soviet leaders endorsed Nehru's Pancha Shilla program on principles of peaceful coexistence, which called for mutual respect for each other's sovereignty and territorial integrity.[2]

Under the Stalin regime the Soviet Union refused to contribute to the development of the former colonial states; by the end of 1966, however, Moscow had allocated almost $3 billion in economic aid[3] and well over $2 billion[4] in military assistance to South and Southeast Asian countries alone.

These relatively large dollar commitments underscore the change in Soviet foreign policy as well as the importance Moscow attaches to South and Southeast Asia. While the region is not the most crucial one in the emerging world for Soviet decision-makers, it nevertheless ranks first among the world's developing regions in Russian economic aid and second in Soviet arms aid. The current positions of Indonesia and India

[1] For the purpose of this study the South and Southeast Asia region comprises Afghanistan, Pakistan, India, Burma, Thailand, Laos, Cambodia, North and South Vietnam, Malaysia, Singapore, the Philippines, Brunei, Indonesia, and Ceylon.

[2] Nehru's five principles of coexistence were originally embodied in the Sino-Indian agreement of April 1954. They were: mutual respect for each other's territorial integrity and sovereignty, non-aggression, cooperation for mutual benefit, non-interference in each other's domestic affairs, and peaceful coexistence.

[3] Aid to North Vietnam is not included. U.S. Department of State, *Aid and Trade in 1966*, p. 2.

[4] Excluding arms aid to North Vietnam. See Table 4-1.

among the four largest recipients of Soviet arms aid contrast markedly with the bitter Soviet denunciations to which their leaders were exposed some two decades ago.

One of the major factors from which South and Southeast Asia derives its prominence in Soviet policy toward the non-aligned world is the triangular competition among the United States, the Soviet Union, and Communist China. Because of its location at China's periphery, South and Southeast Asia became, as the Sino-Soviet split emerged, the region where the three-way rivalry was most intensely felt. Whereas in the fifties Soviet policy in South and Southeast Asia principally aimed at eroding U.S. positions and influence, after 1960–61 Soviet diplomacy and activities also sought to counter Chinese initiatives. More than anywhere else Soviet activities in this area are conditioned by both U.S. and Chinese policies.

Soviet military aid diplomacy in particular experienced the pressures, and usually the conflicting pressures, of American and Chinese postures in South and Southeast Asia. Soviet arms aid initiatives and policies registered Moscow's intentions in its duel with Washington on the one hand and with Peking on the other. An analysis of Soviet military aid provides, therefore, not only a guide for projecting trends in future arms aid, but also a key indicator of the direction of Soviet foreign policy.

SOUTH AND SOUTHEAST ASIA IN SOVIET FOREIGN POLICY

After Stalin's death in March 1953, changes in communist doctrine permitted a greater degree of flexibility in the Soviet approach toward the neutralist nations. The evolving policy of peaceful coexistence called for cooperation with the non-aligned world. At the same time U.S. efforts to enlist allies against Soviet expansionism and to establish at least cordial relations with a number of Asian countries appeared to be succeeding. Pakistan's acceptance of U.S. military aid in 1954 suggested possible realization of the American aim to form a defensive alliance among the northern tier countries. These developments combined to prompt a revision in Soviet policy toward the states of the Asian subcontinent, as well as toward those in other parts of the developing world.

One of the earliest countries singled out for a rapprochement with the Soviet Union was Afghanistan. From a Soviet point of view, the 1,200-mile-long border between the two countries contributed to the selection of Afghanistan as one of the first countries to benefit from the post-Stalin policy of creating close ties with non-aligned nations. Soviet leaders looked upon Afghanistan as a buffer state and wanted to prevent Afghanistan's incorporation in the western alliance structure. Indic- ative of Russian concern was a warning by the Soviet Foreign Minister in early 1954 that U.S. military aid to Pakistan "made it necessary for the Soviet Union to think about our neighbor, Afghanistan's defense, and make sure we [the Soviet Union] are safe."[5]

While Soviet interests in other neutral Asian countries did not reflect such direct national security considerations, Moscow wanted to insure the continued non-alignment of these countries. The Soviet Union had to counter U.S. inroads and increase its own influence if it wished to draw the Asian powers closer to the Soviet orbit. Within this context, India and Indonesia became major targets of Soviet diplomacy. Moscow tried especially to court Indian leaders in the hope that they as major spokesmen for non-aligned Asia would facilitate Soviet access to other members of the so-called Third World.

The new Soviet policy of peaceful coexistence was also applied to the Indochina peninsula, where additional factors prompted the Rus- sians to contribute to the settlement of the French-Indochina war at the Geneva Conference of July 1954. On the one hand, U.S. Secretary of State John Foster Dulles had in early 1954 announced the policy of massive retaliation and was soon thereafter trying to persuade his Euro- pean allies to support "united action" against communism in Indochina. If the Geneva Conference were to have failed, the United States and its allies might well have agreed to escalate the Indochina war, thereby con- fronting the Soviet Union with the choice of becoming involved in the war and risking an armed conflict with the United States, or permitting a defeat of the Vietnamese communists. On the other hand, Moscow had more vital interests in Europe. Some reports suggested that Moscow was prepared to help stop the Indochina war in exchange for France's rejection of the European Defense Community proposal under consid- eration by the French National Assembly at the time. (It was subse- quently defeated.)[6] Most observers agree that strong Russian pressure on the Vietnamese and Chinese communists contributed to their accept- ing the Geneva agreements, under which Laos and Cambodia were neutralized and Vietnam temporarily partitioned at the seventeenth

---

[5] *New York Times*, June 7, 1954.

[6] Whether the French government did make a tacit agreement with the Soviet Union to this effect, as some critics claim, or whether the government was in any case powerless to prevent the defeat of EDC by the National Assembly, in August 1954 the National Assembly rejected EDC without encountering any government intervention aimed at reversing the outcome.

parallel.[7] With the settlement of the Indochina war achieved for the time being, the Soviet Union began to promote its objectives through a peaceful coexistence policy.

ARMS AID INITIATIVES IN NEUTRALIST ASIA

In view of neutralist inclinations in much of South and Southeast Asia, the U.S. policy of sponsoring mutual defense alliances, notably the SEATO pact of September 1954 and the subsequent Baghdad Pact, generally held less attraction for Asian leaders than Nehru's advocacy of the Pancha Shilla program. Soviet endorsement of Nehru's program and Russian efforts to exploit the opposition to western defense alliances found, therefore, a receptive climate in some of the key Asian countries—and in Afghanistan in particular.

Afghanistan viewed with serious misgivings the western-supported defense buildup of neighboring Iran and Pakistan. Kabul's running dispute with Pakistan over the issue of Pakistan's northern frontier province Pushtunistan[8] compounded Afghanistan's concern over U.S. military aid to Pakistan, its major regional opponent. Washington's refusal to provide similar assistance to Kabul made Moscow a logical source for Afghanistan's defense requirements. Because Afghanistan presented the earliest opportunity for Soviet military aid inroads and because its location at the Soviet frontier provided a security incentive for Soviet involvement, Afghanistan became the first Russian arms aid recipient in the region.

The door to Soviet bloc military influence in Afghanistan was opened by Khrushchev and Bulganin during their visit to Kabul in December 1955. Soon afterwards in early 1956 Afghanistan signed formal arms aid agreements with the Soviet Union and Czechoslovakia. The first deliveries on the aid accords arrived the same year and included eleven MiG–15 fighters, one Il–14 cargo plane, two Mi–4 helicopters, mobile radio units, and small arms.[9] Soviet instructors and maintenance per-

[7] See Donald Lancaster, *The Emancipation of French Indochina* (London: Oxford University Press, 1961), pp. 293, 334; and Donald S. Zagoria, *Vietnam Triangle* (New York: Pegasus, 1967), p. 40.

[8] Afghanistan contended that the Pathans who lived in Pakistan's northwest frontier province had a right to decide whether they wanted to form an independent state. Since Pakistan's independence in 1947, Afghanistan had been demanding a plebiscite for Pushtunistan, a demand which Pakistan has consistently rejected. Relations between Afghanistan and Pakistan had deteriorated up to the point that Pakistan in 1955 closed the road to Karachi over which Afghanistan had previously trucked most of its exports. Shortly thereafter Afghanistan arranged its first arms deal with the Soviet Union. See R. K. Ramazani, *The Northern Tier* (Princeton: D. Van Nostrand, 1966), pp. 124-48.

[9] *New York Times*, October 29, 1956; *Christian Science Monitor*, November 24, 1956.

sonnel accompanied the aircraft. A new Russian-built jet airstrip in northern Afghanistan, near the Soviet military base at Termez, was available as a servicing center for the jets shipped to Afghanistan. Substantial Soviet and some Czech arms deliveries reached Afghanistan in the following years; by the end of 1960 the cumulative total of Soviet bloc military aid ran well over $100 million.[10]

In addition to its military assistance program, the Soviet Union undertook a number of economic development projects that also had military implications. The Russians constructed air bases at Mazar and Bagram in the north and at Farah near the Iranian border. A new highway connected the Soviet railway terminal at Kushka with Herat and Kandahar. The most spectacular Russian project in Afghanistan was the highway and tunnel through the heart of the forbidding Hindu Kush mountain range that linked Kabul with the northern provinces and with the Soviet river port on the Oxus. These highways gave the Soviet Union for the first time a year-round, direct access to the Asian subcontinent south of the Hindu Kush.

The Russian decision to grant Afghanistan military aid was a response to the formation of SEATO and the Baghdad Pact. The Soviet leaders perceived the western-sponsored alliances as a threat at their southern border areas. No such security considerations governed Soviet policy toward Indonesia, which is geographically far removed from Soviet borders. Just as Washington had carried the offensive to the USSR in southwestern Asia, so Moscow was on the offensive in Indonesia in early 1958, when the latter obtained the first major credits to procure materiel from Czechoslovakia and Poland.[11] The arms aid Djakarta received in the next two years under the 1958 accords had an estimated value of up to $250 million. The weapons included five Avia cargo planes, some forty MiG–15s, fifty MiG–17s, a number of Il–28 bombers, two submarines, four destroyers, submarine chasers, and small arms.[12]

There were several parallels between the Indonesian and Afghanistani decision to move toward the Soviet bloc and away from the west. Like Afghanistan, Indonesia first turned to the United States for military aid.

---

[10] U.S. Congress, House of Representatives, Subcommittee on Foreign Operations of the Committee on Appropriations, *Hearings for FY 1962*, 87th Cong., 1st Sess. (1961), p. 703.

[11] *Times of Indonesia*, April 19, 1958. Earlier in 1957, the Soviet Union had permitted Indonesia to divert part of an economic loan for the acquisition of four thousand jeeps and two oil tankers for the Indonesian armed forces. *Ibid.*, June 11, 1958. Daniel Wolfstone, "Foreign Aid to Indonesia: From East and West," *Far Eastern Economic Review*, vol. 26, no. 15 (April 9, 1959), p. 508.

[12] Data derived from daily newspaper reports, including *New York Times,* May 28, 1958; *Times of Indonesia*, October 6, 1958; *Nieuwe Rotterdamse Courant*, January 6, 1961.

Afghanistan had argued that the buildup of the armed forces of its traditional rivals posed a threat to its security; Indonesia based its plea for U.S. arms aid on the need to combat rebellions which challenged the existence of the national government in Djakarta.[13] An additional motivation for Indonesia was the desire to lend credibility to its demands that the Dutch surrender control of western New Guinea to the Indonesians. Afghanistan and Indonesia both felt that they had legitimate reasons for requesting American military assistance. Both resented U.S. refusals and turned to Washington's major opponent. The widely held Indonesian conviction that the United States supported the rebels against the Djakarta government precipitated the arms deal with the Soviet bloc.

Receptivity to Russian arms aid overtures also facilitated the establishment of Soviet military aid ties with India. Before the first Soviet-Indian arms aid agreement in November 1960, India filled its defense requirements in western nations—mostly in Britain. Anxious to reinforce its commitment to non-alignment in international relations, India wanted to reduce its dependence on the west for arms and diversify its supply sources. Equally important, India regarded Pakistan as a major threat to its position on the Asian subcontinent and sought to acquire modern equipment to match the weaponry Pakistan received from the United States. According to Indian spokesmen, only the United States and the Soviet Union were able to furnish the heavy transport aircraft and helicopters suited to India's high altitude and climatic conditions.[14] When the Soviet Union proposed to meet Indian demands for considerably less cost than the United States, and when Moscow, unlike Washington, was prepared to receive payment in Indian currency or commodities, India decided to accept the Soviet offer.[15] The arrangement reportedly covered some $31.5 million in Soviet aid and included eight An–12 and twenty-four Il–14 transport planes, ten Mi–4 helicopters, and equipment for the development of communications in India's northern border zone.[16]

[13] Virtually from the beginning of Indonesia's independence, the national government faced a series of rebellions by dissident factions, mostly in areas outside Java, who blamed the Djakarta regime for over-centralization, neglect of outer regions, corruption, and too much leniency toward the communists. Between 1956 and 1958 disaffection on the outer islands intensified. In February 1958 this culminated in the establishment of a rival government in Sumatra. A good summary of the various regionalist challenges to the Djakarta government is presented in Herbert Feith and Daniel S. Lev, "The End of the Indonesian Rebellion," *Pacific Affairs*, vol. 36, no. 1 (Spring 1963), pp. 632-46.

[14] See the defense of the Indian-Soviet arms accord by Defense Minister V. K. Krishna Menon, *Hindustan Times* (New Delhi), April 13, 1961.

[15] *Christian Science Monitor*, October 15, 1960; *Times of India*, October 4, 1960.

[16] *Times of India*, October 4, 1960; *New York Times,* April 2, 1961.

From a Soviet point of view, the establishment of a Russian military assistance presence in India was in part a response to American arms aid diplomacy in the SEATO area. The Soviet Union wanted to offset U.S. weapons aid to Pakistan and to counter American efforts to strengthen the northern tier. Taking advantage of Indian concern over Pakistan's defense buildup, Moscow moved to add New Delhi to its arms aid recipients. By diminishing India's reliance on western military equipment and technology, Moscow hoped to undermine western influence in India and to link New Delhi more intimately with Moscow. Soviet arms aid further served to identify Soviet policy with India's nationalist aspirations. The 1962 accords sought particularly to underscore this point. In early 1962, and again in the summer of that year, India received new credits to finance additional helicopters and transport craft.[17] More importantly, the Soviet Union agreed at the same time to help India build two production facilities. The first would produce and assemble MiG-21s; the second would manufacture engines for a supersonic jet under development in India.[18] The Soviet Union also pledged to deliver a number of MiG-21 jets which India claimed it needed to counter Pakistan's acquisition of F-104 fighters from the United States.[19] Thus American military aid to Pakistan again facilitated a Soviet military aid initiative in India.

Similarly, American military aid activities in Laos helped to bring the USSR into Laos as arms donor. Laos was split into three factions struggling for power: the pro-western "right wing" faction, which included most of the military hierarchy and was backed by U.S. aid; the communist Pathet Lao, which was supported by North Vietnam; and the neutralists led by Premier Souvanna Phouma, who had been ousted by the right wing forces in 1958, but had managed to regain the premiership in August 1960. Souvanna Phouma hoped to reunify the civil-war-torn country under a coalition government of the Pathet Lao, the right wing faction, and the neutralists. But neither the Pathet Lao, which succeeded in consolidating its control over northern Laos, nor the southern-based right wing forces, which continued to receive U.S. military aid, were willing to come to a negotiated settlement. When the right wing forces stepped up their military action and threatened to

[17] *New York Times*, February 1, 1962; *Christian Science Monitor*, August 24, 1962.

[18] *New York Times*, August 18, 1968; *ibid*., August 24, 1962. In September 1961 the Indian government had purchased six Soviet jet engines for the HF-24. Because of India's dissatisfaction with the performance of Soviet engines, however, the agreement to manufacture engines for the HF-24 did not materialize.

[19] *Hindustan Times*, June 24, 1962.

approach the Laotian capital Vientiane with the objective of ousting Souvanna Phouma, the latter in November 1960 turned to the Soviet Union for help. Moscow, which had long been on record as supporting neutralist, "bourgeois-nationalist" regimes such as that of Souvanna Phouma, and opposing the "export of counterrevolution" by the west, complied with an airlift of weapons from Hanoi to Laos.[20]

Shortly thereafter, the right wing army's advance on Vientiane forced Souvanna Phouma into exile and the neutralist troops into a coalition with the Pathet Lao. Russian military aid was redirected to the combined Pathet Lao-neutralist forces which regrouped in north central Laos.[21] Soviet deliveries in December 1960 and in the first few months of 1961 included artillery pieces, anti-aircraft guns, armored cars, ammunition, combat rations, and other war materiel.[22] Personnel of the communist faction were sent to the Soviet Union for training.[23]

The Soviet Union intervened in the Laotian civil war partly to counter U.S. support of the right wing faction. Moscow, however, was also competing with Peking for influence in North Vietnam, which had already encouraged the Pathet Lao in Laos as well as the Viet Cong in South Vietnam. If the Russians had permitted the right wing forces to come into power in Laos, the Chinese, who accused the Russians of betraying the wars of national liberation and who advocated an extremely militant course of action, might have enhanced their influence in North Vietnam at the expense of the Russians. It probably was not a coincidence that almost at the same time, in early 1961, the Soviet Union began an arms airlift to the Viet Cong insurgents at their Laotian border bases.[24]

Moscow's short range goals in Laos were largely achieved with the Geneva Accords of July 1962, which called for the withdrawal of foreign troops (including American military advisers) from Laos, guaranteed the neutral status of Laos, and disassociated Laos from its

---

[20] *New York Times,* November 23, 1960; *ibid.,* December 12, 1960.

[21] For a detailed account of Laotian developments during this period, see Bernard Fall, "The Pathet Lao," in *The Communist Revolution in Asia,* ed. Robert A. Scalapino (Englewood Cliffs, New Jersey: Prentice Hall, 1966), pp. 186ff; Oliver E. Clubb, Jr., *The United States and the Sino-Soviet Bloc in Southeast Asia* (Washington: The Brookings Institution, 1962), pp. 64ff; and Roger M. Smith, "Laos in Perspective," *Asian Survey,* vol. 3, no. 1 (January 1963), pp. 61-68.

[22] *New York Times,* December 15, 1960; *ibid.,* January 4, 1961; *ibid.,* March 3, 1961; *ibid.,* May 18, 1961. In the last two weeks of December 1960, Soviet aircraft flew 184 missions to Laos: see Arthur Dommen, *Conflict in Laos: The Politics of Neutralization* (New York: Praeger, 1964), p. 178.

[23] According to one report, some seventy Laotians were sent to the Soviet Union for training: *Washington Post,* January 15, 1961.

[24] U.S. Department of State, *A Threat to the Peace: North Vietnam's Effort to Conquer South Vietnam,* Publication 7308 (Washington, 1961), p. 42.

former protection under SEATO.[25] The three Laotian factions agreed on the formation of a coalition government under the premiership of Souvanna Phouma. Thus, with Soviet help, a Laotian government was created which was friendly to neither the United States nor to Communist China.

The establishment of a tripartite government did not restore peace to Laos. The three factions retained their separate armies, and by the end of 1962 it had become obvious to the neutralists that the Pathet Lao was the real threat to Laotian stability. In April 1963 fighting broke out again, this time between the Pathet Lao and a coalition of the neutralist and right wing forces.

With the exception of a gift in December 1962 of nine transport planes and one helicopter, to be distributed among the three factions,[26] the Soviet Union halted its aid to the neutralists. A request from Souvanna Phouma for Soviet spare parts and ammunition in the spring of 1964 was turned down,[27] in spite of gradually growing U.S. support for the neutralist-right wing coalition forces.[28] Hanoi, which appeared to be moving closer to Peking, began to take over the role of major arms supplier to the Pathet Lao.

Some Soviet war materiel continued to flow to the Laotian communist guerrillas, but the growing pro-Chinese leanings of the Pathet Lao meant that a communist victory in Laos would enlarge the Chinese sphere of influence. Soviet efforts to aid both the neutralists and the Pathet Lao had yielded significant influence over neither. Increasingly losing its influence even with the Pathet Lao, the Soviet Union terminated all direct aid to Laos in the spring of 1964.

Within the Indochina area the threatening ascendancy of Peking over Hanoi became more and more the object of Soviet concern. Moscow's problems intensified after the Tonkin Gulf events of August 1964 led to a controlled escalation of American involvement in the Vietnamese war. A major objective of the USSR remained the avoidance of an armed confrontation with the United States. It also became increasingly important for the Soviet Union to reverse the pro-Chinese trend in

[25] For a text of the Geneva agreements, see Great Britain, *International Conference on the Settlement of the Laotian Question, Geneva, May 12, 1961 to July 23, 1962*, Laos No. 1, Cmnd. 1828 (London: H.M. Stationery Office, 1962), pp. 15ff.

[26] *New York Times*, December 18, 1962. In June 1963 Moscow agreed to replace two planes which had been allotted to the neutralists, but which had been destroyed in crash landings. *Ibid.*, June 12, 1963.

[27] *Ibid.*, May 30, 1964.

[28] When the Pathet Lao began to push the neutrals from their positions in the Plaine des Jarres in 1963, within a year after the Geneva Agreements, the United States resumed military aid to the Laotian government.

Hanoi, in order to show the world that the USSR, and not Communist China, was the leader of the communist movement.

To achieve the latter goal, the Soviet Union could not compromise on its aid commitment to Hanoi and the Viet Cong. Russian leaders sought, therefore, to emphasize Hanoi's dependence on Moscow by stepping up their arms aid to North Vietnam. The major part of the weapons aid, however, was defensive, such as the SA–2 Guideline missile systems and the anti-aircraft batteries. The first official indication of an increase in arms aid to North Vietnam was given in the Soviet-North Vietnamese joint statement on February 11, 1965, in which Moscow pledged to strengthen the defense capability of Hanoi.[29] Russian military assistance to the Viet Cong insurgents in the south, which had remained limited from the start, was channeled through Hanoi. Ironically, Washington's policy of restraint in the Vietnamese war permitted Moscow to increase its support of Hanoi with a minimum risk of direct involvement and at the same time to offset Peking's anti-Soviet charges.

Efforts to counter both U.S. and Chinese influence were also reflected in Soviet aid policy for Cambodia. Until 1963 Cambodia had managed to pursue a policy that avoided friction in its relations with its traditional opponents Thailand and South Vietnam, and permitted it to accept U.S. military and economic aid despite the protests of its neighbors. By 1963, however, Cambodia's leaders had apparently become convinced that North Vietnam would succeed in defeating its southern counterpart. While they were even more concerned about facing a reunified Vietnam than a divided Vietnam, they expected that a unified Vietnam would be closely allied with, if not dominated by, Communist China. The only power, in their view, that could then offer Cambodia any guarantees against Vietnamese aggression would be Communist China. This evaluation called for an accommodation with China.[30]

Cambodia's President Sihanouk and his followers further believed that Peking would become the most influential power in Southeast Asia. To ensure Chinese support for Cambodia against potential Vietnamese expansionism, and at the same time to protect Cambodia's sovereignty and neutrality against China, Sihanouk began to lean toward Peking and to turn against Washington. A consequence of Sihanouk's policy

[29] *Pravda*, February 11, 1965. The dilemmas the USSR faced in its relations with North Vietnam and Communist China concerning the Vietnamese war are succinctly discussed in Zagoria, *Vietnam Triangle,* Chapter 2.

[30] Cambodia's policy toward its neighbors and China at the time is summarized in Bernard K. Gordon, *The Dimensions of Conflict in Southeast Asia* (Englewood Cliffs, N.J.: Prentice Hall, 1966), Chapter 2. See also Roger M. Smith, "Cambodia," in *Government and Politics of Southeast Asia*, ed. George McT. Kahin (Ithaca, N.Y.: Cornell University Press, 1964), pp. 662-71.

of trying to create a "balance among menaces"—Thailand, Vietnam, and China[31]—was his termination of U.S. aid in November 1963. Both Moscow and Peking were logical substitute suppliers of weapons against Phnom Penh's western-supported neighbors.

From Moscow's standpoint, the Cambodian government's strenuous efforts to steer a neutralist course while courted by both the United States and Communist China made the improvement of Soviet-Cambodian ties politically desirable. Soviet interests would be served by strengthening Cambodia against Thailand and South Vietnam, the allies of the United States. The Russians also wanted to stem the rise of Chinese influence in Cambodia. Cambodia was one of the few countries where the Chinese had managed to outbid the Russians in economic aid.[32] When Cambodia's foreign policy took on a marked pro-Chinese coloring during 1963, the Russians apparently decided to use their military aid instrument to challenge the Chinese in Cambodia. In September 1963 the Soviet Union promised to send Cambodia a small air defense system. The equipment, which consisted of three MiG–17s, twenty-four anti-aircraft guns, a radar station, a jet trainer, trucks, and mobile field units, was delivered in February 1964.[33] Not to be outdone by the Russians, the Chinese a week later agreed to help Cambodia build two jet airbases.[34]

In October 1964 Peking initiated the next round of aid commitments with a pledge of weapons to Cambodia. A month later another supply of Soviet materiel arrived; it included two MiG–17 jets, forty military vehicles, eight 85mm anti-aircraft artillery, and sixteen 67mm artillery pieces.[35] The November 1964 shipment occurred, moreover, at a time when Moscow was coveting support against Peking in its drive to be included in the forthcoming Second Afro-Asian Conference. By the time of the indefinite postponement of the Afro-Asian conference in July 1965, support of North Vietnam had taken precedence over Cambodia's security needs in Soviet military aid policy. The Russians did not furnish any more arms aid to Cambodia until April 1967, at which time they made five more MiG–17s, two An transport planes, trucks,

[31] *Ibid.*, pp. 58-59.
[32] By mid-1963 Cambodia had negotiated two major economic development grants for almost $50 million with China. In contrast, it had accepted a Soviet gift of only $6 million and a loan for another $12 million which the Russians had already offered as far back as 1960. U.S. Department of State, *The Communist Economic Offensive through 1963*, Research Memorandum RSB-43 (Washington, June 18, 1964), pp. 24, 34.
[33] *Washington Post,* February 9, 1964.
[34] *New York Times*, February 18, 1964.
[35] *Ibid.,* November 3, 1964.

and additional anti-aircraft guns and equipment available[36] to demonstrate their sympathy with Cambodia's alarms over U.S. and South Vietnamese incursions into Cambodian territory in pursuit of Viet Cong forces.

Eventually, the Sino-Soviet dispute also had its implications for Russian arms diplomacy in Indonesia, even though it affected Soviet policy there less than in the Indochina peninsula. Nevertheless, competition with both the United States and Communist China influenced Soviet arms diplomacy toward the vast island republic.

When the Sino-Soviet split broke into the open in 1960, Chinese relations with Indonesia were at a low ebb as a result of the discriminatory measures the Indonesian government was taking against the local Chinese population. In contrast, the Soviet Union appeared to be firmly implanted in Indonesia as its principal diplomatic, economic, and military supporter. Moscow had little to fear from inroads by Peking in Indonesia and its aid program mainly aimed at isolating Indonesia from the west. Between late 1960 and 1963 the Soviet Union extended a number of arms credits to Indonesia, with the result that the cumulative total of Soviet arms aid approached the $1 billion mark.[37] Terms for repayment were low, requiring two or two and one-half percent interest, usually for ten years. By furnishing arms without imposing political conditions, without attempting to interfere in Indonesia's defense policies, and without limiting Indonesia's selection of modern and sophisticated weapons systems, the Soviet Union tried to prove its respect for Indonesian sovereignty. In reality, Moscow hoped to ensure Indonesian dependence on the Soviet Union for arms and spare parts and through heavy arms debts to force Djakarta into a closer political and economic relation with its creditor. Another objective of the Soviet weapons assistance program was to diminish the Indonesian army's hostility to communism and thus to win over the most powerful anti-communist sector of Indonesian society. In addition, during 1961 and 1962 Indonesia was engaged in an intensive campaign to drive the Dutch out of West New Guinea (Irian), and the USSR consistently presented its massive weapons deliveries to Indonesia as tangible evidence of Soviet endorsement of the struggle for the national liberation of New Guinea. This justification was directed at refuting Peking's claim that Moscow had abandoned its encouragement of national liberation movements.

After the Irian crisis had been settled, the Indonesian government in 1963 launched its anti-Malaysia policy. Within Indonesia each of the

---

[36] *Washington Post*, April 10, 1967.

[37] *Ibid.*, March 31, 1963; Guy Pauker, "Indonesia: Internal Development or External Expansion?" *Asian Survey*, vol. 3, no. 2 (February 1963), p. 73.

three major rival groups—Sukarno and his clique, the Indonesian Communist Party (PKI), and the army leaders—had a special interest in continuing Indonesia's international crises.[38] For Sukarno, Indonesia's security crises served to divert domestic attention from mismanagement and corruption at home and to rally the heterogenous masses around a common cause against a foreign enemy.

For the PKI, the Malaysia issue provided an opportunity to foment intense anti-western sentiments. It was also important for the PKI to have the army engaged at the Malaysian periphery, thereby reducing the strength of its most serious rival on Java, the main island. Finally, the burden of military expenses was bound to deepen the economic crisis at home and perhaps facilitate the PKI's accession to power.

Indonesian military leaders favored securing Soviet arms, which they needed to strengthen their position in Indonesia, particularly vis-à-vis the PKI. They had a vital interest in creating a powerful military establishment, which the existence of actual or imagined threats abetted. Most army leaders, however, came to recognize that the so-called Malaysia confrontation threatened to enhance the PKI's position at the expense of the power of the armed forces, and of the army in particular. The threat would be greater if sustained fighting were to occur against the British. Although army spokesmen continued to pay lip service to the "crush Malaysia" goal, army troops remained stationed on Java. Djakarta was forced to rely on volunteers and air force troops for guerrilla fighters in North Borneo and Malaya.[39]

The Malaysia issue was a key factor that contributed to a rapprochement between Indonesia and Communist China. The anti-communist views of Malaysia's leader Abdul Rahman had long been known. It could be expected that Peking would not remain indifferent to the creation of an avowedly anti-communist state in an area that the Chinese

[38] In addition to domestic factors that triggered Indonesia's "Crush Malaysia" campaign, there were foreign policy considerations as well. Indonesians generally viewed Malaysia as an instrument of British imperialism. This point is persuasively argued in George McT. Kahin, "Malaysia and Indonesia," *Pacific Affairs*, vol. 37, no. 3 (Fall 1964), pp. 253-70. Other scholars have drawn attention to the aspirations of Indonesian politicians to insure for their nation the leading position in southeast Asia. See Donald Hindley, "Indonesia's Confrontation with Malaysia: A Search for Motives," *Asian Survey*, vol. 4, no. 6 (June 1964), pp. 904-13; and Bernard K. Gordon, "The Potential for Indonesian Expansionism," *Pacific Affairs*, vol. 36, no. 4 (Winter 1963–64), pp. 379-93.

[39] General Omar Dhani, the Indonesian Air Force Chief of Staff, who lacked a domestic power base and whose position depended largely on Sukarno, supported the Malaysia confrontation as well as the creation of the Djakarta-Peking axis. The army leaders generally did not. They quietly pushed instead army civic action programs on Java, partly in order to re-establish army influence at the village level. The results of army civic action efforts contributed to the outcome of the October 1965 countercoup and the army's accession to power.

had traditionally considered to be of major interest to them. Peking became the most enthusiastic champion of the "crush Malaysia" policy which Djakarta pursued from 1963 to 1966.[40] The Malaysia question simultaneously gave Communist China an opportunity to enlist an ally in its rivalry with the Soviet Union in Asia.

The development of the Djakarta-Peking axis during 1963–65 was facilitated by the fact that China's advocacy of armed revolution was much closer to the revolutionary ideology and temper of Indonesia's political leaders than the more cautious policy of the Soviet Union. Another major factor in the growing rapport between Peking and Djakarta was Moscow's reluctance to throw its full weight behind the confrontation policy.

Unlike the West Irian issue, the Malaysia crisis posed some serious policy problems for the Soviet Union. There was a distinct difference between Moscow's enthusiastic support of the Irian policy and its almost reluctant endorsement of the Malaysia confrontation.[41] In 1964 the Soviet Union had embarked on trying to foster a less hostile climate for coexistence with the United States. Soviet backing of Indonesia's Malaysia policy risked jeopardizing the developing détente. The deepening Sino-Soviet rift further upset Soviet policy toward Djakarta. If Indonesia, encouraged by Russian military assistance, went to war over Malaysia, the most likely beneficiary in Indonesia would be the PKI. The latter, which had its own interests to promote in the Malaysia confrontation, sided, however, with Peking in the Sino-Soviet dispute when Soviet hesitation to support Indonesia became clear.

Continued Soviet military aid, on the other hand, could help to reverse Indonesia's increasing affinity for Communist China and to obtain Indonesian support for Soviet policies in the Afro-Asian world. The Russians particularly wanted Indonesia to sponsor Moscow's attendance at the preparatory meeting of the Second Afro-Asian Conference at Djakarta in April 1964 and of the conference itself in 1965.[42] To refuse

[40] The Malaysia confrontation lost momentum after the October 1965 coup and countercoup in Indonesia. The confrontation was officially ended in June 1966, when Indonesia and Malaysia agreed to restore friendly relations.

[41] A discussion of the differences in Soviet statements on the Irian and Malaysia issues is presented in Nadia Derkach, "The Soviet Policy Towards Indonesia in the West Irian and the Malaysian Disputes," *Asian Survey*, vol. 5, no. 11 (November 1965), pp. 566-71.

[42] The Russians were excluded from the preparatory meeting in Djakarta. During the June 1964 visit of Soviet Deputy Premier Anastas I. Mikoyan to Indonesia, Mikoyan reminded Sukarno of Indonesia's arms debts and asked Sukarno to sponsor Soviet participation in the Afro-Asian Conference; see Willard A. Hanna, "The Indonesia Crisis—Mid-1964 Phase," *American Universities Field Staff, Southeast Asia Series*, vol. 12, no. 7 (August 1964), p. 6. The actual conference, sched-

Indonesian requests for arms would have risked the loss of Moscow's dwindling influence in Djakarta and would have increased Peking's influence. The Russians also hoped to move the PKI back toward Moscow.

Russian arms diplomacy in 1963 and 1964 reflected the Soviet dilemma over Indonesia. In late 1963 the Soviet Union signed an agreement with Indonesia which provided for a limited supply of weapons and for a moratorium on arms payments.[43] Moscow's and Prague's negotiations with Djakarta in October 1964 produced additional military aid credits—mostly for An–12 cargo craft, helicopters, and trainers—and another postponement in payments on Indonesia's arms debts.[44] The Russians also agreed to accelerate deliveries of previously promised weaponry. But the 1963 and 1964 accords were noted more for Moscow's political and economic concessions than for new commitments in military hardware.

In spite of its generous aid, the Soviet Union failed to arrest Indonesia's drift toward Communist China. Nor did the Indonesians display any urgency about repaying their more than $1 billion debt to the Russians. These facts, combined perhaps with the change in leadership in the Soviet Union itself, largely accounted for Soviet reluctance to extend another important arms loan to Indonesia in 1965.

The September-October 1965 upheavals in Indonesia eventually resulted in the army's accession to power, the bloody repression of the PKI, and an end to collaboration between Djakarta and Peking. While in the Afro-Asian world Moscow clearly benefitted from Peking's setback, within Indonesia the intense outburst of anti-communism precluded any quick efforts to reassert Soviet influence in Indonesia. The end of the Malaysia confrontation and Djakarta's rapprochement with the Hague suggested that Britain, Malaysia, and the Netherlands were the greatest external gainers of the 1965 coup and countercoup. Indonesia's new leaders, moreover, concentrated on trying to solve their country's immense economic problems and were unwilling to assume any new debts for armaments, except for badly needed spare parts. Under these circumstances Moscow's continued hesitance to offer additional arms aid was not surprising. Although in November 1966 the Soviet Union had virtually no other choice but to consent once more to

---

uled for June 1965 in Algiers, was later postponed as a result of the military coup in Algeria. For Sino-Soviet rivalry with respect to the Second Afro-Asian Conference, see William E. Griffith, *Sino-Soviet Relations, 1964-1965* (Cambridge, Mass.: The M.I.T. Press, 1967), pp. 56-58.

[43] *Washington Post*, December 13, 1963; Hanna, "Indonesia Crisis," p. 5.

[44] *Washington Post*, October 3, 1964; *New York Times*, October 16, 1964.

a rescheduling of Indonesia's arms debts,[45] no commitments for new weapons were made in 1966 or in 1967.

The divergent objectives of Moscow and Peking, prompted in part by different ideological perspectives, but probably in larger measure by opposing national interests, are illustrated in the history of Soviet arms aid to Indonesia. Their conflicting policies are even more dramatically displayed with respect to Russian military aid to India.

During 1958, in spite of earlier declarations of mutual friendship, Sino-Indian relations began to deteriorate. While the reasons for mutual disenchantment were complex, a major point of contention was India's stress on neutralism rather than anti-colonialism, i.e., the anti-American variant of neutralism that China insisted that neutrals follow. China also claimed certain areas of India's Himalayan border region.[46] Chinese forays into Ladakh Province at India's northern border in 1959 created further friction between the two countries.

In addition China deeply resented Moscow's attitude in the Sino-Indian border clashes. The Soviet Union, careful to avoid jeopardizing Soviet-Indian relations, but reluctant to offend China, adopted a neutral position in a conflict between its communist ally and a non-communist power.[47]

The outbreak of the Sino-Indian border war in October 1962 placed Moscow in an even more difficult position, particularly with respect to its military aid program to India. In the summer of 1962 the Russians had made new aid commitments, providing for the supply of MiG–21s and the establishment of MiG–21 factories. Continued Soviet arms aid to India risked serious damage to the already precarious Sino-Soviet relationship at a time when the Russians needed solid communist backing against the west in the Cuban missile crisis. Accordingly, Moscow initially endorsed a Chinese cease-fire proposal.[48] But the Soviet Union also feared that cancellation of its pending arms aid commitments to India would be interpreted as support for Peking against New Delhi,

[45] *New York Times*, November 24, 1967.

[46] Chinese objectives toward India are more fully discussed in William E. Griffith, *The Sino-Soviet Rift* (Cambridge: M.I.T. Press, 1964), pp. 6-8.

[47] The Chinese did not make their resentment public until 1963 when they called the Soviet position in the Sino-Indian border dispute a "betrayal of proletarian internationalism." See Arthur Stein, "India and the USSR: The Post-Nehru Period," *Asian Survey*, vol. 7, no. 3 (March 1967), p. 169.

[48] *Pravda*, October 25, 1962. It is not certain whether the Cuban confrontation and the Chinese crossing of the Indian border were isolated developments. The Russians refuted Chinese claims that they knew of the Chinese action beforehand. One U.S. scholar suggests that the Russians had not expected India's defeat, which forced them to take a position in favor of India and to cut off Soviet military supplies to China. See Arthur Stein, "India and the USSR," p. 31.

which might drive the latter into an alignment with the west. The prompt U.S. response to India's appeal for military aid against the Chinese had, in fact, touched off demands in various Indian circles for a reassessment of India's non-alignment policy. Soviet vacillation with respect to the Soviet-Indian MiG transactions suggested the dilemma the Russians faced.

Soviet sources first indicated that the MiG agreements with India would be shelved.[49] By December 1962 the Russians had shifted their position and announced that a few MiG–21s would be sent as samples and that the licensing arrangements for the production of MiGs in India were still in effect.[50] In the first half of 1963 six MiG–21 fighters and a number of Mi–4 helicopters arrived in India. Negotiations in 1963 and early 1964 led to Soviet agreements for the delivery of An–12 cargo planes and air-to-air missiles for the MiG fighters and for the establishment of a $40 million SA–2 anti-aircraft missile complex in India.[51] By mid-1964 Soviet military sales totalled some $140 million.[52] But the Russians refused to modify the MiG fighter by adding all-weather and night capabilities to meet Indian requirements for an interceptor at the Himalayan border. The implementation of the licensing accord also continued to encounter delays.

The abatement of Sino-Indian tensions helped the Soviet Union out of the awkward position of aiding a communist nation's adversary. Moreover, the widening Sino-Soviet split accentuated Russian interest in bolstering India as a counterweight to China on the Asian continent. In September 1964 the Soviet Union extended a credit to India for some $300 million in arms aid, including forty-four MiG–21 jets, twenty helicopters, and seventy PT–76 tanks.[53] Moscow finally undertook to make the necessary financial and technical arrangements for building MiG–21s in India.[54] The Russians further consented to make the required improvements for turning the MiG into an all-weather and night-flying interceptor. The September 1964 accord indicated that Moscow

[49] *Washington Post*, October 30, 1962. For a discussion of the negotiations on the MiG deals, see Ian C. C. Graham, *The Indo-Soviet MiG Deal and Its International Repercussions,* Rand Corporation P-2842 (Santa Monica, Cal.: Rand Corporation, 1964). For the Indian position in the MiG deals, see Selig S. Harrison, "Troubled India and Her Neighbors," *Foreign Affairs,* vol. 43, no. 2 (January 1965), p. 325.

[50] *New York Times,* December 2, 1962.

[51] *Ibid.,* August 2, 1963; *ibid.,* May 13, 1964; *Washington Post,* May 9, 1964; *Asian Recorder,* April 1-7, 1964, p. 5747.

[52] *New York Times,* September 13, 1964.

[53] *Washington Post,* September 16, 1964; *New York Times,* September 22, 1964.

[54] According to Indian reports, the plants were expected to be in operation by 1968–69. *Hindu Weekly Review,* March 28, 1966. The plants were still under construction in 1968.

was prepared to revert to its earlier policy of extending substantial arms aid to India in order to contain both the United States and China in south Asia.

The eruption of the Indian-Pakistani border war of September 1965 once more placed the Soviet Union's carefully balanced policy in South Asia in jeopardy.

It may be recalled that in the course of 1963 the Soviet Union had initiated a policy of intrusion directed at countries closely identified or formally aligned with the west. As part of this intrusion policy[55] the Soviet Union had also started to try improving its relations with Pakistan. A modest economic aid agreement in August 1963 and a commercial loan to Pakistan in July 1964 were the first steps in this direction. A major obstacle to a Soviet-Pakistani rapprochement remained the Indo-Pakistani conflict over Kashmir, in which Moscow had taken New Delhi's side. The Russians, therefore, began to moderate their previous categorical support of India on the Kashmir issue.[56]

Pakistan had gradually retreated from its alignment with the west in protest over what it regarded as Washington's increasingly pro-Indian policy.[57] American efforts to help shore up the Indian defense forces after the Sino-Indian border war of 1962 had intensified the concern in Pakistan over the reliability of U.S. support in its dispute with India over Kashmir. In consequence, Pakistan's leaders had begun to cultivate relations with the Chinese, whose support could be expected, and with the Russians. Inevitably, relations with Washington suffered. The United States, moreover, was reluctant to contribute to an Indo-Pakistani arms race and delayed a Pakistani request to replace its F–86 fighter-bomber fleet with more up-to-date craft.

When the Indo-Pakistani border fighting broke out in September 1965 and the United States promptly suspended all defense deliveries to the two feuding states, Pakistan accepted a Chinese offer to replace some of its depleted assets with MiG–19 jets, Il–28 bombers, and T–59 tanks.[58] The Russians, unwilling to alienate either the Indians or the Pakistanis, refrained from taking sides and urged a peaceful settlement of the conflict.[59] Moscow furthermore could ill afford to have a war at

[55] Soviet intrusion efforts are more fully discussed in Chapter 2 of this study.

[56] The gradual Soviet switch on Kashmir has been analyzed in Sheldon W. Simon, "The Kashmir Dispute in Sino-Soviet Perspective," *Asian Survey*, vol. 7, no. 3 (March 1967), pp. 176-87.

[57] For a presentation of Pakistani views on U.S. policy toward India and Pakistan, see Khurshid Hyder, "Recent Trends in the Foreign Policy of Pakistan," *The World Today*, vol. 22, no. 11 (November 1966), pp. 482-91.

[58] The agreement with China was reported to be worth between $30 million and $40 million. *New York Times*, September 5, 1967.

[59] *Pravda*, August 24, 1965; *ibid.*, September 12, 1965.

its southern border in which the Chinese threatened to become involved.[60] This partly explains why the Soviet Union assumed the role of peace-maker at the Tashkent Conference of January 1966. Although the perennial Kashmir problem remained unsolved, the Russians succeeded in obtaining an agreement between India and Pakistan for a return to the status quo ante bellum.

Soviet actions did not imply a reversal of Moscow's policy toward India. In contrast to the United States, the Soviet Union did not halt its military aid to India during the war.[61] In fact, while the fighting was still in progress the Russians agreed to supply India with four submarines, Petya class destroyer escorts, and naval patrol craft.[62] At approximately the same time the Indians were also permitted to buy a large number of tanks from the Soviet Union and Czechoslovakia.[63] Although Pakistan's leaders, who recognized their vulnerability in relying on Washington for arms aid, approached Moscow in June 1966 for military aid, the Russians postponed action on Pakistan's request to avoid arousing Indian hostility.

Soviet uneasiness over Chinese inroads in Pakistan, however, progressively intensified. In an effort to counter Chinese influence, Moscow supplied some twelve Mi–6 helicopters to Pakistan in the second half of 1967. A small group of Pakistani airmen was sent to the Soviet Union for training. The total value of Soviet arms aid to Pakistan was reported to be about $10 million.[64] To reassure India, Soviet officials stressed that they would not make any lethal weapons available to Pakistan.[65] A more important gesture to allay Indian fears was the conclusion of negotiations with New Delhi in the latter part of 1967 for the

[60] Soviet writings have emphasized from time to time the strategic location of Kashmir; see S. Mikoyan, "Kashmir: Iabloko Razdora," Literaturnaia Gazeta (Moscow), October 28, 1965, as cited in R. Vaidyanath, "Some Recent Trends in Soviet Policies toward India and Pakistan," International Studies (New Delhi), vol. 7, no. 3 (January 1966), p. 444. The Russians warned the Chinese against any intervention on behalf of Pakistan. Pravda, September 22, 1965; ibid., September 23, 1965.

[61] The question of suspending Soviet military aid to India during the fighting actually did not arise. As one observer noted, it was a fortunate coincidence that the weapons on order were not ready for delivery. Zafar Iman, "Soviet Asian Policy Today," Contemporary Review, vol. 209, no. 1 (July 1966), p. 14.

[62] Indian Express, September 7, 1965. Reports of the inclusion of destroyer escorts were not publicized until 1968. See Sun (Baltimore), April 2, 1968.

[63] Subsequent news releases revealed that India was allowed to purchase more than five hundred Soviet and Czech tanks. New York Times, June 1, 1967.

[64] Ibid., September 5, 1967. Pakistan also received some military trucks. In view of the limited supply of materiel Pakistan received, the actual dollar value of millitary aid was probably half the reported estimate of $10 million.

[65] Washington Post, August 6, 1967.

delivery of some one hundred Su–7 fighter-bombers,[66] which would increase the ground attack capability of the Indian air force. With the Su–7 agreement, cumulative Soviet arms aid to India totalled between $600 million and $700 million.[67] The decision to aid India's enemy in its defense needs nonetheless represented a distinct change in Moscow's south Asian policy and underscored its growing concern over Chinese influence at its southern border.

THE SCOPE OF SOVIET ARMS DIPLOMACY

The early years of Soviet arms diplomacy in South and Southeast Asia reflected an emphasis on orthodox Soviet objectives. These included encouraging a newly independent state to sever its ties with the former European metropole, countering the defense initiatives of western alliances, preventing "reactionary counterrevolution," and consolidating Soviet influence in the recipient state by reducing the military establishment to single dependency for arms buildup and replacement. While not losing sight of these objectives, around 1960–61 Russian arms aid policy was forced to respond to the growing threat of the establishment of paramount Chinese influence in the area. Soviet arms aid activities intensified, particularly in the wake of the November 1960 Conference of Eighty-One Communist Parties in Moscow, where Russian leaders had failed to compose the developing Sino-Soviet controversy. Soviet military aid increased both in terms of dollar value and in number of commitments. After 1964 the Vietnam war progressively became the focus of Soviet attention in the region and affected Soviet policies. Arms aid to non-aligned recipients decreased and became mainly confined to the Asian subcontinent. Nevertheless, Soviet military aid had reached substantial amounts by the end of 1967, as Table 4-1 illustrates.

The distribution of Soviet military aid in South and Southeast Asia shows that Indonesia, India, and Afghanistan were the countries to which Russian leaders attached the greatest importance. Indonesia received by far the largest share of the Soviet arms aid dollar in the region. While aid to Afghanistan in absolute dollar amounts was relatively limited, in relation to the size of the defense budget of a recipient, Afghanistan had received more aid than any other recipient.[68] The

[66] *Ibid.*, January 25, 1968.

[67] This estimate is based on the successive arms deals, as reported in the press, from the first agreement in November 1960. The 1967 agreement for about one hundred Su–7s has been estimated at approximately $100 million since the Su–7 usually costs around $1 million (*Washington Post*, January 25, 1968).

[68] In 1965, for example, Afghanistan's defense budget was only $23 million. U.S. Arms Control and Disarmament Agency, *World-Wide Military Expenditures and Related Data*, Research Report 67-6 (Washington, 1967), p. 10.

Table 4-1.   Estimated Soviet Bloc Arms Aid to South and Southeast Asia: 1956 through 1967 (In Millions of U.S. Dollars)

Afghanistan	$260
Pakistan	5 to 10
India	600 to 700
Indonesia	1,200
Laos	3 to 5
Cambodia	5 to 10
Estimated Total:	$2,185

Sources: Estimates for Pakistan, India, and Indonesia are derived from sources documented in previous pages. Estimates for Laos and Cambodia are based on costs of equipment reported in the press. Costs were calculated on the basis of approximate costs of comparable U.S. equipment and assumed to include support equipment for aircraft, tools, and spare parts. The estimate for Afghanistan is similarly based on equipment costs and on a comparison of bloc economic aid with total bloc aid to Afghanistan as reported in the *New York Times*, May 28, 1967.

transfer of highly sophisticated weapons systems to these three recipients further underlines their significance in Soviet policy. Each acquired the MiG–21 jet; in fact, Indonesia was the first country outside the bloc to receive the MiG–21. India, although receiving less total aid than Indonesia, appeared to be the most privileged recipient among the three states, in that India was the only one to obtain a licensing agreement to produce and assemble MiG–21s at home. All three acquired batteries of SA–2 Guideline missiles. Indonesia and India were the only two countries, other than Egypt, which were able to negotiate agreements for submarines.

Each of the three major recipients in South and Southeast Asia devoted a substantial share of their aid credits to strengthening their air forces. By the end of 1967 the Indonesian air force had acquired at least eighteen MiG–21s and twelve MiG–19s equipped with air-to-air guided missiles, about one hundred older type MiGs, twenty-five Tu–16 bombers armed with air-to-surface missiles, Il–28 bombers, An–2, An–12, and Il–14 cargo craft, and Mi–4 and Mi–6 helicopters. The Indian air force included as a minimum sixty MiG–21s, fifty Il–14 and An–12 transport planes, and sixty Mi–4 helicopters. A few of the Su–7 fighter-bombers had already arrived in late 1967. Afghanistan had received an undisclosed number of MiG–21s, more than one hundred MiG–17s, a small force of MiG–15s, two squadrons of Il–28 bombers, and various transports, trainers, and helicopters.[69] The aircraft types indicate that all three recipients had acquired defensive as well as offensive systems.

Soviet bloc additions to the Indonesian navy similarly showed that Djakarta had been allowed to select ships with both defensive and

[69] Data derived from Institute for Strategic Studies, *Military Balance*, pp. 42-43; Wood, *Middle East*, p. 12; and reports from Indonesian, Indian, and U.S. newspapers.

offensive capabilities. Equipment which the navy received included a nineteen-thousand-ton Sverdlov cruiser, fourteen long range W class submarines, seven Skoryi class destroyers, seven Riga class frigates, eight Kronstadt class submarine chasers, twenty-four motor torpedo boats, seven mine sweepers, twelve Komar class torpedo boats armed with guided missiles, eighteen BK-IV class motor gunboats, submarine support ships, tankers, and other auxiliary and amphibious craft.[70]

While Soviet contributions to the Indonesian navy were substantial, some of the systems did little to improve Indonesia's maritime capability.[71] The young republic lacked a naval tradition. From an operational point of view, it was unlikely that the Indonesian navy could have absorbed such a large number of Soviet ships and provided trained personnel for them. Maintenance and spare parts posed a serious problem for the Indonesian navy. Although most weapons aid deals made some provision for spare parts, the Russians generally failed to deliver them. Of the fourteen submarines Indonesia received, for example, two were used for spare parts.[72] Furthermore, most Soviet-supplied ships, although built in the early fifties, were obsolescent World War II types. The new Komar class torpedo boats were a striking exception and did strengthen the fighting capability of the Indonesian navy.

The Indian navy in 1967 did not show much evidence of Soviet influence. The first Indian-Soviet naval aid agreement had been negotiated as recently as 1965. Only two submarines were ready and some patrol craft had arrived in India by the end of 1967.[73] Further Soviet penetration of India's naval establishment is likely to be encouraged by Britain's withdrawal from the region east of Suez and by continued British and U.S. reluctance to meet Indian requests for warships.

Each of the key recipients also obtained Soviet help in modernizing its ground forces, although in Indonesia the army received only a relatively small share of the weapons deliveries to that country. The Indonesian army acquired only PT-76 tanks, armored personnel carriers, jeeps, anti-aircraft guns, artillery, and light arms.[74] The relative lack of armor for the army reflected partly the environment and partly Indonesian army doctrine emphasizing the significance of guerrilla warfare. There were also strong indications that Indonesia deliberately limited re-

[70] Blackman, ed., *Fighting Ships,* pp. 137-42.
[71] One reason is that the naval revolt in early 1965 seriously undermined the effectiveness of the Indonesian navy.
[72] Blackman, *Fighting Ships,* p. 137.
[73] *New York Times,* April 17, 1967; Institute for Strategic Studies, *Strategic Survey 1967* (London, 1968), p. 33.
[74] Institute for Strategic Studies, *Military Balance,* p. 43.

quests for army equipment.[75] Equipment the Indian army received included more than five hundred light (PT–76) and medium tanks with 56mm and 90mm guns.[76] The eighty-thousand-man Afghan army, like the Afghan air force, was almost completely equipped with communist-fabricated weapons and counted, among others, some one hundred medium T–54 and light PT–76 tanks.[77]

The record of Soviet military assistance diplomacy in the South and Southeast Asia region shows that between 1956 and 1968 the Soviet Union managed to establish a military aid presence from Afghanistan in the northwest to Indonesia and the Indochina peninsula in the southeast. Receptivity to Moscow's initiatives on the part of recipients who had failed to acquire weapons from western sources greatly facilitated Soviet efforts. The balance sheet of Soviet arms aid policies included both gains and setbacks; the record dictated caution in the Asian subcontinent and the Indochina peninsula.

In Afghanistan, the first recipient in the region, the armed forces depended almost entirely on Soviet weapons aid. It seems doubtful whether they can function for any length of time without Soviet spare parts and fuel.[78] While the Russians have not tried to turn Afghanistan into a satellite and have generally avoided open interference in the country's internal affairs, it is highly unlikely that Kabul can pursue any foreign policy to which Moscow strongly objected.

Farther east, Moscow has made considerable progress toward replacing western military influence with its own. The Soviet Union has become India's largest source of military supplies and has succeeded in

[75] Sukarno wanted to build up the air force and the navy to offset the powers of the army. The former Indonesian Army Chief of Staff and Minister of Defense General Nasution and his aides, who negotiated most of the various arms deals, were careful to avoid too much dependence on Soviet military aid where the army was concerned, and were prepared to make the larger share of Soviet credits available to the air force and the navy. Interested above all in consolidating their power in Java, the army leaders did not regard the air force and the navy with the type of weapons each acquired as threats to the achievement of this objective. Nasution could with impunity reserve only a limited share of the aid credits for the acquisition of army materiel because: (1) the cost of army materiel was small compared to that of air and naval craft; (2) when Soviet arms aid began, the army already had a fair amount of small arms and some capability for producing small arms, while the other services had virtually no capability at all; and (3) U.S. military aid was primarily channeled to the army. Nasution's efforts to keep the army free from over-reliance on the Soviet Union were reflected in his emphasizing "berdikari" or self-reliance mission and in his requesting arms workshops from the Russians. See *Indonesian Herald*, May 5, 1965; *ibid.*, May 25, 1965.
[76] *New York Times*, June 1, 1967; Institute for Strategic Studies, *Military Balance*, p. 42.
[77] *New York Times*, May 28, 1967.
[78] See Welles Hangen, "Afghanistan," *Yale Review*, vol. 56, no. 1 (October 1966), p. 66.

creating limited arms aid ties with Pakistan. Yet Soviet military aid policies in these countries turned out to be extremely vulnerable to pressures caused by actual and potential changes in the political-military power constellation on the Asian subcontinent. The potential threat of China in south Asia and the regional conflict between India and Pakistan circumscribed the Soviet Union's freedom of maneuver in its aid policies. The Russian dilemma resulting from the Sino-Indian border war in October 1962 caused delays and obstacles in Soviet-Indian arms aid discussions. When the negotiations were finally resolved in favor of India, it served as a warning to China to restrain its ambitions in the region.

The subsequent rise of Chinese influence in Pakistan led the USSR to intensify its efforts to improve relations with Pakistan, a process already under way as part of a broader endeavor to turn the erstwhile northern tier of western defense into an area open to east-west rivalry. Little perhaps was more galling to New Delhi than Moscow's arms aid agreement with Rawalpindi in 1967. The new Soviet military aid relationship with Pakistan, however, posed serious problems for Moscow in view of the danger of antagonizing New Delhi and the attendant risk of India's turning to the west again. Since Indian good will remains an important asset to the Russians, particularly if Chinese influence grows in the Asian subcontinent, a decision to offer additional Soviet arms aid to Pakistan will probably be accompanied by political concessions to India and by compensatory weapons aid.

The history of Soviet aid activities in the states of the Indochina peninsula demonstrates Soviet capability to react promptly to emergency requests. While military aid generally arrived by ship and with a to-be-expected time lag between the agreement and the delivery date, in Laos the Soviet Union in December 1960 responded immediately with an arms airlift to Souvanna Phouma's request. The Russian airdrop of arms to the Viet Cong in early 1961 also attested to Moscow's rapid reaction capability.

Soviet emergency aid to the coalition of Laotian neutralists and communists helped to bring Souvanna Phouma back into power. But the Russians were unable to consolidate whatever influence they had in Laos or with the Viet Cong. Hanoi began to control the flow of arms, including Soviet arms, to the Pathet Lao and the Viet Cong. In fact, formulating policy for the former Indochina states proved most difficult and complex for Soviet leaders, since it also involved Chinese and American relationships. Moreover, as Hanoi's demands increased, the flexibility of Russia's response diminished. To reject an appeal from a communist ally fighting the major power of the capitalist world carried not only the risk of driving North Vietnam into China's arms, but the threat that such a rejection would erode Soviet influence in other states as well. Under these circumstances the Soviet Union stepped up its military aid to North Vietnam. By the end of 1967, except for a modest military assistance program in Cambodia, Hanoi clearly had priority in the allocation of Soviet arms aid resources for Southeast Asia.

In Indonesia, intensive Soviet military aid diplomacy eventually failed to achieve the Soviet objectives of insulating Indonesia from western influences and turning its government into a supporter of Moscow's policies in the Afro-Asian world. Moscow's lavish arms shipments, persistent encouragement of the Irian policy, and somewhat cautious support of the Malaysia confrontation could neither win the allegiance of Indonesia's army leaders nor alter Indonesia's increasingly pro-Peking position in international relations between 1963 and 1965. Indonesia's return to a more impartial foreign policy after the October 1965 coup was prompted by changes in the domestic power structure and not by Soviet persuasion. Its new military regime, in fact, sought to improve relations with the west rather than with the Soviet Union. It may also have been that the persecution of indigenous communists was too brutal and created a climate too hostile for Indonesia to be able to re-establish close relations with a communist power. The prospects are that Indonesia will pursue a more truly neutralist policy, not only concerning the Sino-Soviet quarrel but regarding east-west relations as well. The Soviet Union's marked disinterest in renewing its extensive military assistance program in Indonesia suggests a recognition by Soviet leaders that for the near future few gains are to be made in Indonesia.

5

LATIN AMERICA

A N ANALYSIS of Soviet military aid policies and operations in Latin America requires a brief appraisal of the region's historical role in Soviet foreign policy. The Soviet Union has traditionally exhibited a low level of interest in Latin America. Not only did the conditions existing in Latin American republics offer little resemblance to the classical requirements for revolution set forth in Marxist-Leninist theory, but the proximity of the United States and its sensitivity to foreign interests in the area have appeared so formidable that Soviet planners have generally considered the region as beyond the pale of external intrusion. Ever since 1823, when the United States issued the Monroe Doctrine, events have served to affirm the determination of the United States to maintain a controlling interest in the area. Soviet leaders had long acknowledged this hands-off-the-western-hemisphere policy, and the communist phrase "geographic fatalism" has been employed to rationalize an inability to spread revolution in the area.[1]

It took the success of a revolution in Cuba, one tolerated by the United States despite its adoption of foreign ties and its anti-American cast, to cause the Soviet Union to probe the U.S. position in earnest. The resulting confrontation, the Cuban missile crisis of 1962, served notice to the world that the United States was determined to be the principal guide of Latin America's destiny. In the opinion of some Soviet observers, it may have stimulated an even greater U.S. concern for the pro-American posture of Latin American governments than had

---

[1] Herbert S. Dinerstein, *Soviet Policy in Latin America* (Santa Monica, California: Rand Corporation, 1966), p. 19.

previously existed.[2] The very success of one Castro has tended to pre-clude the success of another, because it has heightened hemispheric vigilance and made aid to insurgents a matter of extreme sensitivity to the United States and to most Latin American regimes as well. A rec-ognition of geopolitical realities has again influenced Russian leaders.

Limited Soviet Interest. Soviet interest in Latin America did not develop much strength until well after Stalin's death.[3] Stalin generally considered Latin American communist parties as weak and feckless and scarcely bothered to enunciate a propaganda line.[4] Latin America was popularly depicted as "groaning under the yoke of U.S. imperialism," but the Soviet Union did not design a specific strategy for Latin Amer-ican parties. As a rule, they adhered strictly to the dictates of the Soviet Communist party. Almost all Soviet information on Latin America came from Latin America communists, who, in their characteristically faithful fashion, frequently tried to fit Latin American developments into the procrustean bed of Marxist-Leninist revolutionary theory.

The death of Stalin in 1953 marked the beginning of a period of policy reappraisal toward all underdeveloped nations. With the emer-gence of polycentrism in the world communist movement, a greater diversity of opinion among Latin American communist leaders was possible as well. As a result a more differentiated Soviet analysis of Latin America emerged, accompanied by a more sophisticated Soviet policy.

Soviet planners presently make several distinctions between the situa-tion in Latin America and the circumstances existing in the rest of the developing world. Briefly, the USSR analysis recognizes that (1) Soviet (or even Chinese) proximity, which lent impetus to national freedom movements in Afro-Asian countries, is not a factor in Latin America; (2) the national bourgeoisie in Latin America is not as revolutionary or decisively active as in other parts of the world, perhaps because of the long-standing independence of the Latin republics; (3) the bourgeoisie is split between progressive anti-imperialists (or radical bourgeoisie) and an upper class bourgeoisie in collusion with or compromised by im-perialism; and (4) capitalism is far more developed in Latin America, which produces nearly forty-five percent of the entire industrial output

---

[2] *Ibid.,* p. vi.

[3] The Russians did not establish a Latin America Institute at the Soviet Academy of Sciences until 1961.

[4] James M. Daniel, "Latin America," in *Communism and Revolution,* eds. Cyril E. Black and Thomas P. Thornton (Princeton, New Jersey: Princeton Uni-versity Press, 1964), p. 341.

of the underdeveloped countries.[5] For these reasons, Soviet analysts appear to doubt the staying power of radical bourgeois governments in the western hemisphere, unless, as in the case of Castro, the radical bourgeoisie is immediately taken to a "higher stage of development."

The expense and perplexity of the Cuban experience has occasioned a marked and somewhat radical change in Soviet writings on the Third World. It is now admitted that socialist states are not "in a position to provide all requirements for capital, equipment, and technical assistance. A significant portion of their requirements has to be satisfied through the agency of the imperialist states."[6] The Russians have also suggested that the passage of the developing countries from the capitalist world to the socialist world is possible "not only in the form of a comparatively rapid action such as occurred in Cuba in 1959–1960, but also in the form of a prolonged process stretching over many years."[7]

These recent admissions are reflected in Soviet tactics. At present the USSR eschews support for guerrilla forces in Latin America and encourages Latin American Communist parties to pursue peaceful ways of attaining national leadership. Soviet analysts, however, are aware of the limitations of such an approach and probably recognize that it would have a chance of success only in Chile, where the party has the required broad base. In most other countries, a parliamentary accession to power by the Communist party is considered completely unlikely.

Faced with such limited prospects, the Russians have adopted broader goals. Foremost among them seems to be the elimination or weakening of the U.S. monopoly of influence in Latin America. Other Soviet policy goals, such as increasing Soviet influence in the area, a reorientation of Latin American trade toward socialist countries, and the sustenance of the first and only Latin American member of the world socialist movement, are pursued not only for their own sake but also insofar as they contribute to the diminution of U.S. hegemony.

Initial Soviet Activities. The Soviet government was quick to establish diplomatic relationships with Latin American governments when the

---

[5] Analysis developed from Kurt Müller, *The Foreign Aid Programs of the Soviet Bloc and Communist China: An Analysis* (New York: Walker & Co., 1967), p. 26.

[6] V. Tiagunenko, "Current Problems of the Noncapitalist Path of Development," *Mirovaia Ekonomika i Mezhdunarodnaia Otnosheniia* (World Economic and International Relations), no. 11 (November 1964), p. 17, as quoted by Dinerstein, *Soviet Policy,* p. 13.

[7] S. Tiul'panov, "The Basic Problems of the Political Economy of the Developing Countries," *Mirovaia Ekonomika i Mezhdunarodnaia Otnosheniia* (World Economic and International Relations), no. 9, 1965, p. 72, in Dinerstein, *Soviet Policy,* p. 5.

opportunity presented itself.[8] While these relations were occasionally severed, often as a result of alleged Soviet espionage activities, the USSR managed to maintain a significant degree of representation. By the end of 1967 Moscow had diplomatic contacts with a dozen Latin American republics. The East European nations were even more fully represented, and every Latin American country has had diplomatic relations of an official nature with at least one European communist country at some time in its history. Similarly, all of the Latin American nations had carried on some form of trade with the communist world, although in some cases the totals were insignificant. Cuba, Brazil, Argentina, and Uruguay, however, were engaged in substantial commerce with the Soviet bloc. Cuba, whose trade with communist nations had reached eighty-five percent of its total trade by 1964, accounts for much of the total increase in Soviet bloc-Latin American trade.

After the death of Stalin in 1953, Soviet leaders were prepared to further Russian political influence in Latin America more actively, if given the opportunity. Such a situation arose in Guatemala, where the left wing Arbenz government had permitted the local Communist party to obtain increasing prominence and influence. President Arbenz, who drew most of his support from labor unions, teachers, and peasants, became more and more receptive to the idea of creating a popular militia as a bulwark for his regime. Arbenz' envoys had for years tried to purchase arms, first from the United States and, after the United States had placed an embargo on arms shipments to Guatemala in late 1952, from other Latin American nations and Europe. In January 1954 the Arbenz regime succeeded in obtaining five hundred submachine guns from Belgium and in arranging a more secretive transaction with the Czech government.[9] The communist arms shipment was carried in a chartered Swedish vessel which sailed from Poland and unloaded its cargo, under "extraordinary security procedures" at Guatemala on May 15, 1954.[10] The exact nature of the arms and their final destination are still obscure. Most of the equipment, including some rifles, submachine guns, light machine guns, and anti-tank mines, was delivered to the Presidential Honor Guard in Guatemala City, although

[8] Diplomatic relations between the USSR and Mexico were established in 1924, followed in 1926 by an exchange of representatives with Uruguay and in 1935 with Colombia. During the period of wartime solidarity (1942–45), relationships were established with thirteen other countries.

[9] The Czech government would later be recognized as the Soviet Union's proxy in its initial arms dealings with several Middle East and African nations.

[10] *Case Study in Insurgency and Revolutionary Warfare: Guatemala, 1944–54* (Washington: Special Operations Research Office, American University, 1964), p. 87.

some was reportedly delivered from the airport of arrival to other undisclosed locations.[11] This shipment of arms, perhaps the first communist supply of military hardware to enter the hemisphere, did not accomplish what was presumably its goal, the bolstering of Arbenz' faltering regime. In fact, some sources conjecture that the apprehension caused by news of the shipment actually contributed to the government's fall the following month, when a group of Guatemalan exiles led by Colonel Carlos Castillo Armas invaded the country and forced Arbenz to resign.[12] The Guatemalan military promptly swung to the support of Armas and instituted the wholesale arrest of communist and pro-communist members of the former Arbenz government.

Two important lessons for Soviet military aid policy-makers emerged from the Guatemalan episode. The failure of the Guatemalan military to defend the Arbenz regime and the arrest of left wing officials showed the intense opposition in the Guatemalan officer corps to the reported plans to establish a para-military force and to any communist influence. The zeal with which the Latin American military guards its privileged positions and its distrust of left wing elements have remained serious impediments to communist activity and arms diplomacy. In addition, the covert U.S. assistance in effectuating Arbenz' overthrow[13] indicated that the United States was prepared to intervene if a communist government threatened to come to power in Latin America. These two factors help to explain the absence of Soviet military aid agreements with states of the western hemisphere during the next five years. Even when political developments provided another such opportunity in Cuba in 1960, the Soviet response was initially hesitant and very carefully measured.

CUBA: THE FIRST LATIN AMERICAN COLLABORATOR

Soviet activities in Cuba must be considered on two levels, as part of a military aid program through which the Russians hoped to establish a paramount influence in Cuba and as part of a military program through which the Soviet leadership may have seriously attempted to alter the existing strategic power balance between the United States and the USSR. The key distinction between the two endeavors lies not only in the types of arms delivered (small arms vis-à-vis intermediate-range

[11] *Ibid.*, pp. 73, 87.

[12] Ronald M. Schneider, *Communism in Guatemala, 1944–54* (New York: Praeger, 1959), pp. 308-310.

[13] Concerned about the Czech arms delivery to Guatemala, the United States sent emergency arms shipments to Honduras and Nicaragua. Some of the equipment given to Honduras was apparently transmitted to Armas. See J. Lloyd Mecham, *The United States and Inter-American Security, 1889–1960* (Austin, Texas: University of Texas Press, 1961), pp. 446-47.

missiles), but also in their ultimate disposition: The control and owner-ship of the missiles remained in Russian hands throughout. For this reason, the shipment of the missiles to Cuba cannot properly be classi-fied as part of Soviet military aid. Consequently the estimated $750 mil-lion value of Russian arms aid delivered to Cuba[14] from 1960 to 1967 does not include Soviet missiles, nor the Il–28 bombers which were withdrawn after the missile crisis.

The Soviet Program in Cuba. There are several reasons to suggest that the Soviet Union might not have expected the opportunities which resulted from Fidel Castro's ascent to power in Cuba. The Guatemalan incident had strengthened the United States in its determination to pre-vent communist intrusion in the area. Moreover, Cuba was less than one hundred fifty miles away from the U.S. mainland and was the site of the strategic U.S. naval base of Guantanamo. By virtue of Cuba's geographical domination of the Caribbean, it could inhibit the use of the Panama Canal. Soviet planners probably considered Cuba one of the Latin American countries where the United States would be least likely to permit, and most able to prevent, significant internal or external communist influence. Soviet analysts interpreted Castro's movement of July 26, 1959 as a middle class revolution, and one therefore which probably would be influenced or possibly subverted by the United States.

When Cuban-American relations deteriorated during 1959 and 1960, Soviet leaders cautiously began to provide economic aid to and en-courage the new government. Moreover, the Cuban Communist party, which had hitherto been anti-Castro, ceased its opposition to Castro.[15] At the same time, the United States terminated its military assistance program, which had totalled over $10 million during the eight years before Castro. In March 1959 the United States instituted an embargo on American arms to the Caribbean and applied pressure on the British to stop their sale of fifteen jet fighters to the Cuban Air Force. The United States also tried to dissuade Italian, French, and Belgian com-panies from supplying arms.[16] Castro, needing arms for the formation of a militia, turned to the Soviet Union. During Raul Castro's visit to Eastern Europe in the summer of 1960, arms agreements were nego-tiated with the Czech and Russian governments. Equipment began to

[14] *New York Times*, September 5, 1967.

[15] Subsequent trials have brought out that Cuban communists were often ready to betray non-communist revolutionaries to the Batista police. See Leon Lipson, "Castro and the Cold War" in *Cuba and the United States*, ed. John Plank (Washington: The Brookings Institution, 1967), p. 182. Lipson also mentions that Castro had accused the communists of inspiring "counterrevolutionary disorders" in Oriente as late as May 1959.

[16] Edwin Lieuwen, *Arms and Politics in Latin America* (New York: Praeger, 1961), p. 269.

arrive soon thereafter, and by the end of 1960 shipments from Soviet bloc countries were estimated to total $50 million.[17] Deliveries of Soviet military aid continued during the first few months of 1961, and by April 1961 the U.S. Government reported in the United Nations that "in the last few months [Cuba had received] at least fifteen Soviet fifty-ton tanks, nineteen Soviet assault guns, fifteen Soviet thirty-five-ton tanks, seventy-eight Soviet 76mm field guns and over one hundred Soviet heavy machine guns."[18] Soviet and Czech military advisers had also arrived, although they numbered only about one hundred at the time of the Bay of Pigs invasion in April 1961. By the end of 1961, the Soviet Union had contributed an estimated total of seventy to seventy-five MiG fighters, two hundred fifty tanks, one hundred assault guns, one thousand anti-aircraft field guns, five hundred mortars, two hundred thousand small arms, and an unspecified number of patrol vessels and torpedo boats.[19] The buildup continued throughout the first ten months of 1962, culminating in the Cuban missile crisis and the U.S. blockade, after which Soviet bloc shipments substantially decreased.

The Cuban Missile Crisis. The material on the Cuban missile crisis is too voluminous and the scenario of the crucial period from October 22 to November 20, 1962, too well known to bear repetition. The Soviet attempt to place medium-range missiles and jet medium bombers in Cuba was not part of the military aid program, since control of the basically offensive weapons was not given to the Cubans. There can be no doubt, however, that the levels of conventional military aid to Cuba were greatly affected by this Soviet decision.

There is more than one theory as to Soviet strategy during the fall of 1962. Most observers appear to believe that the Russians were actually attempting to change the strategic military balance between the USSR and the United States by obtaining a close-in site from which to aim their deterrent force.[20] Others believe Soviet planners had a lesser objective and had hoped to use the missiles as bargaining points to obtain

[17] U.S. Department of State, *Statement*, November 18, 1960. The arms, delivered on at least twelve Soviet ships, included eight MiG jet fighters, ten Soviet helicopters, forty tanks, thirty rocket launchers, twenty-five field guns, fifty-five howitzers, forty-five thousand Czech automatic rifles, sixty anti-tank guns, and eight anti-aircraft guns.

[18] Lester A. Sobel (ed.), *Cuba, the U.S. and Russia: 1960–1963* (New York: Facts on File, 1964), p. 13. The information was released in connection with United Nations discussions of the U.S. participation in the Bay of Pigs invasion.

[19] Stephen P. Gibert, "Wars of Liberation and Soviet Military Aid Policy," *Orbis*, vol. 10, no. 3 (Fall 1966), p. 853.

[20] See Arnold L. Horelick, *The Cuban Missile Crisis: An Analysis of Soviet Calculations and Behavior* (Santa Monica, California: Rand Corporation, 1963) for a thorough exposition of all such theories.

concessions elsewhere, e.g., the dismantlement of U.S. bases in Turkey or some form of disengagement in Berlin. Still others are of the opinion that the Soviet Union hoped to secure a pledge from the United States not to invade Cuba.[21]

If the latter assumption is true, there would be a valid argument for considering the missiles as part of the Soviet military aid program. The proponents of other theories point out, however, that the missile emplacement entailed too great a risk for such limited objectives as assisting a radical nationalist leader. Nevertheless, the important fact remains that regardless of which strategy the USSR pursued the by-product of the Soviet missile gamble was a rapid buildup in Cuban military might. Perhaps the Russians wanted to provide a smoke screen for the larger weapons which were scheduled to follow. They may also have wished to furnish an ostensible reason for the arrival of the large Russian technical staff required for missile operation. Or perhaps they merely wanted to afford a conventional defensive protection for the missiles while these were being made operational. In any case, the entry of the missiles was preceded by several months of shipments of conventional weapons and supplies. Later, heavy artillery and medium tanks arrived, followed by MiG–15, MiG–17, and MiG–19 aircraft and helicopters. By the spring of 1962, motor torpedo boats and coastal patrol vessels of the Kronstadt class were delivered to the navy. In July and August, SA–2 Guideline surface-to-air missiles arrived and were at least partially deployed by the time the first offensive missiles entered the country in September.[22]

When the United States forced the Russians to remove their forty-two medium-range ballistic missiles (November 8 to November 11) and forty-two Il–28 bombers (December 1 to December 6), all other military equipment and almost all military advisers remained.[23] Eventually, the large number of Soviet personnel was reduced to its present level, estimated at between three to five thousand, including civilians.[24]

[21] This rationale was later implied by Khrushchev himself, as a partial explanation of his insertion as well as his withdrawal of the missiles.

[22] Horelick, *Cuban Missile Crisis*, pp. 38-41.

[23] The number of Russians in Cuba at the height of the missile crisis is disputed. Although U.S. government figures never admitted the presence of more than seventeen to twenty-two thousand, Hanson Baldwin's article "A Military Perspective," in Plank, *Cuba and the United States*, p. 205, cities estimates of from thirty to forty thousand as more probable, including an expeditionary force of more than thirteen thousand men.

[24] *Ibid.*; David Wood, *Armed Forces in Central and South America* (London: Institute for Strategic Studies, 1967), p. 13; U.S. Congress, House of Representatives, Subcommittee on Inter-American Affairs of the Committee on Foreign Affairs, *Communist Activities in Latin America, 1967, Report,* 90th Cong., 1st sess. (July 3, 1967), p. 8.

Strained Soviet-Cuban Relations. United States intelligence sources suggest that the majority of present Cuban military equipment was introduced during the 1962 buildup and that reported shipments in late 1966 "logically could be a phase of the necessary Soviet replacement and resupply program for the equipment introduced in 1962."[25] There are, in fact, indications that Soviet military aid to Cuba has decreased as a result of the growing disagreement between the Soviet and Cuban governments. At the Latin American Solidarity Conference in Havana in August 1967, the Cuban delegation sponsored and won approval for a resolution condemning Soviet bloc economic and technical assistance to "dictators and oligarchies in the hemisphere," an allusion to the agreements which the USSR, Poland, and other Eastern European nations had recently signed with a number of Latin American republics, including Colombia, Brazil, and Chile.[26] The Cubans further insulted the Russians by sending exceptionally low level representatives to the Kremlin ceremonies marking the Fiftieth Anniversary of the Soviet Union,[27] a gesture reciprocated by a Soviet refusal to allow the Cubans to address the assembly.[28]

Whether such strained relations will jeopardize the Soviet military aid program is uncertain. Two vague references to military aid have been made by Soviet officials in recent years. Only two days after the Kremlin's Fiftieth Anniversary ceremony, the acting head of the Soviet mission in Cuba mentioned that the Soviet Union would continue to give military aid and other forms of assistance to Cuba "to strengthen the island's defense."[29] In January 1968 a member of the Soviet Politburo stated that the Soviet Union would continue military and economic aid to Cuba;[30] however, neither statement contained a definite commitment. The Soviet Union's economic aid program—mostly in long-term credits and sugar subsidies, and estimated together with the arms aid at over $1 million a day[31]—seems already to have been affected by the mutual polemics.[32]

[25] *Communist Activities, Report*, p. 8.

[26] *New York Times*, August 10, 1967; *Sun* (Baltimore), August 9, 1967.

[27] *New York Times*, November 5, 1967. Cuba was represented by the Minister of Health and was the only communist country which did not send at least a party chief, titular head of state, or first secretary.

[28] *Washington Post*, November 5, 1967.

[29] *Sun* (Baltimore), November 8, 1967.

[30] *New York Times*, January 4, 1968.

[31] *Ibid.*, November 5, 1967; *Washington Post*, May 17, 1967.

[32] Some observers, noting the purging of pro-Moscow Cuban communists in January 1968, speculated that the action may have been a result of Soviet economic pressures. (Joseph Alsop, " . . . Russian Crackdown on Cuban Ally . . . ," *Washington Post*, January 31, 1968.) A recent Russian-Cuban trade agreement calls for a ten percent increase in trade in 1968, contrasting with a twenty-three percent expansion forecast for 1967. (*Washington Post,* March 23, 1968.)

In spite of the reduction in arms shipments after the missile crisis, the Cuban arsenal remains impressive by Latin American standards. The present Cuban military establishment, still mostly using the Soviet weapons introduced in 1962, includes an army equipped with approximately two hundred Js–2, T–34, and T–54 tanks, Su–100 assault guns, BTR–60 armored personnel carriers, Frog surface-to-surface missiles, and SA–2 Guideline missiles; a navy consisting of approximately twelve Soviet submarine chasers, twelve Komar missile boats, and twenty-four Russian motor torpedo boats; and an air force composed of at least forty-five MiG–21 jet interceptors, twelve MiG–19 jet fighters, twenty-two MiG–17 fighter-planes, fifty MiG–15 jet interceptors, at least fifty Il–14 and An–2 transport aircraft, and twenty-four Mi–4 helicopters.[33]

THE IMPACT OF SOVIET MILITARY AID TO CUBA

The outcome of the Cuban missile crisis was, by some standards, unfavorable to both the USSR and Cuba. The rapidity and boldness of the Soviet involvement reminded other Latin American governments of the true nature of Soviet objectives, while the removal of the missiles upon U.S. demand appeared to many to be a psychological retreat. Although he obtained a formidable arsenal, Fidel Castro lost personal prestige when it became evident how little control he had over the whole situation. Any judgments about the relative advantage or disadvantage the Soviet Union received as a result of its military assistance program in Cuba should take into consideration some other highly relevant factors, such as Soviet relationships with other Latin American countries and Castro's propensity for revolution.

The Export of Castro-Communism. It has frequently been alleged that the Soviet Union used Cuba as a staging point for the further exportation of revolution to Latin America. In actuality, however, the initiative for such subversion seems to have come directly from Fidel Castro. Small rebel forces embarked from Cuba to other Latin American republics in 1959, well before any Soviet personnel or weapons had reached Cuba and before Soviet influence was established there. The first invasion in 1959 was aimed at Panama. An expeditionary force of approximately one hundred, containing more Cubans than Panamanians, was equipped and organized by Castro followers and led by a Castro army officer.[34] It was quashed within hours by local Panamanian forces. In June 1959 the Castro government sent a small force to the Dominican Republic to launch a guerrilla movement against

---

[33] Wood, *Central and South America*, pp. 12-13, and daily newspaper reports.
[34] Tad Szulc, "Exporting the Cuban Revolution," in Plank, *Cuba and the United States*, p. 79.

Trujillo. In this instance, as in others to follow, Castro used exile groups which had been trained in Cuba, but he did not commit Cuban troops themselves. Trujillo's troops routed the Dominican exiles, who received no support from the native population, within a few days. Similarly, Cuban-sponsored invasions by tiny exile groups in Nicaragua, Guatemala, and Haiti were totally unsuccessful and did not arouse much concern even within the governments at which they were directed. These failures are generally conceded to have ended the first or "starry-eyed" phase of Castro's plan to export revolution to Latin America.[35]

The second phase, which coincided with the influence the Soviet Union was gaining in Cuba through its military aid program, was a more sophisticated endeavor that consisted of disseminating propaganda, training subversives, encouraging Latin American leftists to visit Havana, and hosting revolutionary conferences. Yet during the next seven years, despite growing censure and consternation about the "exporting of Castro-communism," only one case in which Cuban weapons were exported to other parts of Latin America was verified.[36] This involved a shipment of three tons of weapons to Venezuela in November 1963.[37]

The circumstances surrounding this weapons shipment indicate that it was undertaken by Castro as a free agent rather than as a proxy for the USSR. The arms were apparently landed in November 1963, a period when Soviet-Cuban relations were still suffering from what Castro had felt was a general disregard for his position during the missile crisis one year earlier. The arms cache, located on the ocean coast of Falcon State, consisted of eighty-one Belgian automatic rifles, thirty-one Belgian submachine guns, five U.S. mortars, twenty U.S. bazookas, and nine U.S. recoilless rifles.[38] Although Venezuela is generally conceded to be Castro's chief target in Latin America, this one shipment remained the only evidence of direct arms aid from 1960 to 1966. Neither the OAS Special Consultative Committee on Security, convened to study the Venezuelan accusations, nor the findings of U.S. intelligence agencies, provided proof of any other direct Cuban aid to insurgent groups during

[35] *Ibid.*, p. 78.
[36] Not until 1967 would another such case occur. In May, a clandestine landing of Venezuelan insurgents was accompanied by four Cubans, two of whom were killed and two captured, providing the first instance in recent years "in which direct Cuban military involvement could be proved." Statement by Brig. Gen. Burton R. Brown before the U.S. Congress, House of Representatives, Subcommittee on Inter-American Affairs of the Committee on Foreign Affairs, *Communist Activities in Latin America, 1967, Hearings*, 90th Cong., 1st sess. (May 16, 1967), p. 22.
[37] *Castro-Communist Insurgency in Venezuela* (Washington: Georgetown Research Project, 1964), pp. 108ff.
[38] *Ibid.*, p. 111.

this period.[39] A U.S. government spokesman stated in March 1963 that "we have evidence that in principle Cuba is not sending identifiable quantities of weapons to Latin American insurgents at present." He further affirmed that "Cuba is willing to furnish funds, training, and technical assistance [to militants]." Any reference to weapons is pointedly omitted.[40] Cuban instructors apparently require guerrilla warfare students to procure weapons from security forces at home. In 1965 another U.S. government statement reiterated that "Havana now generally prefers to provide the money for arms purchases rather than the arms themselves."[41]

The existence of a Soviet military aid program in only one Latin American country[42] and the lack of evidence of any significant re-exportation of arms do not exclude the possibility of Castro-communist intrusion into the rest of the hemisphere at some point in the future. The Tricontinental Conference of January 1966[43] and the Latin American Solidarity Conference of August 1967 have clearly established a Cuban commitment to aid insurgent groups. There are two factors militating against more active Cuban support at present. The most obvious one relates to the low level of activity and dim prospects for success which currently characterize the guerrilla movements. The rebel groups in Guatemala and Venezuela have in recent years suffered serious military setbacks, while the military in Peru and Bolivia have succeeded in virtually eliminating the insurgency in their countries altogether. In Bolivia, the military in 1967 also captured and killed the Latin American revolutionary Che Guevara, who, because of his continental theories of revolution and his former ties with the Cuban government, had come to symbolize the exportation of Castro-communism.

---

[39] Szulc, "Exporting the Cuban Revolution," p. 84.

[40] U.S. Congress, House of Representatives, Subcommittee on Inter-American Affairs of the Committee on Foreign Affairs, *Castro-Communist Subversion in the Western Hemisphere, Hearings,* 88th Cong., 1st sess. (1963), p. 67.

[41] U.S. Congress, House of Representatives, Subcommittee on Inter-American Affairs of the Committee on Foreign Affairs, *Communism in Latin America, Hearings,* 89th Cong., 1st sess. (1965), p. 121.

[42] Charges of direct Soviet bloc military aid to any Latin American insurgents have never been taken seriously by responsible observers. On February 20, 1963, a Cuban exile leader testified before the U.S. House Subcommittee on Inter-American Affairs that the Russians had established secret air bases in two countries, Paraguay and Brazil. Subcommittee on Inter-American Affairs of the Committee on Foreign Affairs, *Castro-Communist Subversion,* p. 87. Such references to direct Soviet bloc involvement in Latin American countries other than Cuba have never been verified and are considered highly unlikely.

[43] A gathering of revolutionary groups from Latin America, Africa, and Asia in Havana.

The other factor inhibiting Cuban aid to insurgency is the lack of Soviet support for such enterprises. In October 1966 *Pravda* published two commentaries on Che Guevara's death and failure in Bolivia, in which such adventurism was equated with "Maoism," and "sad results" were predicted for all "revolutionary adventurists" who forget the true principles of "proletarian internationalism."[44] Latin American communist parties allied to Moscow have attacked Castro-communist subversion tactics with a severity usually reserved for imperialist activities. The Soviet Union has also shown some restraint in its support of Castro. Soviet military aid to Cuba has afforded the Castro government a rather limited offensive capability, in spite of its quantity. Although Cuba almost completely lacks naval transport facilities and has very little in the way of air transport capability, the Soviet Union has not attempted to correct this deficiency through its military aid program.[45] Without an adequate airlift or amphibious transport capability, Cuba's offensive power with regard to other Latin American countries is limited.[46]

Soviet Relationships with the Latin Republics. Soviet economic aid and trade with Latin American governments have expanded in recent years. Castro has vehemently denounced USSR trade agreements made with Chile in August 1966, with Venezuela and Colombia in March 1967, and with Brazil in June 1967. Even Peru, which has never recognized the Soviet Union, has proposed the exchange of trade consulates with socialist countries, if such can be accomplished without establishing diplomatic relations.[47]

That economic relations have frequently preceded military aid in Soviet dealings also brings up the possibility that one of the Latin American governments might approach the Soviet bloc for a purchase of military equipment. The Latin American governments are currently engaged in a miniature arms race. The traditional monopoly of the U.S. government in arms sales to Latin America has already been broken by

[44] As quoted in the *Washington Post*, January 31, 1968.

[45] While the Soviet Union had delivered some missile boats and other small coastal craft in 1962, the only large-draft warships in the Cuban navy are three U.S. frigates of 1947 vintage. John L. Sutton and Geoffrey Kemp, *Arms to Developing Countries: 1945–1965* (London: Institute for Strategic Studies, 1966), p. 22. The Soviet-made transports delivered to the Cuban air force were predominantly light transports, Il–14s and An–2s. William Green and Dennis Punnett, *MacDonald World Air Power Guide* (Garden City, New York: Doubleday & Co., 1963), pp. 8-9.

[46] Baldwin, "A Millitary Perspective," p. 203. Baldwin rates Cuban naval transport strength even lower, " . . . one ancient and obsolete vessel (a so-called frigate). . . . "

[47] *La Prensa* (Buenos Aires), February 1, 1968.

French willingness to sell certain items, such as supersonic jets, which the United States has long refused to introduce into the area. Peru has purchased a squadron of fourteen French Mirages and seventy-eight French AMX–13 light tanks;[48] Brazil has expressed an active interest in the supersonic Mirages; and Argentina is negotiating for modern French AMX–30 tanks.[49] In view of the strong anti-communist bias of Latin military establishments, it is extremely doubtful that Soviet weaponry will be politically acceptable in the immediate future. The possibility cannot be completely discounted, however, that in the case of certain categories of military equipment, notably in non-lethal transport and communications, a Soviet offering may prove sufficiently attractive to lead to an outright purchase. It has been rumored, for example, that the Colombian government has placed an order for helicopters.[50] More concrete is the announcement that a leading Peruvian airline has acquired a twin-turbine, twenty-eight-passenger helicopter, known as the B–8, from Avia export of Moscow.[51]

Other Russian-built helicopters, the Mi–10 and Mi–8, have been bought by private commercial oil companies for use in Bolivia.[52] The Mi–10 is described as the world's largest and will make possible the lifting of oil rig equipment twice or triple the weight presently carried. Another Soviet plane, the YAK–40, a workhorse jet designed for short-haul work, has been estimated by airline executives to have a particular utility for Africa, Latin America, and the Far East; they predict a good market for it there.[53] The successful performance of such equipment in Latin America could easily lead governments to consider similar purchases from the Soviet bloc.

There are also rumors of transactions involving conventional military equipment. Latin American governments fear that the economic agreements made with the Soviet Union by other countries may contain secret provisions for military equipment. The Peruvians, themselves purchasers of military equipment from France, have accused the Chileans of having imported missiles and tanks from the Soviet Union under the guise of "agricultural purchases."[54]

---

[48] *New York Times*, April 21, 1968.
[49] *Washington Post*, February 6, 1968.
[50] *Marcha* (Montevideo), September 1967.
[51] *Peruvian Times* (Lima), October 6, 1967, p. 2.
[52] *Peruvian Times* (Lima), November 24, 1967, p. 3.
[53] *Time*, June 9, 1967.
[54] *El Comercio* (Lima), October 5, 1967. In March 1968, there were rumors regarding arms negotiations between the USSR and the Uruguayan army, subsequently denied by the Uruguayan Defense Minister. The previous month, however, the Ministry of the Interior made a $570,000 arms purchase from

Future Alternatives for Soviet Military Aid Policy. There are several theories that could be developed from the failure of the Soviet Union to promote an aggressive military aid program in Latin America. It could be argued that the Soviet Union, as part of its attempted détente with the United States, does not wish to take any action in Latin America which might jeopardize Soviet-American relations. Or, the Soviet Union might be acting upon its own theories about the "peaceful alternatives" to armed revolution in Latin America and therefore concentrating on united front tactics. Finally, one could conclude that the hazardous association with Fidel Castro has discouraged the Soviet Union from considering a possible repetition. Each of these theories contains elements of wishful thinking about Soviet intentions.

First, the Soviet Union is not likely to be restrained from taking any action which it deems advantageous to its interests merely out of consideration for a Soviet-American rapprochement. Russian activities in the Middle East after the June 1967 war are a case in point. It is more likely that the Russians fear that communist penetration of another Latin American country, or even the threat of this, will be met by firm and probably successful U.S. intervention.

Second, the notion that the Soviet Union has renounced the use of force and denied that revolutionary methods could be successful in Latin America is correct only from a short run point of view. The Russians do feel that the Cuban Revolution is not a good example for the rest of Latin America to follow and that the lack of cohesive leadership and ideological unity among guerrilla movements has for the time being doomed them to failure. Soviet strategists, however, remain convinced of the revolutionary potential of the continent and strongly imply that when "conditions are ripe," a return to subversion and revolution will be feasible.[55]

Finally, it is misleading to conjecture that Soviet disenchantment with Fidel Castro has led them to harbor thoughts of disengagement from that alliance. While Castro's purges of pro-Moscow communists and his continued advocacy of aid to insurgent movements present the Soviet Union with a constant dilemma, "the Soviet Union would presumably rather have these worries . . . and the controversies . . . than have no

---

Czechoslovakia to equip the police force. INTERPRESS dispatch filed from Caracas, March 27, 1968. The police purchase consisted of ten thousand Dehgrues revolvers, fifty light machine guns, and five hundred thousand rounds of ammunition.

[55] The Russians did sign the agreements arrived at during the January 1966 Tricontinental Conference of Havana, calling for insurrection throughout Latin America.

Castro."[56] While the Soviet Union does profit from its increased contact with other Latin American governments, the advantages of having an ally in Cuba (even at the $1 million-a-day price tag) appears to be valued by the USSR highly enough to justify its investment.

Cuba still remains of military significance to the Soviet Union. In spite of past failures and the historical evidence discussed before, it could be argued that Cuba remains a potential missile base. Cuba is also a potential naval base and refueling stop, which would permit Soviet vessels to remain on station longer in the Caribbean. It is even now an invaluable intelligence center for monitoring U.S. missile range activities in Florida and Texas and will shortly be used as a tracking station for Soviet space shots. The use of Cuba as a military diversion is also occasionally mentioned,[57] although at present Cuban diversionary potential would amount to little more than harassment.

Even though the net benefit that the Soviet Union has received from its association with Castro has been substantial, there are indications that the Soviet Union would not at present be as enthusiastic in its response to a request for military aid if another bourgeois revolution should succeed in Latin America.

Cuba is likely to retain for some time its exclusive status as the only Latin American nation receiving Soviet bloc military aid. The sensitivity of the U.S. government and the anti-communist tradition of the Latin American military are major obstacles to new Soviet military aid inroads in the western hemisphere. But if and when any additional Russian arms aid agreements are made in the region, they will be modest and will probably take the form of inter-governmental transactions rather than covert assistance to anti-government groups. Agreements are unlikely to include weapons of a primarily offensive nature but may involve transport and communications equipment. In these categories commercial purchasing practices, rather than political considerations, are apt to guide Latin American governments, leading to possible trade or aid in Soviet military equipment which has a competitive edge in price or quality over similar offerings from western governments.

The Soviet course in the later 1960s, although ambiguous enough to draw substantial criticism from Maoists and Castroites, enables the

<hr/>

[56] Leon Lipson, "Castro and the Cold War," p. 199.

[57] Baldwin even believes that the United States has had to divert a "sizeable fraction" of its military establishment to what is essentially a static, defensive task on its own doorstep. Baldwin, "A Military Perspective," p. 220.

Soviet Union to pursue a gradualist policy of helping to overturn the U.S. monopoly of influence in the Latin American region. The continuing, if reduced, military assistance program in Cuba, while not imperiling the success of this major policy, may still afford the Soviet Union long-term opportunities for the support of militant revolution in Latin America.

6

SOVIET BLOC AID DIPLOMACY:
POLICY ALTERNATIVES

SINCE 1954 foreign aid has been a principal element of statecraft in the Soviet Union's dealings with the less-developed nations of the non-aligned world. The Soviet government's initial decision to embark upon ruble diplomacy, taken in 1954 with economic aid to Afghanistan, was the first of many vital policy determinations made by the Soviet leaders. As military aid followed economic aid, the list of Soviet aid recipients expanded, costs of the programs mounted, and the diplomatic involvement of the USSR with the less-developed world increased. Among the major questions raised by the basic decision, four stand out. Was the communist military aid offensive in the Third World to be solely a Soviet thrust, or was it to be a concerted effort by the entire Warsaw Pact group of nations? How were foreign assistance efforts to be divided between economic and military aid? To what extent were economic aid and military assistance complementary to each other? Finally, how did military and economic aid and trade instruments relate to the achievement of Soviet foreign policy objectives?

To some degree, of course, these questions could not be solved exclusively by either the Soviet government or by the USSR and the other Warsaw Pact countries, since foreign assistance necessarily operates within the constraints imposed by the recipient as well as by the donor nations. These constraints, however, did not relieve the Soviet Union of the necessity for facing such problems if it were to pursue a rational aid strategy. Although evidence is fragmentary, it is the purpose of this chapter to suggest the broad principles which appear to have guided Soviet aid policy in these important questions.

THE CHOICE OF DONORS: WHICH MEMBER OF THE WARSAW PACT?

The East European allies of the Soviet Union, particularly in the Stalinist period, tended to pursue very similar policies toward the outside world. Their policies followed those of the Soviet Union and were undoubtedly dictated by the objectives of Soviet policy. Although the monolithic character of the Soviet bloc began to change after the death of Stalin—especially after the Hungarian revolution in 1956—in general a relatively high degree of consensus has continued to characterize the foreign policies of the Warsaw Pact members. To some extent, similar approaches to foreign policy are a characteristic feature of any alliance system. With the Warsaw Pact this natural propensity was reinforced by the preeminent position of the USSR relative to its satellite East European states. Given such a situation, it was to be expected that the East European nations would follow in the Soviet Union's footsteps when military aid assumed prominence in Soviet relations with Middle Eastern, Asian, and African states.

Surprisingly, the evidence on East European participation in Soviet military aid diplomacy suggests that the Warsaw Pact members are only marginally involved in this major area of Soviet foreign policy. A quantitative look at the Soviet bloc aid programs shows Moscow as the principal communist aid donor in all bloc-aided countries. There is no state for which the combined total of East European military aid contributions equals that of the Soviet Union. In fact, the Soviet government furnished approximately ninety percent of the estimated total of communist bloc arms aid to the less-developed world between 1955 and 1968. Of the remaining ten percent, nearly all came from Czechoslovakia. Minor aid contributions representing only a tiny fraction of bloc aid were provided by the other Warsaw Pact nations, in particular by Poland and East Germany.[1]

The Soviet Union has not only been the principal bloc contributor of military aid, but has also furnished most of the economic aid to the less-developed countries. Participation of other Warsaw Pact nations in economic aid, however, has been significant. Of a total of slightly more than $8 billion in economic aid provided Third World countries by the Warsaw Pact countries, Eastern Europe contributed approximately twenty-six percent and the USSR approximately seventy-four percent.

---

[1] The percentage figures were estimated from the documentary data utilized in Chapters 2 through 5 of this study. Precise dollar estimates for the small amounts of aid furnished by Poland and East Germany were not available. The percentage estimates refer only to the Warsaw Pact nations and do not include aid by Communist China.

While every military aid recipient received more military aid from the USSR than from other East European nations, Ghana, Nigeria, Sudan, Brazil, Ecuador, Uruguay, Burma, and Ceylon have received more economic aid from Eastern Europe than from the Soviet Union. The remaining thirty-two economic aid recipents received more economic aid from the USSR, but other East European states have been significant contributors to Indonesia, India, Syria, United Arab Republic, Guinea, Mali, Morocco, and Tunisia.[2]

There were occasions when the Soviet leaders had reason to minimize their military aid effort and to work through intermediary nations. Since the recipient states would compromise their "neutrality" by too close an involvement with either the Soviet Union or the United States, they too on occasion preferred assistance from smaller nations rather than from one of the two superpowers. In such cases, it was expedient for one of the other Warsaw Pact members to act as military aid donor. These motivations probably were present in the very first instance of Soviet bloc arms aid diplomacy, the accord signed between Egypt and Czechoslovakia in the fall of 1955. This agreement covered Soviet weapons as well as Czech equipment. The parties of the agreement could have included the Soviet Union, since the bulk of the arms were probably of Russian origin. It must be assumed either that the Egyptians preferred to deal with Czechoslovakia, or that the Soviet government was not yet prepared to become openly a source of arms for Third World nations. The latter interpretation seems plausible since the next Soviet bloc arms deals in the Middle East—the agreements with Syria and Yemen in early 1956—were also made with Czechoslovakia instead of directly with the USSR. Also, in 1958 Czechoslovakia was a party to an arms aid arrangement with Afghanistan. This case differed from the other three instances in that the Soviet government also signed the Afghan arms aid accords. In addition, Czechoslovakia furnished weaponry to Indonesia in the early years of the bloc aid program there and subsequently to India in 1965. More recently, in 1967, the Czechs provided military assistance to Morocco and Nigeria. Except for those two cases, no other instance was reported during 1967 of East European participation with the Soviet Union in arms aid accords with the less-developed world.

The participation of East European countries other than Czechoslovakia as military aid donors has been of little significance. Indonesia, it is true, received some naval equipment from Poland, and Egypt and

Tanzania obtained an undetermined but probably very limited amount of arms aid from East Germany.

As these examples indicate, the participation of the Warsaw Pact nations in communist military aid programs has not followed a set pattern. The quantities of aid furnished were unimportant compared to the Russian contribution. In the early Egyptian, Syrian, and Yemeni deals, the Soviet leaders probably preferred to remain in the background. In the case of Morocco, which was one of the few recent Czech arms aid recipients,[3] it seems likely that the Russians wished to minimize their involvement to avoid offending Morocco's North African rival Algeria. In the Tanzanian case, the involvement of East Germany probably was meant to convey a gesture of appreciation to Tanzania for its diplomatic recognition of the German Democratic Republic. Poland's participation in supplying naval weapons to Indonesia may simply have resulted from the fact that Poland has tended to specialize in naval craft. Finally, Czechoslovakia's preeminent role as an arms donor undoubtedly reflected that country's important position in arms production and its comparatively high level of industrialization.

Participation by the Warsaw Pact nations in communist arms diplomacy, then, was conditioned by the special circumstances prevailing at the time, usually reflecting the economic specialization and level of industrialization of the individual East European nations. In some instances, the equipment furnished to the recipients was of Soviet manufacture, with the East European donor in essence acting only as an intermediary. Despite this fact, there is no evidence of a fully articulated Soviet-East European military aid plan that provided for a coordinated bloc-wide approach to arms aid diplomacy and selected the donors on the basis of established foreign policy criteria.

THE CHOICE OF INSTRUMENTS: MILITARY OR ECONOMIC AID?

Just as the Soviet government had to determine whether or not its East European allies should participate in arms aid diplomacy, so it also had to determine whether aid programs should consist exclusively of military aid, or of economic aid, or of a mixture of both. In making these decisions on a country-by-country basis, Moscow appears to have been guided more by political considerations, such as the degree of neutrality of the aid recipient and the particular interest group in the

---

[3] After the Arab-Israeli war of June 1967, the Soviet Union apparently facilitated a Czech-Moroccan agreement for tanks and field artillery up to an amount of some $16 million. See *New York Times*, July 16, 1968. Czech-made equipment started to arrive in Morocco in November 1967. *Africa Report*, vol. 13, no. 1 (January 1968), p. 33.

country the USSR wished to influence, than by economic considerations, such as the relative costs of the alternative aid instruments to the Soviet Union.

In a few cases the Soviet objective was to strengthen the military capability of the recipient against an actual or potential military threat. In these instances the USSR offered military aid irrespective of whether the country was receiving Soviet economic assistance.

Political Criteria: Allocating Military and Economic Aid. A key factor in determining whether recipients receive military or economic aid seems to be the position of the aid recipients in international affairs. It appears that the Soviet government ranks aid recipients with respect to their degree of identification with Soviet foreign policy positions in world politics. Those nations most closely associated with the Soviet Union, or most hostile to the United States, receive Soviet approval in the form of both economic and military aid. Countries which are less closely associated with Soviet views on world politics, but which are nevertheless considered potential targets for Soviet influence, tend to receive economic aid only, whereas most countries hostile to the Soviet Union or in military alliance with the United States are likely to obtain neither military nor economic aid.[4]

Table 6-1 lists the twenty-five Soviet military aid recipients from 1955 through 1967. Except for Iran and Pakistan, none of them are members of U.S. alliance systems. It is perhaps worthy of note that Iran's original alliance with the west through the instrumentality of the Baghdad Pact (later CENTO) is no longer viable. Similarly, there has been a marked deterioration in Pakistani-American relations, particularly since the Pakistani-Indian border war of 1965, which stimulated strong Chinese support for Pakistan.

In contrast to military aid recipients, a few countries receiving only economic aid from the USSR have been allies of the United States, and some have tended to be pro-western in their neutralism. Table 6-2 lists countries which obtained only economic aid, with estimates of the amounts of aid received. Compared to the Soviet military aid recipients presented in Table 6-1, most of the economic aid-receiving countries in Table 6-2 are decidedly less closely associated with the Soviet Union. To illustrate, Argentina and Brazil, members with the United States in the Organization of American States, obtain only economic assistance from the Soviet Union. Cuba, on the other hand, bitterly hostile to the United States, has received both military and economic aid from the

---

[4] For a detailed discussion of the relationship between receiving Soviet arms aid and identifying with Soviet world policy positions see Chapter 8.

Table 6-1. Estimated Soviet Bloc Assistance to Military Aid Recipients: 1955 through 1967 (In Millions of U.S. Dollars)

	Military Aid	Economic Aid
Afghanistan	$ 260	$ 582
Algeria	200	254
Cambodia	5 to 10	30
Congo-Brazzaville	1	9
Congo-Kinshasa	1 to 2	0
Cuba	750	N.A.*
Cyprus	28	0
Ghana	10 to 15	191
Guinea	at least 6	98
India	600 to 700	1,948
Indonesia	1,200	635
Iran	100	386
Iraq	at least 500	184
Laos	3 to 5	N.A.
Mali	at least 3	78
Morocco	20	79
Nigeria	10 to 15	14
Pakistan	5 to 10	234
Somalia	35	72
Sudan	N.A.	49
Syria	at least 300	377
Tanzania	5 to 10	26
UAR	1,500	1,573
Uganda	N.A.	16
Yemen	100	109
Total Up To:	$5,770	$6,944

Sources: Data presented on military aid are based on sources documented in Chapters 2 through 5; see especially Tables 2-1, 3-1, and 4-1. Soviet bloc military aid to the Middle East countries (Algeria, Iraq, Morocco, Syria, UAR, and Yemen) provided after the June 1967 war is not included. The economic aid data includes aid from 1954 through 1967. See U.S. Department of State, *Aid and Trade in 1967*, pp. 2-3.
* Because much of the economic aid to Cuba takes the form of "hidden aid," such as subsidies of Cuban sugar exports to the Soviet Union, it is difficult to present an accurate estimate of Soviet economic aid to Cuba. For a discussion of Soviet bloc economic relations with Cuba, see Goldman, *Soviet Foreign Aid*, pp. 160-67.

Soviet Union. A similar pattern is repeated in other regions. In Africa the Ethiopians, associated with the Americans, receive only economic assistance from the Russians; the Somalis, more friendly to the Russians, obtain military as well as economic assistance from the Soviet government. In the Middle East, Turkey and Tunisia, both identified with the United States in east-west relations, are the only Soviet economic aid recipients in the region that do not also receive Russian arms aid. In South and Southeast Asia, Burma, one of the countries in the region which perseveres most strongly in its neutralism, is the recipient of merely economic aid from the Soviet Union. The same applies to non-aligned Ceylon.

In some instances countries which have obtained Soviet economic but not military aid undoubtedly could have acquired Soviet arms assistance had they chosen to do so. Since, however, the receipt of military aid is

Table 6-2. Estimated Soviet Bloc Economic Aid to Developing Countries Receiving Economic
Aid Only: 1954 through 1967 (In Millions of U.S. Dollars)

Country	Total	From USSR	From East Europe
Argentina	$ 49	$ 45	$ 4
Brazil	312	85	227
Burma	40	14	26
Cameroon	8	8	0
Ceylon	82	30	52
Chile	55	55	0
Ecuador	5	0	5
Ethiopia	119	102	17
Kenya	44	44	0
Mauritania	3	3	0
Nepal	20	28	0
Senegal	7	7	0
Sierra Leone	28	28	0
Tunisia	54	34	20
Turkey	218	210	8
Uruguay	10	0	10
Zambia	6	6	0
Totals	$1,060	$699	$369

Source: U.S. Department of State, *Aid and Trade in 1967*, pp. 2-3. For an excellent and com-
prehensive study of Soviet economic aid, see Goldman, *Soviet Foreign Aid*.

commonly viewed as compromising neutrality, these countries may have
preferred economic to military assistance. Soviet economic aid recipients may fear that the acceptance of Russian military assistance, in
addition to economic aid, might jeopardize their relations with the
United States. This seems especially true in Latin America.

Soviet policy-makers also select their aid instruments on the basis of
which power group they hope to cultivate in the recipient country.
Military aid programs create opportunities for influencing the military
elites of the Third World. It is important for the USSR to obtain the
good will of these elites because of the powerful role and influence they
have in the political life of emerging nations. The political leadership
of developing countries generally finds the support of military officers
indispensable; in fact, it frequently draws its members from military
ranks. The high incidence of military coups in the developing countries
reinforces this observation.

The usual practice has been to offer military aid after an economic
aid program has begun, but there are also examples in which the process
was reversed and an initial grant of arms aid led to subsequent economic
aid. If, however, a principal objective of the Soviet Union is to establish
a hold on the military elites, the USSR is likely to make use of its military aid instrument to promote that objective.

Economic Criteria: The Costs of Aid. Both Soviet military and economic aid normally take the form of long-term (ten to twelve years),

low-interest-rate loans, repayable by the recipient in convertible currencies, in commodities, or in local funds. Although these arrangements are referred to as Soviet "military aid" or "economic aid," the technically more accurate term would be "military loans" or "economic loans." Nevertheless, the terms of the aid agreements are generally sufficiently favorable to the recipients that the aid is equivalent to partial grants. While twelve-year repayment periods impose a burden on recipients, the two or two-and-a-half percent interest rate charged by the Soviet government amounts to a limited subsidy.[5]

The magnitude of the subsidy, however, has to be interpreted in terms of prices placed on the items granted and on goods received in payment, as well as in terms of the exchange rates. To the extent that prices of Soviet goods were higher than the market prices, and to the extent that exchange rates reflected an overvaluation of the Soviet ruble, the low interest rates charged to aid recipients were partly offset. Some Soviet aid actually might have been very profitable to the Soviet Union because of exorbitant prices charged for Soviet goods. The Indians, in particular, have complained of the high cost of replacement parts for Soviet machinery.[6]

In the earlier years of the Soviet military assistance program, weapons aid may have been less costly to the Soviet government than economic aid. In Syria, for example, the Soviet bloc initially supplied a number of reconditioned World War II model tanks which, although probably satisfying Syrian military requirements, were obsolete in terms of Soviet army utilization. The cotton the USSR received in payment for these weapons yielded in all likelihood a net profit. The majority of the arms shipped to African states was of little utility to the Soviet armed forces, and commodities received in payment may have represented profitable transactions for the Soviet Union. Since about 1961, however, when Russian arms deliveries included more modern weapons still in use by the Soviet military forces, the cost differential between economic and military aid has declined and perhaps vanished altogether. The more privileged countries among Soviet recipients, notably Egypt, Indonesia, Cuba, and India, have acquired sophisticated weapons systems in standard use by the Soviet armed forces.

[5] Occasionally, Soviet terms are longer than twelve years. In the case of Afghanistan, fifty-year loans were made, with twenty-five-year grace periods. In these cases, the loans were practically equivalent to grants. Afghanistan also is the only country which has received a substantial economic grant from the USSR. See U.S. Department of State, *The Communist Economic Offensive through 1964*, Research Memorandum RSB-65 (Washington, August 4, 1965), p. 7.

[6] Michael P. Gehlen, *The Politics of Coexistence* (Bloomington, Indiana: Indiana University Press, 1967), p. 182.

In the long run, military assistance is likely to be more expensive to the USSR than economic aid of a similar dollar value. Unlike economic aid, military aid does not contribute to the economic infrastructure and production capability of recipients, nor does it enhance the ability of recipients to meet future repayments. Arms aid, moreover, may stimulate the recipients to undertake an unwise allocation of resources. Large scale military aid may contribute to maintaining a large military establishment which constitutes a drain on the recipients' economies, thereby causing defaults in repayment schedules. This situation already seems to have developed in Indonesia; it may be an element in the reluctance of the Soviet Union to extend new military aid to Indonesia.

As in the case of most creditors, Moscow is undoubtedly aware of the costs of its foreign policy instruments. There is, however, no evidence to show that the relative cost to the Soviet Union has been much more than a marginal consideration in the choice of instruments. The doubtless poor repayment prospects which faced the Soviet Union in its decision to aid Sukarno did not prevent the huge arms aid program in Indonesia, nor did costs appear to be a deterrent to the rapid restocking of Arab arsenals after the Middle East war of June 1967. Similarly, Soviet aid to Cuba probably constitutes an uneconomic enterprise in view of recent Cuban export shortages and poor sugar crops. Thus while the Soviet Union may use cost-effectiveness accounting to decide upon the merits of a specific economic aid project or upon the size or shape of a particular military aid program, it is likely that the question of whether economic or military aid should be used hinges on other than economic considerations.

The Interrelationship of Military and Economic Aid

Just as the Soviet government considers the comparative advantages of economic and military assistance, so do the recipients consider the impact of the two forms of aid on their economies. From the recipient's budgetary point of view, military aid and economic aid may be potentially interchangeable. Third World countries generally have very limited resources available to provide for large armed forces, to invest in capital goods, and to produce consumer articles for their populations. Accordingly, foreign aid of whatever content may release some resources for purposes other than that for which the aid was received. Military assistance, by releasing domestic or foreign exchange resources originally earmarked for defense, enables the recipient country to allocate more funds to the consumer sector or to capital investment. In similar fashion, economic aid permits recipients to allocate more resources to the acquisition of military equipment and the maintenance of armed forces.

It is not possible to know how a military aid recipient might have used its resources in the absence of Soviet arms assistance. It might be that the failure to obtain military aid would have left its economic development program unaffected. For example, the government concerned could have chosen to do without the desired military equipment rather than to divert scarce resources from economic to military purposes. It is also possible that a nation was already allocating the maximum feasible resources to military procurement and that Soviet military aid would have been used to maintain forces far beyond the recipient's capacity to do so in the absence of aid. Soviet arms aid would not in such cases replace the efforts of the recipient to maintain its military establishment but would merely supplement them. In addition, a nation might not resort to budgetary interchangeability between military and economic aid without first seeking arms aid from donors other than the USSR.

The extent to which budgetary interchangeability is possible varies from case to case and depends upon such factors as the recipient's holdings of foreign exchange and the degree to which the government can allocate resources. If the Soviet Union demands repayment of its arms aid in convertible currency, less foreign exchange will be available for purposes of economic development. A similar disadvantage exists in the case of economic aid repaid in hard currency. Repayment in specified commodities for economic or military assistance also tends to restrict the recipient's budgetary flexibility. To illustrate, Egypt's repayment of Soviet aid in cotton reduced Egypt's ability to earn foreign exchange through the export of cotton to other foreign markets. For this reason, grants, in contrast to loans, maximize the recipient's ability to engage in budgetary interchangeability between military and economic aid.

While economic aid and military aid are thus interchangeable to only a limited extent, economic aid can contribute to the military potential of the recipients. Economic aid in trucks, transport aircraft, and ships, and in the form of building or improving airports, harbors, and telecommunications lines is highly useful to the armed forces of the recipients in internal security as well as in national defense missions. Guinea, Ghana, and Mali received credits for the purchase of Soviet passenger aircraft, which could be converted into troop transports. Although provided under the rubric of economic assistance, transportation and communications aid may be viewed as affording both economic and military utilities to the recipients.

A further relationship between military and economic aid is relevant in long range terms. To the extent that economic aid is directed into industrial investment or provides social overhead capital, such assistance necessarily enhances the long term potential of the recipient to produce military hardware. Construction of steel mills, power plants, dams, and roads, as well as the training of technicians and students, can all be viewed as economic aid. Nevertheless, some of these programs increase a recipient's ability to produce its own military supplies in the future and to earn foreign exchange to purchase military equipment abroad. Particularly where Soviet economic aid is used to establish or improve heavy industries, such as the Bhilai steel works in India, the potential arms manufacturing capabilities of the recipient are distinctly advanced.

By the same token, military aid can make a long range contribution to economic development through the role that arms aid plays in maintaining internal security and stability, a necessary prerequisite to economic progress for any developing country. If, however, military aid encourages a recipient to devote a larger share of its resources than it can sustain to maintaining a huge military establishment, its economic growth can be seriously retarded.

ECONOMIC AID AND THE SOVIET MILITARY POSTURE

Soviet economic aid in the form of transportation and communications may have military utilities, not only for the recipient countries but also for the Soviet Union.

In the field of civil aviation, Soviet assistance has been used to build or improve landing strips capable of accommodating jet aircraft in Guinea, Yemen, Somalia, the UAR, and Afghanistan. In return for its assistance, the Soviet bloc has obtained landing, refueling, or overflight rights from some recipient countries. Soviet bloc civil airlines serve Algiers, Conakry, Bamako, Accra, Khartoum, Cairo, Dar es Salaam, Mogadishu, and Sana.

A major portion of Soviet bloc economic aid for transportation purposes has been devoted to the improvement of maritime port facilities in some of the recipient countries. The types of improvements have generally been those which the nation involved requested in order to meet the needs of its own merchant, fishing, and naval vessels. Maritime ports that have been developed with Soviet bloc aid include Hodeida in Yemen, Berbera in Somalia, Basrah in Iraq, and Tema in Ghana. A port survey has been carried out in Tangiers, Morocco, and facilities to support the Egyptian navy at Alexandria have been improved.

The possible availability of Soviet-aided aviation and port facilities to Soviet aircraft and ships may be a goal of Russian aid efforts. In fact, it seems likely that the extensive road-building programs and harbor, airport, and railroad improvements and construction in the Middle East and Africa have been reviewed by Soviet military planners in the light of potential Soviet strategic interests. Soviet economic development projects in Afghanistan have a particular potential to contribute to the Soviet military posture; the road and tunnel through the Hindu Kush mountains provide the USSR with a long coveted all-weather access route into the Indian subcontinent.

In discussing the utility of economic aid in potentially enhancing Soviet logistic capabilities in less-developed countries, the acquisition of bases has to be distinguished from arrangements to use transportation and communications facilities. To date, the only known Soviet attempt to acquire a military base in the territories of aid recipients is in Cuba. This particular adventure was inconsistent with the apparent caution which the Soviet Union has exhibited in trying to enhance its military posture through the utilization of overseas bases. Except for the Cuban failure, there is no indication that the Soviet Union actively seeks control of overseas bases as a means of promoting its strategic goals. Such a policy would entail serious risks for the Soviet Union in view of its provocative impact on the west. Although Soviet naval forces in the Mediterranean have markedly expanded since June 1967, it is likely that the USSR will continue to be restricted to the use of the port facilities of Egypt, Syria, and Algeria and will not try to acquire naval bases. The permission to use these bases, however, has improved Soviet maritime logistic capabilities.

The substantial Soviet economic and military aid programs in India and Pakistan have opened up the possibility that the Soviet Union might expand its naval operations in the Indian Ocean area. There has been particularly close cooperation between the Indian and Russian navies, and recently Moscow made four submarines available to the Indian navy. Soviet advisers are training Indian submarine crews. In return it has been rumored that India will provide the USSR with a naval base in the Indian Ocean, but to date this has not occurred.[7]

TRADE AND AID

Soviet bloc trade with the Third World seems to be both economically and politically motivated. From an economic point of view, Third World countries provide the Soviet bloc with needed raw materials and

[7] *Christian Science Monitor*, November 30, 1968.

agricultural products such as wheat, cotton, rubber, grain, tea, and cocoa. The Soviet bloc exports machinery and equipment, particularly complete plants and installations. Such exports have few buyers in the industrial countries but are in demand among the less-developed nations. Third World countries find in the Soviet bloc a market for their agricultural raw materials and foodstuffs. Thus trade between the Soviet bloc and the developing countries has a sound economic basis.[8] Nevertheless, in 1966, the last year for which complete trade data is available, communist trade, including both the Soviet bloc and China, accounted for only six percent of the total trade of the developing countries and about ten percent of aggregate communist world trade.[9]

Trade is related to economic and military aid in that exports from Third World countries to the Soviet bloc to some extent reflect repayments in commodities for the assistance received. It also reflects the desire of the less-developed nations to engage in bilateral trading to conserve their limited foreign exchange holdings.[10]

Beyond the economic logic of trade between the Soviet bloc and the Third World, political motivations for trade appear to be present as well. Two of the largest military aid recipients, India and the United Arab Republic, accounted for forty-one percent of the USSR's trade with developing countries in 1966. Of the sixteen largest importers of Soviet goods in 1966, thirteen were military aid recipients. Nine of the fifteen largest Third World exporters to the Soviet Union also were military aid recipients. Among the major trading partners of the USSR, only Argentina, Brazil, Ceylon, Malaysia, and Turkey did not receive military assistance. Malaysia was the only major trading country with the Soviet bloc that received neither military nor economic aid.[11] Stated differently, almost all Soviet bloc aid recipients are also major Third World trading partners with the Soviet bloc. Thus receipt of military or economic assistance correlates very highly with the volume of trade between the Soviet bloc and Third World nations.

The interconnections between military aid and trade and the partially politically inspired basis for each are suggested by Soviet-Indonesian and Soviet-Pakistani relations. Following the change of government in Indonesia in 1965, not only did the Soviet Union sharply curtail military assistance to Indonesia, but Soviet exports to that country plunged from their 1965 total of $54 million to approximately $5 million. This $5

[8] Milton Kovner, "Soviet Trade and Aid," *Current History*, vol. 49, no. 290 (October 1965), pp. 231-33.

[9] U.S. Department of State, *Aid and Trade in 1967*, p. iv.

[10] *Ibid.*, p. 15.

[11] *Ibid.*, pp. 14-23.

million in exports marked a low point in Soviet-Indonesian trade, contrasting sharply with Soviet exports of $163 million in 1964.

Pakistan and the Soviet Union concluded their first military aid agreement in August 1967, after Pakistan had already received some military assistance from Communist China. Consistent with these developments, Pakistan's imports from the Soviet Union rose from $13 million in 1965 to $39 million in 1966. Pakistan's exports to the USSR rose even more dramatically, from $4 million in 1965 to $29 million in 1966. The increasing involvement of Pakistan with the communist countries was evident the following year. The total value of communist trade with Pakistan rose from about $70 million during the first half of 1966 to about $120 million during the first six months of 1967.[12]

Both the Indonesian and Pakistani examples, as well as the close correspondence between trade partners and aid recipients, suggest that Soviet military assistance and volume of trade will tend to rise and fall together. Military aid, economic aid, and trade may be viewed as a composite politico-economic barometer of Soviet relations with Third World countries.

[12] *Ibid.*, pp. 13, 19, 22.

7

WARS OF LIBERATION
AND MILITARY AID POLICY

FUNDAMENTAL TO Soviet foreign policy in the last decade has been the concept that international politics may be viewed in terms of the "correlation of world forces." This phrase apparently means that Soviet decision-makers appraise Soviet foreign policy moves in the context of their impact on total Soviet political, economic, and military strength in relation to that of the United States and other possible adversaries, and in terms of an assessment of the worldwide distribution of power among communist, capitalist, and the new "nationalist-bourgeois" states. Current Soviet doctrine maintains that the correlation of world forces has shifted decisively in favor of the USSR since World War II. This development was brought about primarily by the successful national liberation movements, which destroyed western colonial empires. The newly emerging states, although not communist, support the "socialist camp" headed by the Soviet Union, in opposition to the declining "imperialist camp" led by the United States. Neutralist states, emerging from former western colonial areas as the result of successful "wars of national liberation," constitute a "zone of peace." Countries comprising this zone of peace assist the Soviet Union, as head of the "international camp of socialism," to exert greater influence on the course of world politics.

These doctrinal developments are logically related to the Soviet Union's repudiation of the long-standing communist theory of the inevitability of war between world capitalism and world socialism. Now that the international camp of socialism had become so strong, so the reasoning went, the capitalist camp would not dare attack it. Even the United States, with its vast armaments, was deterred from committing aggression against the socialist nations. The era of "capitalist encirclement" of the USSR had come to an end; the balance of forces in the world had shifted decisively and irrevocably in favor of the international camp of socialism; Soviet political, economic, and military supremacy was steadily increasing.

Changes in the Soviet world view have been accompanied by a stress on the theme of "peaceful coexistence." Communists everywhere are now required to "struggle for peace," and the possibility, even certainty, that world-wide communism can be achieved without general war is constantly emphasized. Taken at face value, it would seem that the Soviet government has renounced the use of force to achieve world communism. Closer examination, however, reveals that peaceful coexistence refers only to the renunciation of certain kinds of wars, rather than the repudiation of all use of force in international politics. It must be assumed that distinctions between approved and condemned uses of force condition, if not determine, other aspects of Soviet foreign policy and in particular Soviet military aid policy. Hence an analysis of Soviet military aid as a significant instrument of approved force through wars of liberation must address itself first to distinguishing between approved and disapproved wars in Soviet doctrine.

CONCEPTS OF WARS IN SOVIET DOCTRINE

Soviet doctrine distinguishes three basic types of wars: (1) general and strategic war; (2) local-limited war; and (3) wars of liberation. Soviet spokesmen strongly condemn the first two types of wars but emphasize the duty of communists to support wars of liberation. Soviet sources, however, are somewhat ambiguous in distinguishing between the various types and are occasionally even contradictory. While Soviet doctrine is fully developed as regards general and strategic war, other types of war concepts are not fully articulated. Accordingly, Soviet policy toward non-strategic wars, whether local wars or wars of liberation in doctrinal terms, must be interpreted not only from Soviet statements but also through empirical analysis of Soviet behavior toward these conflicts.

The category of general and strategic war includes any war directly between the Soviet Union and the United States, irrespective of whether such a war might be limited in geographical scope and level of intensity. Any war involving the Soviet Union and the United States, even if fought with conventional weapons, is classified as general and strategic. Although recent Soviet writing suggests some possibility for revisions in Soviet thought, ordinarily any wars involving Europe and any wars in which nuclear weapons are employed, even if only tactical, are also classified as general and strategic. All of these types of general and strategic wars are condemned by Soviet spokesmen, and Soviet doctrine requires communists to "struggle against" such wars.

Local-limited wars may be divided into several subcategories: (1) local-limited wars between capitalist states; (2) local-limited wars initiated by capitalist states against newly independent states, or against nationalist-bourgeoisie elements within a state struggling for "freedom" against capitalist states; (3) local-limited wars initiated by capitalists against communist states other than the Soviet Union; and (4) civil wars between capitalist elements within a state.

As for the first type of local-limited war, until the death of Stalin, Soviet doctrine held that the struggle for world markets would cause war between capitalist states. At the Nineteenth Communist Party Congress in 1952, it was asserted that the diminishing area available to the capitalists for colonialist exploitation would lead to war between capitalist countries. Present doctrine, however, appears to discount that possibility; other capitalist countries are now viewed as virtual satellites of the United States and thus incapable of resisting American domination. About civil wars between capitalist factions within a country, Soviet doctrine has little to say. This is understandable since Soviet theory expects civil war situations to develop between capitalists and non-capitalists rather than between groups representing the same socioeconomic class.

Hence the persistent admonitions to "struggle against" local-limited wars are confined to those wars initiated by capitalists against newly independent states, a nationalist-bourgeois group within a state, or communist states other than the Soviet Union. These types of wars are strongly condemned. Soviet condemnations are frequently accompanied by threats to escalate such conflicts into general and strategic nuclear war, or warnings that they will inevitably escalate, regardless of Soviet intentions.

In no area of discussion about the use of force to achieve international objectives are Soviet statements more vague and more contradictory than in the case of wars of liberation. It is frequently assumed that these types of wars refer solely to conflict initiated by communists or other revolutionary elements within a society, usually the so-called national bourgeoisie, against a capitalist-colonialist incumbent government. This interpretation, in fact, has been given credence by Khrushchev's extensive review of world politics in a speech before a group of world communist leaders meeting in Moscow in January 1961.[1] Other Soviet statements seem to suggest, however, a much broader definition of wars of liberation.

A 1964 article written by two Soviet army colonels identifies Soviet military aid to incumbent governments in Indonesia, Egypt, and Algeria as aid to "national liberation movements."[2] Another article justified Soviet military aid to newly independent nations as necessary to assist these nations in their "fight against colonizers."[3] This theme, that *incumbent governments* are also forces of national liberation, was repeated in a 1965 commentary which stated that the Soviet Union grants new nations "long-term credits at favorable terms . . . to strengthen their national-liberation armies and provide them with modern military technology."[4] The military of the new nation-states are regarded as forces of national liberation in conflict with capitalism and colonialism, whether at home or abroad. Military aid to these incumbent revolutionary-type governments is justified, since the "armed forces of these countries have acquired an anti-imperialist character" and are struggling to free themselves from foreign control.[5]

These statements, coupled with Soviet aid behavior, suggest a broad interpretation of wars of liberation, which includes at least three distinct elements: first, struggles by revolutionary elements, communist or not, within a state against an incumbent capitalist government; second, conflicts of communist states in the less-developed world against capitalist governments; and third, wars by non-communist but left-oriented new states against capitalist nations. All three types of wars of liberation are to be supported and encouraged by the Soviet Union through the provision of military assistance. These wars are "holy wars," "just wars"—legitimate instruments for hastening the day of world communism.

The distinctions drawn between general and strategic nuclear war, on the one hand, and local-limited wars and wars of liberation, on the

---

[1] See Charles Burton Marshall (ed.), *Two Communist Manifestoes* (Washington: Washington Center of Foreign Policy Research, 1961), *passim*.

[2] Lt. Col. G. Eckov and Colonel Prilepskii, "World Socialist System: A Decisive Contemporary Factor, *Kommunist Vooruzhennykh Sil* (Communist of the Armed Forces), no. 22 (November 1964), pp. 34-41.

[3] Colonel S. Kukonin, "The Character of our Epoch and the General Line of the World Communist Movement," *ibid.*, no. 21 (November 1964), pp. 15-22.

[4] "Contemporary Stage of the National Liberation Movement," *ibid.*, no. 6 (March 1965), pp. 67-71.

[5] Colonel E. Dolgopolov, "Armies of Liberated Africa," *Krasnaia Zvezda* (Red Star), September 25, 1965, p. 3.

other, are reasonably clear, despite the murkiness of Soviet doctrine. The definitions of local-limited wars and wars of liberation, however, do not permit a ready distinction between these two types of conflicts. The basic difficulty lies in the fact that they are not contrasted by measurable military criteria such as scope and level of violence, but by political and socio-economic standards. These standards appear to include appraisal of a particular conflict situation in terms of the political and socio-economic attributes, objectives, and the foreign policy orientations of the contestants.[6]

Employing such political rather than military criteria, the Soviets have condemned as local-limited wars the Israeli-French-British attack on Egypt in 1956, French military action in Indochina until 1954, and present American military actions in Vietnam. Additional local-limited wars, according to Soviet spokesmen, include those waged by the United States and the United Nations in Korea, by the British in Malaya, the Dutch in New Guinea, and the French in Algeria. The opponents of these western forces, however, were considered to be the forces of national liberation. Thus Soviet-approved wars of liberation were fought by the Algerians against France, the Pathet Lao against the incumbent Laotian government, and the Indonesians against the Dutch and the Malaysians. Currently, the most critical war of liberation is being conducted in Vietnam by the Viet Cong.[7]

In short, recourse to war by the western powers or their allies is condemned as local-limited war; recourse to arms by the newly independent or "colonial" peoples, or by communist states or guerrilla forces in opposition to western or western-oriented regimes, ordinarily receives Soviet approval as a war of liberation. The *same war* may be labeled a war of liberation by the Soviet Union when reference is made to the belligerent that the USSR supports and may be classified as a local-limited war in reference to the western-oriented combatant. This distinction between the two types of wars merely reflects Soviet preferences as between the protagonists. It is a propaganda one only and it should

[6] According to Colonel General N. A. Lomov, "The only correct criterion for defining the character of wars is their socio-political content." Quoted in Thomas W. Wolfe, *Soviet Strategy at the Crossroads* (Cambridge: Harvard University Press, 1964), p. 289.

[7] Some commentators have contrasted wars of liberation and limited wars by noting that Khrushchev emphasized the intergovernmental character of local wars, while wars of liberation are proxy wars and generally intragovernmental. For discussion of this point, see *ibid.*, pp. 118-29. Wolfe notes (p. 289) "signs of doctrinal difficulty" in distinguishing between local and national liberation wars.

not be taken as serious socio-political analysis.[8] Appreciation of this central fact leads inescapably to the conclusion that peaceful coexistence signifies something other than the absolute renunciation of force as a means to world-wide communism.

Reference to Soviet approval of wars of liberation would not be complete without noting, in a speculative way, the possible relationship between Soviet doctrinal support for such wars and the Sino-Soviet ideological conflict. The Chinese have accused the Russians of "revisionism" in urging the thesis of the peaceful attainment of communism and have implied that the Soviet government was fearful of a military clash with the United States. The Soviet Union has replied that it never renounced all use of force to achieve communism, but only general and strategic nuclear war and local-limited war. Soviet support for wars of liberation, the Russians argued, proved that the USSR was fully prepared to hasten the inevitable triumph of world-wide communism through military means. The Sino-Soviet dispute suggests that Soviet distinctions between local-limited wars and wars of liberation were formulated, at least to some extent, in order to answer Chinese criticisms.

Whether or not the distinctions arose for this reason, the fact is that Soviet military aid has been given to some twenty-five nations, many of which, at one time or another during the history of the aid program, have been involved in conflicts which could be called wars of liberation under the broad meaning the Soviet government has assigned to that term.

WARS OF LIBERATION POLICIES

Once the Soviet Union has determined to prefer one group of contestants over an opposing group in a "hot" or sublimited conflict—that is, has determined which combatant is the war-of-liberation force in terms of political, socio-economic and foreign policy analyses—its support of the favored protagonist through military aid appears to take into account several factors. Criteria for Soviet support include: (1) the risk to the USSR should the war escalate; (2) the probabilities of suc-

---

[8] The U.S. position on this question is that wars of liberation are intragovernmental only. On this basis official U.S. sources cite fourteen major wars of liberation between 1946 and 1968. See U.S. Department of State, *Vietnam Information Notes: Wars of National Liberation*, no. 12 (Washington, June 1968), p. 3. Based on Soviet statements justifying military aid, however, it seems to the authors of this study that the Soviet Union has not consistently followed this limited definition of wars of liberation. Accordingly, a broader definition of wars of liberation which includes certain intergovernmental conflicts has been adopted in this chapter.

cess for the Soviet-backed forces; and (3) the effect of Soviet support, whether or not Soviet-backed forces are successful, on the international political situation in general, and on the position of the leading western countries and Communist China in particular. The problem for Soviet aid policy, however, is that the rough standards employed are seldom met in all essentials. While some elements in the situation may be favorable from the Soviet point of view, others may be unfavorable.

Theoretically, it is possible to establish a continuum ranging from the most favorable to the least favorable situation. The most favorable situation would be one with the following attributes: (1) Soviet appraisal of the contestants would result in a distinct Soviet preference for one side against the other; (2) the favored side would enjoy a high probability of success; (3) such a success would be a clear net gain for the USSR at the expense of the western powers and of China; and (4) in the process of achieving this success, the danger of escalation directly involving the Soviet Union would be minimal or nonexistent.

At the other end of the continuum, the least favorable situation would have these characteristics: (1) Soviet appraisal of the contestants would yield dissatisfaction with the foreign policy orientations, socio-economic bases, and political outlooks of both, thus making a choice between them difficult; (2) the favored side would have little hope of achieving success; (3) the outcome of the struggle might produce U.S. or Chinese gains at the expense of the Soviet Union; and (4) the risk of war escalation involving the USSR would be substantial.

Most of the situations in which the Russians have had to decide whether to grant military aid in support of wars of liberation have contained a mixture of favorable and unfavorable aspects and hence cannot be placed at either end of the spectrum. Because Soviet policy-makers have had to make aid decisions under conditions of uncertainty, they have been compelled to establish overriding priorities or considerations which help them to make a determination. To reach any general conclusions about the criteria employed by Soviet decision-makers, and to determine whether certain criteria may be decisive, it is necessary to test these standards against specific Soviet military aid policies in particular situations. Although the Soviet Union's decisions to grant or withhold military aid are certainly not based solely on its wars-of-liberation strategy, this analysis will assess only the wars-of-liberation criteria governing such decisions.

The Soviet Union, since its stated aim is to foster world communism, would clearly prefer the recipients of its aid to be communists or Marxist-Leninists. This standard, however, has not been decisive in determining Soviet military aid allocations. Cuba, the Viet Cong, and the Pathet Lao could be termed communist or Marxist-Leninist. A number of others may be described as Marxist-Leninist oriented, ranging from ultra-leftist to moderate-leftist. These include Iraq in 1958 and again in 1964, Egypt, Indonesia, Laos, Cambodia, Algeria, Tanzania, Guinea, Ghana, Mali, Cyprus, Somalia, and the Lumumba and Stanleyville regimes in the Congo. This list indicates that the USSR has tended to proffer its aid to left-oriented recipients. On the other hand, the Soviet Union has extended military aid to regimes that range from moderate-reformist to ultra-rightist or semi-feudal. These include Syria in 1956 and 1963, Yemen under the Imamate, Afghanistan, and Morocco. In Soviet theory, the leaders of all of these governments are considered national bourgeoisie and therefore antipathetic to imperialist powers.

In some cases, military aid was continued to recipients who suppressed communist or ultra-leftist movements within their borders. For example, Soviet aid was at times employed in a counterrevolutionary manner by Iraq, Egypt, Syria, Morocco, and Algeria. The compelling conclusion is that Soviet decisions to provide military aid to particular countries were prompted by the desirability of assisting all national bourgeoisie governments deemed hostile to western interests. Neither the classical Marxist-Leninist attributes of the aided recipients nor their internal policies toward indigenous communism seem to have been overriding considerations. Accordingly, Marxist-Leninist socio-economic criteria must be largely discounted.[9]

The Soviet government would prefer, of course, to back recipients who have some reasonable chance of winning their wars of liberation. At the same time, Soviet decisions must also take into account the opponents of the wars-of-liberation forces. Thus the Russians might support even a losing side if the other combatant were a western country or strongly oriented toward the west. On the other hand, they would not support a preferred but losing side in a case where neither protagonist was closely linked to the western powers. With these standards in mind, it should be noted that the Soviet Union has not supported indigenous communist movements in wars of liberation against anti-colonialist, nationalist-bourgeois regimes when it appeared that the communist forces could not possibly succeed. Examples of this policy of restraint include Soviet disinclination to aid communists in Egypt and

---

[9] It should be noted, however, that the Soviets have attempted to reconcile aid to the national bourgeoisie with communist doctrine by creating concepts such as the zone of peace and by classifying many aid recipients as in the first stage of a two-stage struggle to establish a "people's democracy."

Indonesia against friendly regimes or even Indian communists against the neutralist government of India.

In instances where insurgents faced neutralist regimes not friendly to the USSR, but where the insurgents had little chance of success, the Russians have displayed some ambivalence but generally have opted for the winning side, notably in Iraq. Despite frequent strains in Soviet-Iraqi relations, particularly in the 1960–63 period, the Soviet Union did not materially assist the Kurdish insurgency except by attempting to persuade Iraq to seek a negotiated settlement with the Kurds. In 1964, when Iraqi policy became more favorable to Moscow, Kurdish aspirations were disregarded; both Iraq and Syria received Soviet military aid for almost certain employment against Kurdish wars-of-liberation forces.

In those cases where insurgents, whether communist, leftist, or moderate nationalist-bourgeois, faced regimes clearly hostile to the USSR, they benefitted from Soviet support, at least on a limited basis, even if they had little probability of success. Hence Soviet arms arrived for Lumumba and his followers in the Congo in their efforts to liberate territory controlled by the Belgians. The chance of success in this conflict was minimal. Illustrative of the same policy would be the limited amounts of weapons supplied to clandestine, sublimited warfare operations in Portuguese Africa.

From the Soviet point of view, favorable situations would be those in which the recipients would have both a high probability of success in their wars of liberation, and those in which the opponents of liberation were western regimes or governments strongly oriented toward the United States. In such cases, unless there were other overriding considerations, wars-of-liberation forces have received Soviet military aid. Important examples that come to mind include Soviet aid, both directly and through Egypt, to the Algerian rebels against France, and to Indonesia in its struggle to take areas held by the Netherlands.

The Soviet government is concerned with the possibility that military aid might encourage escalating conflicts to dangerous levels; however, Soviet statements regarding war escalation have been ambiguous. In urging a struggle against local-limited wars, the USSR has stressed the risk of war escalation and has warned the western powers that pursuit of local-limited wars is dangerous for that reason. In addition to the inevitable tendencies of local-limited wars to escalate into general war, Soviet spokesmen have clearly implied that the Soviet Union might deliberately escalate a local-limited war conducted by capitalist-colonialist forces against movements or governments friendly to the USSR.

Insofar as escalation may be the result of deliberate Soviet policy, it is obvious that the Russians may apply their subtle propagandistic distinctions between local-limited wars and wars of liberation to control escalation. But to the extent that there are inevitable tendencies for a localized conflict to escalate, mere political or theoretical distinctions between local-limited wars and wars of liberation will not suffice to ensure this control. Accordingly, if the USSR is concerned about the danger of localized conflict escalating into general war, Soviet leaders will take this factor into account in supporting wars of liberation. In fact, the entire rationale behind Soviet support for such wars is that they are a means of hastening through military conflict the inevitable triumph of world communism without incurring the risks involved in general and strategic nuclear war. Thus proxy wars, such as wars of liberation, are *ipso facto* techniques designed to minimize the danger of escalation. It follows logically that awareness of the escalation problem should be reflected in the Soviet military aid program.

An appraisal of the types and quantities of military aid given to wars-of-liberation forces provides some evidence that the USSR has attempted, in most cases, to avoid escalating wars of liberation into general conflicts. For example, the Soviet government has not given nuclear weapons to such major aid recipients as Egypt and Indonesia.[10]

In the earlier years of the Soviet aid program, weapons acquired by wars-of-liberation forces, although perhaps suitable for the particular recipients, were not sufficiently sophisticated to pose a threat to the principal western powers in the conflict area. Before 1961 Soviet aid furnished to Egypt in its campaign to liberate the Middle East and Africa from western influence was in the form of weapons primarily suited for limited insurgency operations and for Egyptian defense against Israel. Not until 1961 did Egypt begin to receive equipment somewhat comparable to that of the Soviet army, modern fighters equal to those acquired by Israel from France, and surface-to-air rockets. Only in recent years has Egypt received the kind of assistance it needed to threaten western positions in the Middle East. Even in this case, Yemen and Egypt have not received the amounts and kinds of aid and military training which would enable them to risk conflict with Britain in South Arabia.[11]

[10] Even before the intensification of the Sino-Soviet conflict, the Soviet-Chinese 1957–59 nuclear agreement apparently did not result in significantly advancing Chinese acquisition of nuclear weapons, nor were nuclear warheads given to Castro's Cuba. Furthermore, Soviet adherence to the Nuclear Test Ban Treaty suggests that the USSR is concerned about the spread of nuclear weapons with its attendant dangers of escalation.

[11] For a full discussion of aid to Egypt and the Middle East, see Chapter 2.

WARS OF LIBERATION 121

Soviet policy in Africa has also been cautious. African countries have not received the kinds and massive amounts of assistance that might encourage them to attack western-oriented states such as the Union of South Africa. The assistance given pro-Soviet Congolese forces has not been sufficient to enable them to gain control of the former Belgian Congo. Revisionist governments such as Somalia, while benefitting from Soviet aid, have not been enabled to escalate the border conflicts with French Somaliland, Kenya, and Ethiopia into major confrontations. It is also instructive to note that when the clash occurred between Egypt and Israeli-French-British forces in 1956, the Il–28 jet bombers that the USSR had supplied to Egypt were flown away from the combat zone.[12] Furthermore, although Soviet leaders threatened escalation by missile attacks on England and France, such threats were voiced only after it was reasonably clear that Moscow would not have to implement them. The Soviet Union also threatened—as it has done on other occasions—to send Soviet "volunteers," but in fact such volunteers have seldom been employed outside of areas immediately under control of the Soviet army.[13]

In Asia, with the exception of Indonesia, Soviet policy again appears to have been designed to lessen the risks of escalation. Neither the Pathet Lao nor the North Vietnamese-Viet Cong forces have received aid in kinds and amounts that would encourage a stark confrontation of Soviet and American military might. Although the USSR has strongly condemned U.S. action against North Vietnam and has constantly implied that the increasing American involvement in South Vietnam's struggle against the liberation forces runs the danger of escalating into general war, North Vietnamese and Viet Cong forces have continued to receive only those kinds of weapons useful in fighting a limited conflict. Despite the increasing American military commitment in Vietnam throughout 1965 and 1966 and the resumption of air attacks against North Vietnam in February 1966, Soviet policy has remained cautious. In 1967 U.S. troops committed to the Vietnam war rose to approximately five hundred thousand, and Soviet military aid deliveries increased. Nevertheless, the USSR has continued to limit its involvement in the war.[14]

[12] J. M. Mackintosh, *Strategy and Tactics of Soviet Foreign Policy* (New York: Oxford University Press, 1963), pp. 185-186.

[13] The only proved instance of Soviet "volunteers" being engaged in combat missions, as well as in "advisory" operations, occurred in Yemen.

[14] One reason for this may be the difficulty the USSR apparently has experienced in shipping aid for North Vietnamese and Viet Cong forces through Chinese territory. The Chinese have stated that at the end of 1965 about forty-three

Indonesia has been a recipient of large-scale Soviet military aid. This aid has included, especially since 1961, sophisticated equipment, with an emphasis on weapons suitable for offensive purposes, such as heavy and medium bombers, air-to-surface missiles, long-range W class submarines, and amphibious craft. Thus Indonesia is the exception to the general rule that in Asia the Soviet government has pursued a policy of reducing the risk of escalation. Possibly Soviet decision-makers found it difficult to ignore the strident claims of Indonesian nationalism. Perhaps the presence, until October 1965, of a very large Chinese-oriented communist party in competition with the Soviet-equipped forces and the unusually intense Sino-Soviet competition in Indonesia influenced the USSR to adopt an adventuresome military aid policy. The remoteness of Indonesia from the Soviet Union and the concomitant minimization of escalation risks directly involving Soviet forces may have contributed to an apparently bold military aid policy. Nevertheless, by assisting a revisionist and belligerent Indonesia to liberate areas held by western or western-oriented states, and by providing its armed forces with a large number of modern offensive-type weapons, the USSR has courted at least some risk of a confrontation with the western powers.[15]

To recapitulate, in terms of quantities and types of weapons furnished, with the exception of Indonesia and Cuba before the missile crisis, the Soviet Union has avoided giving military aid which could cause a war of liberation to escalate into general and strategic nuclear war. But the probabilities of escalating a war of liberation into a direct Soviet-American clash can also be affected by the manner in which the wars-of-liberation forces are supplied. Moscow may supply the wars of liberation directly or make the Soviet challenge ambiguous by supplying them through third countries.

Have the Soviet leaders chosen to play down their involvement with wars-of-liberation forces by engaging in indirect supply—providing third countries with surplus Soviet weapons to re-export? The record here is a mixed one. Where there was no convenient way to supply recipients other than directly, the USSR has been the direct source of arms. In some instances the Russians have been direct suppliers even when re-export possibilities existed. On the other hand, Moscow has frequently preferred to supply wars of liberation through the medium of third

---

thousand tons of Soviet arms had been shipped through China to Vietnam. Soviet deliveries via the port of Haiphong have been harassed by American planes, according to Soviet sources. The closing of the Suez Canal in June 1967 created further logistical problems for the USSR. Finally, the type of war being waged has resulted in a need for small arms rather than for major Soviet weapons.

[15] For a full discussion of Soviet aid to Indonesia, see Chapter 4.

countries. An outstanding example of the indirect method was the use of Egypt as an intermediary supplier of Soviet weapons destined for the Algerian rebels before Algeria's independence. Egypt has also been the intermediary for the supply of arms to the Congo and other areas of Africa. The Viet Cong have received Soviet weapons through North Vietnam. Algeria was used as an intermediary to supply Congolese rebels in 1964. Guinea, to a limited degree, has supplied Soviet arms to insurgents in Portuguese Guinea and Angola, as has Tanzania to Mozambique. In general, the record reveals that the USSR has preferred to remain in the background and employ re-export arrangements, although the Russians have not hesitated to supply military aid on a direct basis when it was expedient to do so.

Military aid seems to be viewed by the Soviet government as an important tool of foreign policy. The overriding goals of Soviet diplomacy remain the twin objectives of insuring Soviet security and altering the world correlation of forces in such a manner as to advance world communism and the international position of the USSR. Hence it is to be expected that the Soviet Union will give strong consideration to the foreign policy implications of support for a particular war of liberation.

In making these judgments, Soviet leaders are concerned with certain specific problems. Foremost appears to be an assessment of the effect of Soviet support in the context of the general Soviet effort to influence the non-committed world. Specifically, how will the decision further Soviet influence in the less-developed world at the expense of the United States and Communist China? Will Soviet support for a given war of liberation create difficulties for its two main rivals? Should a particular war of liberation be successful, will such a success be a gain for the USSR and a loss of influence by the United States or China? Negatively, should the Russians fail to support a contestant, will Soviet influence be reduced?

The answers to these questions are seldom self-evident, and the outcomes of Soviet policy decisions are shrouded in uncertainty. Moscow has apparently adopted a general policy line to support wars of liberation but is prepared to abandon the general policy in particular instances where circumstances are not favorable. Considering these standards, it is possible to make certain statements about the foreign policy factor in Soviet decisions concerning wars of liberation.

First, Soviet spokesmen have viewed wars of liberation in broad terms, not only through classification of various conflicts as wars of liberation but also in supporting incipient or sublimited as well as "hot" wars of liberation. Thus they have granted military aid to certain friendly countries and engaged in confrontations with other states short of actual war, with little regard for the fact that Soviet support might escalate such a sublimited conflict into full-scale war, the outcome of which might adversely affect the Soviet Union. Certainly Russian aid to Nasser greatly encouraged Cairo to pursue a provocative policy toward Israel and directly contributed to the outbreak of the June 1967 war in the Middle East. Here the escalation risk of a Soviet-American confrontation was avoided primarily by the swift Israeli victory.

Second, where the conflict had passed from the incipient or sublimited stage to actual warfare, and where one of the opponents was a western nation, the USSR has tended to support the contestant fighting the western power, even when the Soviet-supported side had little chance of success. An example of this policy was Soviet support for Yemeni war-of-liberation forces against Britain in the South Arabian area.

Third, the USSR has supported certain key countries in given areas, even if such support was opposed by other non-committed states. Key countries, such as Cuba, Egypt, India, and Indonesia have been supported wholeheartedly, even at the risk of antagonizing other nations in the area. But support for less important countries has been more tentative when such support would antagonize other neighboring non-committed countries. The USSR has been cautious in assisting irredentist nations in Africa such as Somalia, for strong Soviet support for Somalia's wars of liberation would alienate other African countries.

Fourth, the USSR has limited its support where a stepped-up war of liberation might result in a net gain for either China or the United States. The outstanding case here is the North Vietnam-Viet Cong war of liberation. Should the USSR encourage an intensification of this struggle, two things might occur, both of which would be unfavorable to the Soviet Union. The United States might actually invade North Vietnam, forcing the Russians either to commit themselves fully to North Vietnamese-Viet Cong forces or to allow them to be defeated; or in an intensified war situation an increased Communist Chinese commitment would, if the liberation movement succeeded, result in a gain for Communist China and not the Soviet Union. Whichever side won, the Russians might emerge as the loser.

Finally, in a situation in which a recipient engaged in a war of liberation policy might secure help from either the USSR or China, the Soviet Union has usually attempted to be the principal arms supplier. In the case of Indonesia, Soviet policy has been to grant substantial military aid, despite some risk, in order to gain influence in Indonesia at the expense of China.

Thus it appears that the foreign policy motivation for Soviet support or non-support of wars of liberation, and the degree of such support, has been conditioned by the Soviet government's appraisal of the international situation in terms of the following: (1) the effect of granting the aid on Soviet influence with the particular recipient; (2) the hostility or approval with which other non-committed countries will view Soviet support and the relative importance of the recipient in his area of the world; (3) the effect of such support on western and Chinese influence in the recipient country or adjoining areas; and (4) the effect on Soviet versus American and Chinese positions should Soviet support for a war of liberation increase the intensity of the conflict. These factors vary from situation to situation; accordingly, although Soviet foreign policy in general is to support the aspirations of the non-committed countries even to the extent of military aid for wars of liberation, in specific cases the USSR may withhold support or grant only very limited military aid. Policy appears geared to a case by case assessment by the Soviet government.

POLICY ASSESSMENT

After reviewing more than a decade of Soviet aid in support of wars of liberation, can any conclusions be drawn about the factors that appear to influence Soviet decisions? Probably the most evident one is that the attitudes and policies of recipient countries toward indigenous communism are of minor importance. Possibly more significant, but still not of great concern to Soviet decision-makers, is the question of socio-political orientation—whether the recipients are ultra-leftist, moderate-leftist, or rightist. A more important consideration is the Soviet estimation of which side in a struggle appears to be the likely victor; unless the struggle is against a western or western-oriented power, the Russians show an understandable propensity to support the winning side. By all odds the paramount criterion for the USSR, in engaging in arms diplomacy, is whether support for wars of liberation will weaken the position of the western powers, bind the recipient more closely to Moscow, and reduce or eliminate the influence of Peking. The USSR does not intend to contribute to the success of a war of liberation if that success results in a Chinese- rather than a Soviet-oriented regime.

The problem for the Soviet Union in increasing its influence through arms diplomacy is difficult and complex, and the factors conditioning Soviet decisions vary from country to country. Although the Soviet government proclaims its support in theory for all wars of liberation, in practice each individual case is judged on its own merits. In making this assessment, the dangers of war escalation, which military aid helps to create, are of prime concern. The USSR is careful not to contribute toward escalating conflicts and is not apt to embark on reckless adventures.

There is no such thing as a consistent Soviet theory of wars of liberation. Instead, the Soviet government is utilizing this vague concept to engage in a conservative and cautious effort to further Soviet foreign policy objectives through arms diplomacy.

8

CHALLENGE AND RESPONSE:
SOVIET-AMERICAN MILITARY AID COMPETITION

IN THE beginning of the post World War II era there was nothing subtle about Soviet foreign policy. Openly revisionist, it was designed to create a belt of satellite nations around the borders of the USSR. The military might of the Soviet government was the principal instrument of this policy, and areas occupied by the Soviet army, from Berlin to North Korea, were brought quickly under the sway of communist regimes dependent upon Moscow. In the Mediterranean-Middle East area, however, Soviet expansionism was thwarted. In the first test case, that of Iran, the United States countered the Soviet challenge with political pressure backed up by stern warnings and UN support.

It was in Greece and Turkey in 1947, however, that the United States first began employing foreign aid as a means of bolstering the recipient country's resistance to Soviet policies. Turkey, emboldened by American economic and military aid, and by American diplomatic support, refused to accede to Russian demands concerning the Dardanelles and the Turkish eastern territories. In Greece, American assistance helped prevent a communist-supported insurgency from toppling the Greek government. Thus in the very early years of the cold war was born an American policy instrument, subsequently employed all around the periphery of the communist world, of creating alliances and mutual assistance pacts and supporting the members of these arrangements with both economic and military aid.

When some six to seven years later the Soviet Union began to reappraise its policy toward the less-developed nations, American aid diplomacy received the supreme compliment of imitation. As it had been for the United States, foreign aid became a principal foreign policy instrument of the Soviet Union. First hesitatingly with limited economic aid, then more boldly with military aid as well, increasing the number of recipients and the amounts involved, Soviet aid diplomacy began to compete with the United States in the less-developed world.

The Soviet government's decision to engage in aid diplomacy was brought about only in part by the failure of communist insurgencies in the less-developed countries. It also resulted from the growing realization among Soviet military leaders that nuclear confrontation with the United States must be avoided. During the period of the Korean war, when the United States launched an extensive expansion of its military forces, Soviet leaders began to acknowledge that a clash between the two superpowers might destroy both, a thesis that Communist Chinese leaders denied then and continue to deny. The Soviet Union searched for methods to continue the offensive against the western powers in the former colonial areas without risking nuclear war. Ideologically, this took the form of a differentiation between types of wars that condemned nuclear strategic war and limited wars and supported wars of liberation. Pragmatically, this policy decision resulted in Soviet entrance into foreign, particularly military, aid diplomacy.[1]

In later years the decision of Soviet leaders to offer military aid to less-developed countries was also conditioned by the growing tension between the Soviet Union and Communist China. The Chinese regarded the downgrading of militant revolutionary struggle as a betrayal of Marxist-Leninist principles and proceeded to join, albeit in a limited way, the competition for influence in the less-developed countries. Unlike the Soviet Union, however, Communist China viewed military aid in the more ambitious light of fostering revolutionary takeover in the recipient countries. Whereas the Soviet government was prepared to aid neutral and even rightist regimes, the Chinese tended to support more militantly leftist groups and hoped to foster communist uprisings in the less-developed world. Accordingly, the Soviet Union had to consider its military aid decisions not only in the light of its competition with the United States, but also in terms of the Chinese Communist challenge. In view of Communist China's internal problems and its relatively under-developed economy, the Soviet Union could regard the limited military aid that China could afford as posing a lesser threat than western aid. But there is no doubt that the Soviet military aid program has been conditioned by competition with China as well as with the United States.

By 1967 it was clear, as the Arab-Israeli conflict starkly revealed, that military aid had become a principal instrument for the major powers

[1] The use of military aid to support wars of liberation is discussed more fully in Chapter 7.

in their desire to influence the course of events in Asia, the Middle East, Africa, and Latin America. Challenge and response, competition and coexistence, intrusion and penetration—these became the key terms describing the motives of the Soviet Union, the United States, and Communist China in their world-wide military aid diplomacy. Since the principal competitor of the USSR is the United States, this section is concerned with estimating the effect of American military aid diplomacy on Russian arms aid policies.

PRIORITY REGIONS IN SOVIET AND AMERICAN MILITARY AID PROGRAMS

Both the Soviet Union and the United States have concentrated a large part of their military aid in those countries which are proven allies or satellites. Significant amounts of Soviet aid have gone to Eastern European countries, North Korea, and in earlier years to Communist China. Currently an undetermined but undoubtedly substantial amount of aid is being furnished to North Vietnam. The United States formerly directed the bulk of its military aid to its West European allies and to Japan. More recently, the principal recipients of American military aid have been the Republics of Korea (South Korea), China (Taiwan), and South Vietnam. Any comparisons of the American and Soviet arms aid programs must begin, therefore, by emphasizing that the observations are limited to the less-developed, relatively uncommitted countries of Asia, the Middle East, Africa, and Latin America. It is in these nonaligned or Third World countries that the military aid programs of the two superpowers are in competition.[2]

Table 8-1 lists fifty-four Third World countries which received American military aid during the period from 1956 through 1967. Large recipients included Brazil, India, Iran, Laos, Pakistan, the Philippines, and Turkey. Currently Thailand is the Third World country receiving the largest share of U.S. military aid allocations. Its total aid is still slightly less than that of Iran and Pakistan, however. It is much less than that of Turkey, the largest Third World recipient.[3]

[2] Since the objective here is to analyze military aid diplomacy in the Third World, countries completely identified with either the Soviet bloc or the United States have been omitted. These include North Korea, Mongolia, North Vietnam, South Korea, South Vietnam, and Nationalist China. Had these countries been included, of course, the aid totals would have been larger than those presented in this chapter.

[3] The current emphasis on so-called forward defense countries in U.S. military aid allocations will raise Thailand's total even higher. Of $500 million requested for FY 1969, $365 million was allocated to countries "which, because of their geographical proximity to the USSR and Communist China, are exposed to the direct threat of Communist aggression." See U.S. Department of Defense, *Military Assistance Facts* (Washington, March 1968), p. 7.

Table 8-1. Estimated United States Military Aid to Third World Countries: FY 1956 through 1967 (In Millions of U.S. Dollars)

Country	Amount	Country	Amount	Country	Amount
Afghanistan	$ 3.2	Guinea	$ 1.0	Morocco	$ 26.7
Argentina	23.5	Haiti	3.2	Nicaragua	8.4
Bolivia	15.8	Honduras	5.0	Niger	0.1
Brazil	160.8	India	200.0	Nigeria	1.0
Burma	35.0	Indonesia	59.8	Pakistan	750.0
Cambodia	87.1	Iran	627.6	Panama	2.3
Cameroon	0.2	Iraq	41.3	Paraguay	5.1
Chile	67.2	Israel	52.0	Peru	63.8
Colombia	57.9	Ivory Coast	0.1	Philippines	262.5
Congo-Kinshasa	16.1	Jamaica	0.8	Saudi Arabia	33.0
Costa Rica	1.7	Jordan	48.0	Senegal	2.6
Cuba	7.5	Laos	150.0	Sudan	0.7
Dahomey	0.1	Lebanon	8.8	Thailand	600.0
Dominican Republic	14.1	Liberia	4.9	Tunisia	16.3
Ecuador	29.0	Libya	12.4	Turkey	1,735.5
El Salvador	4.7	Malaysia	0.4	Upper Volta	0.1
Ethiopia	95.8	Mali	2.8	Uruguay	33.8
Guatemala	10.8	Mexico	1.5	Venezuela	6.4

Source: Compiled from U.S. Department of Defense, *Military Assistance Facts*, pp. 14-15. Figures for countries whose aid totals could not be adapted from this document were derived from articles in the press, principally the *New York Times*.

Table 8-2 illustrates the regional emphases in the American and Soviet military aid programs. Disregarding Soviet aid to other communist countries, and examining Soviet arms aid allocations only to the relatively uncommitted states of Asia, the Middle East, Africa, and Latin America, it is clear that Soviet assistance has been directed principally toward the Middle East and south and southeast Asia. Cuba is the only country in Latin America that has received Soviet military aid. In Africa, on the other hand, the small amount of Soviet aid has been disbursed among nine countries.[4]

There are some interesting similarities and contrasts between the Soviet and American military aid programs. The regions are ranked in the same order for the two superpowers in terms of amounts of military aid allocated. For both countries, the Middle East has been the area of most importance, whereas Africa has received from both donors the least amount of military aid. The fact that the Middle East and South and Southeast Asia have received more than eighty percent of the total U.S. and Soviet military aid allocations suggests the importance which the two superpowers accord to these regions in their competition for influence in the Third World.

[4] While the regional discussion of Soviet arms aid in Africa in Chapter 3 lists ten rather than nine recipients, the analysis here excludes Congo-Kinshasa⁻ because the recipient was only very briefly a part of the Congolese government and later became an insurgent faction. Excluding Congo-Kinshasa, the total number of Soviet military aid recipients in the Third World comes to twenty-four. For a listing of Soviet military aid recipients, see Table 6-1.

Table 8-2. Comparison of Regional Priorities in Soviet and United States Military Aid

Region	Estimated Total Aid		Percentage of Total Program		Number of Recipients	
	USSR	U.S.	USSR	U.S.	USSR	U.S.
Middle East	$2,748	$2,602	48%	48%	8	10
South-Southeast Asia	2,185	2,148	38%	40%	6	10
Latin America	750	523	13%	10%	1	21
Africa	85	126	1%	2%	9	13
Totals	$5,768	$5,399	100%	100%	24	54

Sources: Soviet aid figures were compiled from data in the regional sections, Chapters 2 through 5. Aid to Congo-Kinshasa is omitted. United States aid figures were compiled from Table 8-1. All amounts given in millions of U.S. dollars.

A second comparison of the two aid programs indicates the relative concentration of Soviet military aid efforts, in contrast to the relative dispersion of American military aid. Although the total amounts involved are nearly the same for each country for the twelve-year period, the Soviet Union has concentrated its $5,768 million in only twenty-four recipients, or an average of approximately $240 million per recipient. The United States, on the other hand, has spread its $5,399 million among fifty-four recipients, with an average of approximately $100 million per recipient. These figures suggest that the Soviet goals differ from the goals pursued by the United States. The USSR chooses recipients who may be expected to agree with Soviet policies or to maintain friendly relationships with the Soviet Union. United States aid goes not only to countries allied with or sympathetic to American goals and aims, but also goes to countries which would be likely to oppose U.S. policies. The United States, of course, expects that such countries receiving American aid will at least preserve their own independence and thus contribute to a stable, non-communist world.

Logically, it can be expected that large amounts of aid tend to give the donor country greater influence in the recipient country than a small amount of aid. If this is true, it would appear that Soviet aid is designed to secure for the Soviet Union a position of significant influence in a limited number of recipient countries, while American aid appears designed to maintain at least a minimum aid relationship with a large number of countries. Of course such conclusions must be very tentative in that analysis of the two competing aid programs must take into account qualitative as well as quantitative factors. But that the USSR and the United States tend to pursue somewhat different aid strategies is quite evident.

To some extent, the relative dispersion of American military aid and the relative concentration of Soviet military aid are related to the special position occupied by Latin America in the foreign policies of the two countries. The United States appears determined to maintain its pre-eminent influence in Latin America, and the Soviet Union seems to accept this status. It has frequently been argued that Soviet foreign policy may be distinguished from Czarist Russian diplomacy in that the former is unlimited in scope and world-wide in its interests and ambitions, whereas Czarist aims centered on areas of the world geographically adjacent to Russia. Karpovich supports this point of view. He argues that "pre-revolutionary Russian imperialism was essentially no different fom the imperialism of the other great powers," but that the foreign policy of the Soviet Union is radically different in that it is global in scope, "seeking to achieve a number of aggressive aims simultaneously in various corners of the earth. This alone sharply distinguishes Soviet policy from the policy of the Tsars, who, as a rule, pursued limited aims . . ."[5] It is true that Soviet theorists proclaim a world-wide policy of spreading communism. The military aid program indicates, however, that Soviet policy, like that of imperial Russia, still emphasizes regions adjacent to the Soviet Union and is still cautious about moving into distant areas such as Latin America. In this light Soviet aid for Cuba appears as an exception to the general conduct of Soviet foreign policy, for in aiding Cuba the Soviet government sought to extend its influence thousands of miles from the Russian homeland.

American aid to Latin America during the period 1956 to 1967 has totalled only $523 million. Every Latin American country, however, received at some time or another during those years at least token aid from the United States. This contrasts with other regions of the world where American aid has been much more selective. The inclusion of all Latin American countries in the U.S. military assistance program does much to explain the relative dispersion of U.S. military assistance efforts. In fact, if Latin America were excluded, the U.S. military aid program would resemble that of the USSR more closely in its aid concentration. This also suggests the importance the United States accords to maintaining good relations with the countries of the western hemisphere, especially since there is no rational need to arm Latin America.

Africa, like Latin America, appears to be a region of low priority in Soviet military aid diplomacy. To some degree the small amounts contributed to black Africa by the United States and the Soviet Union—less than two percent of their total combined military aid allocations—are the result of the inability of relatively backward societies to absorb large

[5] Michael Karpovich, "Russian Imperialism or Communist Agression?" in *Readings in Russian Foreign Policy* (New York: Oxford University Press, 1959), pp. 659-60.

amounts of military aid. The generally small armed forces of the African countries lack sufficient training to utilize sophisticated and costly weapons systems. The token aid Africa has received from Washington and Moscow also reflects Africa's geographical remoteness from both donors and its inability to affect drastically the military security of the two superpowers. The USSR has extended a total of $85 million to nine African countries; the United States has contributed approximately $126 million to thirteen African recipients. Both Washington and Moscow appear to accept a situation in Africa where neither is predominant and where competition is muted and hence cheap in terms of military aid. Only in the Horn of Africa, with respect to Ethiopia and the Somali Republic, have the two superpowers confronted each other in military aid diplomacy.[6]

In terms of military aid diplomacy the competition of the United States and the Soviet Union is most intense in the critical regions of the Middle East and South and Southeast Asia. It is to those two regions that the bulk of each donor's military aid flows, and it is there that the two superpowers compete for influence and prestige. These are the regions of the world where there is the most serious risk that military aid policies will contribute to escalating local conflicts into a clash between the two superpowers. In South and Southeast Asia the presence of Communist China, hostile to both the United States and the Soviet Union, complicates an already dangerous rivalry. Nevertheless, both superpowers continue to accord high priority to the Middle East and South and Southeast Asia. Eighty-eight percent of the American military aid commitment to the less-developed world has gone to these regions, as has eighty-six percent of the total Soviet military aid program.

The substantial amounts of arms aid which the Soviet government has allocated to the Middle East and to South and Southeast Asia argue against the view that the Soviet Union, unlike Czarist Russia, pays little heed in its foreign policy to geographical considerations. On the contrary, most Soviet aid has gone to countries adjacent or close to Russian borders. The only major recipient in the Middle East and South and Southeast Asia which is far removed from the Soviet Union is Indonesia. Through military aid the Soviet government appears determined to extend its influence throughout the Russian rimlands in the south and east, and to exclude, if possible, the United States from these areas.[7]

---

[6] The special case of the Horn of Africa is more fully discussed in Chapter 3 and subsequently in this chapter.

[7] For more detailed discussions of Soviet military aid to the Middle East and to South and Southeast Asia, see Chapters 2 and 4.

The extensive U.S. military aid commitments in the Middle East and in south and southeastern Asia were designed to bolster the containment-encirclement policy pursued by the United States toward the Soviet Union for the past twenty years. The creation of military alliances such as CENTO and SEATO, accompanied or followed shortly by American military aid, has been the principal technique by which the United States has sought to contain communist expansionism. Neither of the two protagonists appears willing to concede these two vital world regions to the predominant influence of the other. It is to be expected that this regional emphasis on military aid programs will continue into the foreseeable future. On this assumption, the analysis of Soviet-American rivalry and competition must turn to the sources of aid on a country-by-country basis, noting how challenges of one are met by responses from the other.[8]

THE SOURCES OF MILITARY AID

From the inception of the Soviet military aid program in 1955 to the extensive rearmament of the Middle Eastern countries following the June 1967 Arab-Israeli war, the Soviet government has aided twenty-four less-developed, non-aligned countries. During approximately the same number of years, from 1956 through 1967, the United States extended military aid to fifty-four Third World nations. In Latin America, the United States has been the sole source[9] of military aid for twenty of the twenty-one recipients. After Castro achieved power, the USSR became the sole source of military aid for Cuba, and the United States discontinued its Cuban program. In other world regions, however, neither of the two superpowers has achieved the position of sole military aid donor. Table 8-3 cites the number of countries in each region which received military aid from either or both of the two donor countries and indicates the number of sole-source versus dual-source nations in each world area.

It will be observed from Table 8-3 that the Soviet government has been the sole source of military aid to only ten of the sixty-four aided countries; of the total of twenty-four countries receiving Soviet arms assistance during these years, fourteen also received military aid from

[8] It should be observed that many other countries in addition to the U.S. and the USSR furnish military aid to Third World countries. Since, however, this chapter is concerned with the competition between the two largest donors and principal cold war rivals, military aid policies of other donors are not included in this analysis.

[9] "Sole source" as used here refers only to the United States and the USSR and does not include third donor countries such as Britain, France, Germany, and Communist China.

Table 8-3. Number of Countries within Regions Receiving American and Soviet Aid: A Comparison of Two Sources of Aid, 1956 through 1967

Source of Aid	Middle East	South and Southeast Asia	Latin America	Africa	Totals
Soviet Union Only	5	0	0	5	10
United States Only	7	4	20	9	40
Both U.S. and USSR	3	6	1	4	14
Totals	15	10	21	18	64

the United States. It is assumed that donor countries wish to achieve maximum influence in recipient countries. If it is further assumed that donors enhance their influence by becoming the sole source of military aid for the recipient, then the United States has been much more successful than the Soviet Union.[10] Forty of the total of sixty-four countries relied solely on the United States for military aid. Expressed differently, fifty-eight percent of the Soviet military aid recipients also received American military aid, while only twenty-six percent of the countries receiving U.S. military assistance also received aid from the Soviet Union. Again, however, the U.S. achievement of a sole-source position is primarily due to the fact that all Latin American countries received U.S. assistance at some time or another in the history of the aid program, while only Cuba has been a Soviet recipient. In contrast, three of the fifteen aid recipients in the Middle East obtained military aid from both donor countries. None of the South or Southeast Asian countries relied solely upon the Soviet Union. In Africa, four of the eighteen countries obtained military aid from both donors.

Although there are several important exceptions to the general rule, it is usually true that countries tend to rely on one or the other donor rather than on both. As Table 8-3 indicates, fifty of the sixty-four aided countries relied on a single aid source. Of course, if military aid to the close associates of the donors were considered—the aligned in contrast to the Third World countries—the tendency toward sole-source aid would be even more striking. Viewed from that perspective, it is remarkable that so many countries rely on one or the other military aid donor. The commonly held belief that neutrality enables countries to blackmail both the United States and the USSR and hence receive

[10] It might be postulated that influence of the donor is a function of achieving a situation in which the donor is the sole source of military aid to a recipient. Measured by this standard, the U.S. military aid program has been more successful than that of the Soviet Union. On the other hand, if it is assumed that influence is a function of the size of the donor's program in the recipient country, then the USSR has been more successful than the United States, since Soviet programs are on the average about twice as large as those of the United States.

aid from both is certainly a myth in terms of military aid commitments in the past dozen years. Most countries, willingly or not, have chosen sides.[11]

The fact that the United States has aided all twenty-one Latin American countries whereas the Soviets have aided only Cuba in Latin America is of significance in explaining why most countries have chosen sides in terms of aid donors. Accordingly, it is useful to disregard small aid recipients and consider only those countries that have obtained substantial amounts of military aid. Eight of the fifty-four U.S. aided countries and eleven of the twenty-four Soviet aided nations have received more than $100 million in aid. Of these substantial aid recipients, only two, India and Iran, have obtained more than $100 million from both aid donors. This seems to indicate that competition between the United States and the Soviet Union over India and Iran is especially acute.

In contrast to India and Iran, nearly all of the remaining twelve mutually aided countries have received preponderant aid from one or the other superpowers. Afghanistan, for example, received $260 million from the USSR but only $3 million from the United States. Iraq received $500 million from the Soviets but only $41 million from America. Moscow furnished Indonesia $1200 million, in contrast to $60 million provided by Washington. Pakistan obtained $750 million from America but only between $5 and $10 million from the Soviets. Stated differently, even in those instances where recipients have not chosen sides, that is, have received aid from both superpowers, recipients have relied in essence on either the United States or the Soviet Union, but not on both. This fact makes the position of India and Iran all the more unusual.

Why have aid donors chosen certain countries to aid and not others? Why have aid recipients tended to choose aid from Moscow or Washington, but ordinarily not from both? To answer these questions, it is necessary to look at the three types of aid recipients as revealed by Table 8-3: those countries that received aid only from the USSR; those that received aid only from the United States; and those that received aid from both. What criteria determined the choices made by the donor countries? Are there regional differences which affect the selection of recipients?

[11] The same point is made by David Beim, "The Communist Bloc and the Foreign Aid Game," *Western Political Quarterly*, vol. 17, no. 4 (December 1964), pp. 795-99. In recent years, however, certain countries have succeeded in getting aid from both the USSR and the United States. Among the important countries aided by both sides are Pakistan, India, and Iran. The special circumstances involved in these three cases are discussed in Chapters 2 and 4.

In Latin America it is clear that the two donors have come to perceive the situation in similar terms: since the Cuban missile crisis both sides regard Latin American countries as suitable recipients only for U.S. military aid. Latin America offers an example of an area where neither protagonist competes in the same country. If the United States aids a Latin American country, the USSR does not. Conversely, if Moscow aids a Latin American country, Washington does not. Since the United States has given every indication in recent years that it will not tolerate another situation like the Cuban one in Latin America, it seems probable that there will be no aid competition between Washington and Moscow in Latin America. In fact it seems likely that the Soviet government, faced with such a hostile response from the United States, might even continue to moderate further its military aid program with Cuba. Latin American countries, accordingly, will not be likely areas of military aid competition in the cold war. In such a situation, the stakes will be low for each side, and the amounts of military aid received by Latin American countries will remain small. The United States, of course, finds it more difficult to exert pressure on Latin American countries receiving aid from American military allies, such as France, Germany, or the United Kingdom. To the extent, therefore, that military aid to Latin American countries is stepped up by the United States, it is likely to be as a result of competition with western nations, not the Soviet Union.[12]

As in the case of Latin America, black Africa has not been the scene of intense Soviet-American arms aid competition. With the exception of arms aid to Ethiopia and Somalia, military aid programs have been inconsequential. Most African countries have relied on one of the two donors, but not on both. Five African countries (Congo-Brazzaville, Ghana, Somalia, Tanzania, and Uganda) have received aid only from the Soviet government, nine (Congo-Kinshasa, Cameroon, Dahomey, Ethiopia, Ivory Coast, Liberia, Niger, Senegal, and Upper Volta) only from the United States, and four (Guinea, Mali, Nigeria, and Sudan) from both donors. As in the case of Latin America, the fact that most recipients in Africa have aligned themselves, in terms of military aid, with one or the other protagonist does not seem to have resulted in their receiving substantial amounts of military aid. Africa, like Latin America, is accorded low priority in the aid diplomacy of both donor countries.

Soviet and American military aid competition has been particularly intense only in the Somalia-Ethiopia region of east Africa. There Soviet-aided Somalia and American-aided Ethiopia confront each other with military forces far superior to those which either could sustain were it

---

[12] For further discussion of Latin America, see Chapter 5.

not for the military aid rivalry between the two superpowers. The Soviet assistance program in Somalia is larger than that in any other sub-Saharan country. This is especially significant, since the largest American recipient in Africa is Ethiopia, the chief target of Somalia's irredentist ambitions. Somalia sought western aid during the 1960-1963 period, but the response was not acceptable to Somalia, primarily because the western offer was conditioned upon Somalia not accepting aid from other sources.[13] Somalia instead accepted a larger and unrestricted Soviet offer of arms. The United States continued to aid Ethiopia. Thus the pattern of one rival receiving military aid from Moscow and the other from Washington was once more repeated.

South and Southeast Asia and the Middle East differ from Latin America and Africa not only in quantities of military aid received, but also in terms of the intensity of the competition between the donor countries. In South and Southeast Asia, Washington has been the sole source of aid for four (Burma, Malaysia, Philippines, and Thailand) of the ten recipients, but none of the countries has received aid solely from Moscow. Six (Afghanistan, Cambodia, India, Indonesia, Laos, and Pakistan) of the ten Asian recipients have obtained aid from both the United States and the Soviet Union. In the Middle East the United States has been the sole donor to seven countries (Israel, Jordan, Lebanon, Libya, Saudi Arabia, Tunisia, and Turkey), the Soviet Union to five (Algeria, Cyprus, Syria, the U.A.R., and Yemen), and both countries have aided three (Iran, Iraq, and Morocco). Thus while the Middle East follows the Latin American and African pattern, in that the majority of recipients chooses sides, South and Southeast Asia form the one region where the number of mutually aided countries exceeds the number of sole-source countries. This raises an interesting question: What special situation exists in South and Southeast Asia that results in a relatively large number of mutually aided countries? It seems probable that the answer is that both donors face a common threat to their positions of influence in Asia. It is the perceived threat of China which has influenced the United States and the Soviet Union to aid a number of the same recipients in Asia. Three of the largest non-communist Asian countries—India, Pakistan, and Indonesia—have received military aid from both the Soviet and American governments. Both donor governments have to some extent viewed this aid as a means of bolstering opposition in these countries to the influence of China or possibly even against Chinese aggression or penetration of the recipient countries.

[13] *New York Times*, December 17, 1963. For further discussion of Africa see Chapter 3.

Regardless of whether these fears are real or imagined, and whether the recipient governments share these views, concern over China has prompted both donors to furnish large amounts of military assistance to Asian countries.

Pakistan has not only benefitted from American-Soviet military aid rivalry to secure assistance from both donors, it has also obtained aid from Communist China as well. During the Indian-Pakistani border war in 1965, while both the United States and the Soviet Union attempted to remain neutral and to settle the conflict as expeditiously as possible, Communist China openly backed Pakistan and voiced veiled threats of renewing the Sino-Indian border war. China also sent Pakistan approximately eighty MiG–19 fighters, some bombers, and tanks.[14] In August 1967 the Soviet government began to provide military assistance to Pakistan.[15] With this agreement Pakistan apparently accomplished the impossible. It had succeeded in securing aid from China despite its adherence to the SEATO alliance, which was directed against China. Further, it had succeeded in securing aid from the Soviet Union, despite the Soviet commitment to India. Finally, it remained an important ally of the United States, despite the fact that both Communist China and the USSR had become active in Pakistan. No better illustration of the successful playing off of the United States, the Soviet Union, and Communist China could be found. This was possible only because all three rivals saw the subcontinent as vital to their military and political positions in Asia.[16]

The Middle East has been the largest aid recipient region for both donor countries. It is clear that both view the Middle East as an extremely important region in the world-wide struggle for influence. But since Communist China is not a threat in the Middle East, the pattern in the Middle East tends to follow that of the lesser priority areas, in that most Middle Eastern countries are aided by one or the other of the two superpowers; relatively few are aided by both. To a significant degree this situation has been brought about by the special situation of Arab-Israeli hostility. The intensity of the Arab-Israeli struggle has resulted in a situation in which it is difficult for the two donors to avoid choosing sides. The Soviet government has clearly done so: Its aid has gone primarily to those countries most hostile to Israel—especially to Egypt, Iraq, and Syria. American aid has tended to go to those countries less aggressively oriented toward Israel, such as Iran and the

---

[14] Institute for Strategic Studies, *Military Balance,* p. 32.
[15] *Washington Post,* August 6, 1967.
[16] For further discussion of this situation, see Chapter 4.

conservative Arab powers. Iraq, the second largest Soviet aid recipient in the Middle East, was initially aided by the Soviet Union to wean Iraq away from the American alliance system.

Just as the donor aid programs have been complicated in Asia by the presence of Communist China, donor aid policies have been complicated in the Middle East by the Arab-Israeli confrontation. Where an external regional adversary, from the the point of view of the donors, exists as China does in Asia, the military aid programs tend to be large and to some degree mutual. When from the point of view of the recipients an intra-regional enemy exists, the donors tend to compete for the role of exclusive source of aid, and the aid programs are also large. Where one area is clearly in the military sphere of influence of one or the other superpower, as in Latin America, the absence of genuine competition limits the total aid program. Finally, where recipients face neither indigenous nor external rivals, as in Africa, the aid donors tend to limit their aid. This is especially true if the area under consideration is viewed by the two donor countries as of marginal importance in world politics.

FOREIGN POLICY ORIENTATIONS OF MILITARY AID RECIPIENTS

Both the United States and the Soviet Union have declared that their military aid programs are intended to support their foreign policy objectives in Third World countries.[17] To measure their success, an analysis of roll-call voting in the United Nations by Third World countries which have been the recipients of American and Soviet military aid programs has been undertaken. The approach consists of comparing the positions of Third World military aid recipients on important roll-call votes in the United Nations with the positions taken by the Soviet Union and the United States. This method rests on the belief that a government's voting record on questions before the United Nations is as objective a measurement of its international political position as can be devised.[18]

[17] See, for example, U.S. Department of Defense, *Military Assistance and Foreign Military Sales Facts* (Washington, May 1967), p. 7; T. Bulba, "International Significance of the Development of Communism in the USSR," *Kommunist Vooruzhennykh Sil* (Communist of the Armed Forces), no. 24 (December 1964), p. 37; and unsigned editorial, "Fifty Years of the Great October Socialist Revolution; Thesis of the Central Committee, CPSU," in *ibid.*, no. 14 (July 1967), pp. 37 and 41.

[18] Obviously measuring the degree of identification on U.N. roll calls between aid donors and aid recipients is only one method of estimating the military aid-foreign policy nexus. The test implies correlation only, not causality, since it cannot be ascertained whether aid recipients agreed with aid donors because they received aid, or received aid because they agreed with aid donor policies.

The test was applied to roll-call voting in the United Nations by Third World countries during the period 1958 to 1964 and considered two categories of issues: political and security issues affecting nations generally; and trusteeship and colonial questions of particular interest to Third World governments.[19]

Table 8-4 lists all fifty-four Third World nations which received military aid valued at $1 million or more during the 1958-1964 period. It then compares the "scores of agreement"[20] between aid donors and recipients. It will be observed that, except for Cyprus, the ten countries aided exclusively by the USSR agreed with the Soviet Union the majority of the time. Algeria, with an agreement score of eighty-one, was the Third World nation most in agreement with the USSR on political and security issues.

Except for Laos, the nine countries aided by both the Soviet Union and the United States agreed more often with Moscow than with Washington.[21] While it was to be expected that governments aided exclusively by Moscow would have high agreement scores with the Soviet Union, it is surprising that nearly all mutually aided nations had higher scores of agreement with the Soviets than with the United States.

---

[19] Roll calls selected were from both committee and plenary sessions of the General Assembly. In order to be included a roll call had to meet at least one of the following criteria: (a) the division on the roll call was such that twenty percent or more of the voting governments were opposed to the majority position; and (b) the Soviet Union and the United States voted differently on the issue. These criteria were designed to ensure that only politically significant roll calls were included in the sample and to screen out roll calls on which there was little or no disagreement. The distinction between political and security roll calls and those concerning non-self-governing territories and trusteeships, hereafter referred to as colonial roll calls, is that of the U.N. Secretariat, as reported in the annual volumes of the *Yearbook of the United Nations*.

[20] The "scores of agreement" presented in Table 8-4 are a measure of the percentage of times nations agreed with the Soviet Union or the United States on the one hundred two roll calls examined. The method employed assigns weight to abstention votes as against positive and negative positions. It also corrects for the fact that not all governments voted on all one hundred two roll calls, since several were not U.N. members throughout the entire period and since there were occasional absences. The formula used to compute the scores of agreement is that devised by Arend Lijphart, "An Analysis of Bloc Voting in the General Assembly: A Critique and a Proposal," *American Political Science Review*, vol. 57, no. 4 (December 1963), pp. 909-10.

[21] The fact that Cyprus has not supported Soviet policy in the United Nations, despite receiving military aid, perhaps is explainable because Cyprus did not become an aid recipient until 1964. The Laos case was also exceptional in that some Soviet aid went to the neutralist incumbent Laotian government, some went to the combined neutralist-Pathet Lao forces, and some went to the Laotion communist guerrillas.

Table 8-4. **Scores of Agreement between Aid Donors and Aid Recipients on Political and Security Roll Calls in the United Nations: 1958 through 1964***

Aid Recipient	Aid Donor	Percentage Agreement with USSR	U.S.
Algeria	USSR	81	19
Cyprus	USSR	41	62
Ghana	USSR	62	40
Guinea	USSR	80	22
Somalia	USSR	57	48
Sudan	USSR	64	37
Syria	USSR	73	27
Tanzania	USSR	75	25
U.A.R.	USSR	72	30
Yemen	USSR	71	30
Afghanistan	USSR-U.S.	71	34
Cambodia	USSR-U.S.	59	44
Cuba	USSR-U.S.	69	32
India	USSR-U.S.	62	43
Indonesia	USSR-U.S.	68	35
Iraq	USSR-U.S.	71	30
Laos	USSR-U.S.	28	74
Mali	USSR-U.S.	80	28
Morocco	USSR-U.S.	75	26
Argentina	U.S.	17	84
Bolivia	U.S.	27	74
Brazil	U.S.	25	78
Burma	U.S.	64	41
Chile	U.S.	23	81
Colombia	U.S.	17	84
Congo-Kinshasa	U.S.	40	60
Costa Rica	U.S.	18	83
Dominican Republic	U.S.	21	83
Ecuador	U.S.	24	77
El Salvador	U.S.	23	81
Ethiopia	U.S.	57	46
Guatemala	U.S.	20	83
Haiti	U.S.	27	74
Honduras	U.S.	16	86
Iran	U.S.	34	72
Israel	U.S.	19	81
Jordan	U.S.	51	51
Lebanon	U.S.	54	47
Liberia	U.S.	35	68
Libya	U.S.	59	42
Mexico	U.S.	37	66
Nicaragua	U.S.	9	92
Pakistan	U.S.	35	68
Panama	U.S.	24	78
Paraguay	U.S.	15	87
Peru	U.S.	17	84
Philippines	U.S.	25	77
Saudi Arabia	U.S.	64	38
Senegal	U.S.	39	61
Thailand	U.S.	23	87
Tunisia	U.S.	54	48
Turkey	U.S.	18	88
Uruguay	U.S.	19	84
Venezuela	U.S.	25	77

* Includes all Third World nations which received military aid valued at $1 million or more from either the Soviet Union or the United States during the 1958-64 period. The Aid Donor column lists the source or sources of aid for the 1958-64 period. Scores of agreement may total more than 100 percent since the USSR and the U.S. were not in total disagreement on all roll calls. Aid relationships after 1964 are not included.

Considering the thirty-five Third World nations aided exclusively by the United States, it was found that twenty-eight had higher scores of agreement with Washington than with Moscow. Six, on the other hand, agreed with the Russians more than with the Americans despite the fact that the United States was the exclusive military aid donor. Jordan was precisely neutral in its voting.

The results presented in Table 8-4 indicate a strong relationship between military aid policy and attitudes, as expressed in U.N. voting, on political and security issues. The Soviet government has tended to be rewarded by military aid recipients to a somewhat greater degree than has the United States. Foreign policy attitudes definitely correlate with receipt of military aid.

While cold war problems may be of paramount importance to the Soviet Union and the United States, Third World nations perhaps are more intensely concerned with the colonialism issue than with the problems of international political security. With few exceptions, Third World countries are former colonies of European powers. This legacy has tended to make the issue of colonialism and national self-determination one in which emotions are high and feelings intense. Just as the cold war has split the United Nations, so has the conglomerate of problems labeled colonial questions. In recognition of the importance of these issues, Table 8-5 presents the scores of agreement between the Soviet Union, the United States, and Third World military aid recipients on colonial roll calls in the United Nations. Following the same procedures as with the political and security roll calls, twenty-one important votes on colonial issues from 1958 to 1964 were selected for analysis of the positions of the two aid donors and the aid recipients.

All ten nations which received military aid exclusively from the Soviet bloc had high scores of agreement with the Soviet Union on colonial votes. The aid recipients mutually assisted by Moscow and Washington also showed strong agreement with the USSR. Laos, the one Soviet recipient which was not in majority agreement with the Soviet Union on political and security questions, had a relatively low agreement score on colonial roll calls.

The thirty-five nations receiving aid solely from the United States did not show high scores of agreement with Washington. While only six of the thirty-five failed to agree with American positions on political and security questions, most of the thirty-five sharply disagreed with the United States on colonial issues. Three Latin American nations and Turkey, the Third World recipient which has been beneficiary of the largest amount of U.S. military aid, were in substantial agreement with the United States.

Table 8-5. Scores of Agreement between Aid Donors and Aid Recipients on Colonial Roll Calls in the United Nations: 1958 through 1964*

Aid Recipient	Aid Donor	Percentage Agreement with USSR	Percentage Agreement with U.S.
Algeria	USSR	100	0
Cyprus	USSR	88	25
Ghana	USSR	93	21
Guinea	USSR	97	23
Somalia	USSR	100	0
Sudan	USSR	93	18
Syria	USSR	93	7
Tanzania	USSR	100	0
U.A.R.	USSR	95	15
Yemen	USSR	91	22
Afghanistan	USSR-U.S.	98	17
Cambodia	USSR-U.S.	81	20
Cuba	USSR-U.S.	90	26
India	USSR-U.S.	91	24
Indonesia	USSR-U.S.	95	16
Iraq	USSR-U.S.	95	19
Laos	USSR-U.S.	61	60
Mali	USSR-U.S.	100	22
Morocco	USSR-U.S.	95	19
Argentina	U.S.	67	38
Bolivia	U.S.	66	56
Brazil	U.S.	55	50
Burma	U.S.	95	20
Chile	U.S.	68	48
Colombia	U.S.	55	45
Congo-Kinshasa	U.S.	89	11
Costa Rica	U.S.	68	53
Dominican Republic	U.S.	61	50
Ecuador	U.S.	68	50
El Salvador	U.S.	50	50
Ethiopia	U.S.	87	29
Guatemala	U.S.	67	38
Haiti	U.S.	74	26
Honduras	U.S.	50	63
Iran	U.S.	85	25
Israel	U.S.	63	37
Jordan	U.S.	91	22
Lebanon	U.S.	91	22
Liberia	U.S.	88	26
Libya	U.S.	95	19
Mexico	U.S.	76	38
Nicaragua	U.S.	20	80
Pakistan	U.S.	83	31
Panama	U.S.	65	40
Paraguay	U.S.	64	36
Peru	U.S.	47	59
Philippines	U.S.	88	26
Saudi Arabia	U.S.	96	32
Senegal	U.S.	91	9
Thailand	U.S.	72	43
Tunisia	U.S.	92	18
Turkey	U.S.	25	85
Uruguay	U.S.	74	32
Venezuela	U.S.	76	38

* Includes all Third World nations which received military aid valued at $1 million or more from either the Soviet Union or the United States during the 1958-64 period. The Aid Donor column lists the source or sources of aid for the 1958-64 period. Scores of agreement may total more than 100 percent since the USSR and the U.S. were not in total disagreement on all roll calls. Aid relationships after 1964 are not included.

Table 8-5 demonstrates that on the important issue of colonialism the views of the Soviet Union and most Third World nations generally coincided. While Soviet military aid recipients tended to have high scores of agreement with the USSR, nations aided by the United States were only slightly less in agreement with the Soviet Union. It is clear that political attitudes are related to military aid diplomacy, but the issue of colonialism is so intensely felt as to override other considerations. Aid recipients may modify their positions on international security questions to conform to those of the donors of aid; they do not do so on colonial problems.

Comparing the findings on both political and security questions and on colonial roll calls for the United States and the Soviet Union, it is obvious the USSR has succeeded in identifying itself with the positions of the less-developed countries on colonial questions, but not to the same degree on roll calls involving political and security issues. For the United States the opposite situation holds true. The U.S. positions on political and security questions were very similar to those taken by Third World countries. There was, however, virtually no identity in positions of the United States and Third World countries on colonial issues. For the United States as well as for the Soviet Union military aid appears to be a significant but not a decisive factor in affecting the foreign policy orientations of aid recipients.[22]

TWELVE YEARS OF AID COMPETITION

An analysis of twelve years of American-Soviet military aid competition in the Third World reveals a rather remarkable degree of similarity between the two superpowers in their arms diplomacy in the less-developed nations, despite some differences in strategy and objectives. Perhaps the close resemblance of the two policies reflects a recognition on the part of both the USSR and the United States of certain common phenomena which affect arms aid decisions. Whatever the case, it is clear that the approaches of the two donor countries to military assistance are sufficiently alike to permit generalizations applicable to the foreign policies of both in the Third World.

The Soviet and American governments have invested approximately the same dollar value in military aid over the twelve-year period from 1955 to 1968. Viewed in terms of dollar amounts, regional priorities have been very similar: Africa and Latin America are low priority regions while South and Southeast Asia and the Middle East receive the

[22] For discussion of variables other than military aid which correlate with voting positions in the United Nations, see Bruce M. Russett, *Trends in World Politics* (New York: The Macmillan Co., 1968), Chapter 6.

great bulk of Soviet and American weapons. The reasons for area priorities also seem to be similar. Both the United States and the Soviet Union appear to regard Latin America as within the U.S. sphere of influence; both donors appear to believe that Africa is too underdeveloped and geographically remote from their respective power centers to warrant providing African states with more than token military aid. Further, both superpowers appear sufficiently concerned about Communist China to engage in very active military aid programs in south and southeast Asia. Finally, both the USSR and the United States seem to believe that the Middle East is of sufficient importance to justify active and at times risky competition in that region of the world.

Most countries of the world have in the past relied on one or the other donor country but not on both. This was partly because the donor countries seemed to have insisted on this situation as a price for military aid, partly because the recipient countries tended themselves to choose sides in the cold war, and partly because both donor countries tended to aid nations which were friendly to them. Not that the donor countries have not attempted to maintain relationships with countries which they did not aid militarily. Neither donor country has irrevocably committed itself in the less-developed world.

A common problem faced by both donors is that the weapons furnished by them may be used against third countries with which the donors are attempting to maintain good relations. The United States has furnished large amounts of weapons to Pakistan and more limited supplies to India; the USSR has reversed the order and furnished large amounts of military aid to India and limited aid to Pakistan. Neither the United States nor the USSR has any interest in seeing the weapons they furnish used by Pakistan and India against each other. Both donor countries prefer that the subcontinent be strong against possible Chinese influence or penetration, but neither donor can prevent the recipient countries from using the weapons against each other. This is the most serious difficulty faced by both military aid donors: The purposes for which they give military aid frequently do not coincide with the purposes for which the recipients desire the aid, nor the uses to which the recipients put the weapons. The numerous and intense rivalries in the Third World inevitably drag the donor countries into local quarrels in which they have no interest. This explains why both superpowers tend not to commit themselves fully to Third World causes and why they maintain relationships through economic aid and other instruments even when heavily arming rival protagonists.

The original motive for the American military aid effort was to contain Soviet expansionism along the rimlands of Russia, particularly in the eastern Mediterranean region. Today American military aid is still justified in terms of containing communism. But apparently the Soviet threat has receded in the minds of many recipients. The Soviet government has encouraged this development by adopting more conciliatory policies toward certain American military aid beneficiaries in the southwest Asian-Middle Eastern areas. This more flexible Soviet approach has taken the form of extending Soviet aid to Iran, offering economic assistance to Turkey, and providing at least token military aid to Pakistan.

Voting trends in the United Nations suggest that as more countries become recipients of Soviet military aid programs, there will be a tendency for these countries to become greater political allies of the Soviet Union in world politics. They will be more likely to identify with the Soviet side in voting on colonial issues and will tend to defer to Soviet opinion on political and security questions affecting nations generally.

After twelve years of Soviet and U.S. military aid rivalry in the Third World, no conclusive statement can be made as to which government is winning the struggle. The one point which stands out is that the Soviet Union for many years has been expanding its military aid programs to the Third World, whereas the United States in 1967–69 entered a period of military aid retrenchment in Latin America, Africa, and the Middle East that will give the Soviet government more leeway for maneuver. In the normal course of events, further aggrandizements of Soviet military influence in the Third World must eventually lead to a U.S. reaction. This reaction may take the form of stepping up American military aid to the Third World. More hopefully, the United States will choose instead to develop alternative instruments of competition tailored to solving the truly desperate social and developmental problems facing most Third World nations. This policy will not be possible, however, unless the United States can persuade the less-developed countries to decline "opportunities" to obtain Soviet military assistance. Third World nations must be convinced that maintaining large military forces diverts scarce resources from more pressing needs. Unless they come to this conclusion, and accordingly seek economic and other forms of aid rather than arms, Soviet-American military aid competition seems destined to remain a characteristic feature of the struggle for influence in the Third World.

9

SOVIET ARMS AID DIPLOMACY IN PERSPECTIVE

I N THE years after the first Egyptian arms aid agreement with the Soviet bloc in 1955, the Soviet Union succeeded in establishing a military aid presence throughout the Third World. By 1968 the USSR counted twenty-four states—twenty-five, if the brief episode of Russian arms aid to the Lumumba government in the Congo is included—that received at one time or another military assistance. As events unfolded in the history of Russian arms aid diplomacy, Soviet objectives became crystallized and certain broad patterns, characteristics, and recurrent themes in Soviet military aid policies emerged. This does not mean that every Soviet arms aid initiative can be neatly placed in a particular category. Nor does it imply that the USSR designed and adhered to a master plan in executing its arms assistance policies. On the contrary, although Soviet military aid polices were deliberate and aimed at achieving certain goals, perhaps their most striking aspect was their quality of opportunism. Military aid to a militant Arab state like Egypt, to the socialist-inclined Touré government of Guinea, or to the virulently anti-colonial Sukarno regime in Indonesia fitted Soviet ideological precepts of the post-Stalin era. Arms aid to the Imam of Yemen, to Iran, Nigeria, and Morocco, however, epitomized the considerable ideological flexibility of the Soviet Union in furthering its goals. Nevertheless, although the Soviet government did not follow any preconceived grand strategy, its policies were purposeful and reflected an awareness of the political circumstances and conditions bearing upon its arms aid initiatives.

AID PATTERNS, CHARACTERISTICS, AND THEMES

Soviet military aid was designed to promote two basic long range and closely related political objectives. The defensive aim was the impairment of western, especially American, influence in the states and regions receiving aid. Besides the resolve to compete with the west, this goal originally also reflected a security concern. The early arms aid programs in states adjacent or close to the Soviet border, such as in Afghanistan, Egypt, and Syria, were partly developed in response to western efforts to contain Soviet expansionism by encircling the USSR with a ring of defensive alliances. In most subsequent Russian arms aid policies the goal of eroding western positions became the principal motivating factor.

The offensive objective in Soviet arms assistance was the extension of Russian influence into the developing world. The USSR used its military aid instrument to demonstrate its support of the national independence of recipient states, and expected in return to enhance its stature and influence in the Third World.

Soviet leaders pursued these defensive and offensive objectives in two distinct patterns of aid relations. The most pronounced pattern which has existed throughout Soviet arms aid relations can generally be defined as an aggressive pattern. This pattern was basically the result of east-west competition in the very hostile climate of the early cold war period. Soviet arms aid sought to encourage the recipient to maintain an anti-western or anti-American posture in international affairs; to strengthen the recipient's military capability vis-à-vis its local opponents, particularly if they received western support; and to encourage the recipient in sustaining a militant or aggressive policy toward such adversaries. By retaining a high level of tensions the Soviet Union hoped to increase the recipient's dependence on the USSR for weapons and to undermine western interests in regional stability. Soviet military aid policies in Indonesia and India, and in the majority of Middle Eastern and African recipients, display this aggressive pattern.

The second pattern, which can be defined as a policy of intrusion, was the result of a set of conditions that began to influence Soviet foreign policy in 1963 and 1964. The most important of these was the development of intercontinental ballistic missiles, which decreased the deterrence value of the western mutual defense pacts along the Soviet border. Accordingly, the USSR could afford a more conciliatory approach toward developing states aligned with the west. With the passing of time Soviet militant ideology appeared to have lost some of its urgency, and after the Cuban missile crisis the USSR embarked on promoting a climate conducive to less hostile coexistence with the United States. Unlike Communist China, Soviet spokesmen no longer emphasized the "world communist revolution." These factors gradually facilitated a new Soviet policy toward emerging countries identified with the west.

Indicative of the new intrusion approach were economic agreements with Pakistan in 1963 and 1964, the upsurge in economic aid to Iran in

1965, the marked increase in trade with Japan in 1965 and 1966, and trade agreements with a number of Latin American republics in 1966 and 1967. The pattern of intrusion was further evidenced by the arms aid deals with Iran, Pakistan, and Nigeria in 1967 and by Soviet bloc defense aid to Morocco in 1966 and 1967. Russian long range goals remained the weakening of western ties, although in some cases, such as in Pakistan, other aims were probably more important. But the immediate goals were more modest. The USSR sought to introduce a limited presence in areas previously dominated by western or American influence and to encourage more neutralist foreign policy positions in the target states. This policy was relatively cheap for the Soviet Union, both in financial and political terms, and yet it appeared to offer prospects of greatly increasing the number of countries over which the USSR exercised some influence.

As the rift with China developed, Moscow's military aid policy turned toward countering Chinese penetration of the Third World, thus adding one more dimension to the twin objectives of eliminating western influence and replacing it with Soviet influence. While the differences between Moscow and Peking were expressed most vociferously in ideological terms, the Soviet government's chief trump card in its competition for the good will and allegiance of the developing countries was its capacity to extend much more economic and military aid than could China. Sino-Soviet rivalry was most intense in areas on the periphery of China, and in consequence affected most directly Russian military aid policies to Vietnam, Laos, Cambodia, India, and Pakistan. It influenced the formulation of Russian arms aid programs in black Africa to a somewhat lesser extent. Competition with China influenced little, if at all, the patterns of Soviet arms aid relations in the Middle East and Latin America.

A major characteristic of Soviet military aid diplomacy is its relatively high degree of continuity. While the Soviet Union was frequently quick to exploit an opportunity for establishing a military aid presence abroad, once arms aid ties had been formed, the USSR was usually prepared to continue such relationships. In only one significant case—in Iraq in 1963—did the Soviet government decide to suspend its program temporarily. In the few instances in which Russian military assistance was terminated or drastically reduced, the decisions were made primarily by the recipients rather than by Moscow. Neither Ghana nor Indonesia, after their respective anti-western presidents had been ousted by more moderate army leaders, was eager to assume large new Soviet arms debts. Between 1962 and 1966 neither Morocco nor Guinea obtained Soviet bloc military hardware. Morocco preferred to fill most of its defense requirements in the United States and France; Guinea distrusted

Soviet motives after it had had a taste of communist subversion in 1961. As a rule, Moscow rarely withdrew of its own volition from an arms aid relationship.

The flow of arms, however, varied from period to period, for Russian weapons aid does not ordinarily follow the American approach of annual allocations to particular on-going programs. A decrease in weapons shipments did not necessarily indicate a comparable decline in Soviet interest in the recipient. Indeed, the continuation of Russian military training missions in countries where there had been reductions in arms deliveries suggests an abiding Soviet commitment. On occasion, the decreased flow of weapons resulted from the fact that the military establishments of the recipients had reached a point of saturation and could not usefully absorb additional equipment.

Another basic characteristic of Russian arms aid policies was the relative ease with which the Soviet Union was prepared to dispense with ideological principles in taking on another military hardware customer. In most Middle Eastern and African recipients domestic communist parties were proscribed and, at times, harshly repressed. Also, in spite of its alleged commitment to wars of national liberation, the USSR has been cautious in its support of such forces with military aid. Neither the ideology of the recipient, nor its policies toward indigenous communist movements, seems to have significantly affected Russian military aid decisions.

A recurrent theme in Soviet arms aid diplomacy has been non-interference with the defense and other internal policies of the recipients. Not until the disastrous defeat of the Arab armies in 1967 did Moscow openly press for reorganization and reforms in the Egyptian armed forces and become involved in operational advice, basic individual personnel and officers' training, and unit tactical training. In its relations with most other recipients, especially before the June 1967 war, the Soviet Union limited its military role to technical advice and specialist training. Even since the Arab-Israeli war, Soviet military technicians have remained insulated from the Arab population, and Russian spokesmen stress the theme of non-interference in the domestic affairs of arms aid recipients.

Moscow also sought to avoid pressuring its prospective clients into selecting particular kinds of weapons. With some qualifications a distinction can be made between Russian arms aid before and after 1961. Much of the weaponry delivered before 1961 was obsolete or obsolescent by the standards of the major powers, while after 1961 more modern first line equipment began to reach recipients capable of absorbing it. Nevertheless, the arms provided in the earlier period met, on the whole, the requirements of the recipients as they perceived them. The terms "obsolete" and "obsolescent" should not be judged by Soviet or American criteria. The post-1961 shipments of MiG–21s, the Komar and Osa class patrol boats, and other advanced systems were partly in response to the demands of the client states for more sophisticated weapons. The USSR had to meet these requests if it did not wish to risk losing its influence with them.

This does not suggest, however, that Moscow indiscriminately agreed to deliver every item on the shopping list of its customers. With the exception of the Cuban affair, the most powerful restraint on the Soviet Union in its arms aid policies was the concern to limit the risk of an armed encounter between the superpowers. The USSR restricted its aid to developing countries to conventional weapons. The Egyptian request for nuclear weapons in 1965 was quickly rejected. Even in the Cuban venture in 1962, the Soviet government retained control over the missiles deployed in Cuba. After experiencing the American reaction, the Russians withdrew not only the offensive missiles, but also the Il–28 bombers from Cuba. In its subsequent arms aid to Havana, Moscow moved cautiously and refrained from strengthening Cuba's offensive capability. Similarly, to limit the chances of a direct confrontation with the United States, the USSR did not take up Arab charges of Anglo-American complicity in the Middle East war of 1967. Nor did Moscow intervene with troops on this or on any other occasion on behalf of its Arab or other arms aid clients.

If, however, the general theme in the story of Soviet arms aid diplomacy is one of caution, both the volume and kind of military assistance supplied to Middle Eastern countries tended to compromise this policy of restraint. It is in the Middle East that Moscow pursued its objectives most aggressively. To be sure, the importance of the region as the nexus between Europe and Asia and as a prime area of the western defense system has somewhat declined for America and its western allies. But the region's geographical proximity to Soviet borders and its lure of warm water ports for the Russian navy go far to explain the enduring interest of the USSR in the Middle East. The Soviet government used its military aid instrument most extensively there. In Soviet-American rivalry for influence in the Third World, the Middle East represents for the Russians the highest stakes. Of the major Third World regions, the Middle East, because of the unique conditions deriving from the Arab-Israeli conflict, offers Russia the best chance to replace the United States as the predominant foreign power. It is, therefore, the most likely scene for a clash between the superpowers.

ACHIEVEMENTS, FAILURES, AND THE FUTURE OF ARMS AID DIPLOMACY

While the United States, and later China, were the major opponents which the Soviet Union had to consider in its military aid diplomacy, its successes and failures were, of course, also conditioned by the policies of the recipients. Each situation constituted at least a "three- or four-person game" for the Soviet Union, thereby rendering the maximization of gains more complicated and the payoff more uncertain.

In the Middle East, the implacable Arab hostility to Israel contributed to the fact that success outweighed the setbacks in Soviet military aid diplomacy. As a result of the Arab-Israeli war in 1967, Soviet arms aid policies did experience a setback because Moscow's vast weapons supplies did not prevent the smashing defeat of the Arab forces. The Russians, moreover, proved unwilling to intervene directly on behalf of the Arabs. Also, despite its political and military support to the Arab nations immediately after the war, the USSR could not reverse the new political map of the Middle East.

The Soviet Union, on the other hand, scored a major success because the dependency of the militant Arab states on Soviet political and military backing had markedly increased, and Soviet leverage in the Arab world had grown. After the war, furthermore, the rapid expansion in the number of Russian military advisers, and their increased role in the military establishments of the Arab states, provided the Soviet Union with more effective opportunities for influencing the military elites and the defense policies of its protégés. The Soviet government also adroitly exploited the Arab defeat by establishing for the first time a considerable naval presence in the Mediterranean.

Egypt's defeat paved the way for an expansion in the Russian military aid presence in Yemen, at the southeastern entrance to the Middle East. The Soviet commitment there will probably remain limited. Soviet leaders apparently do not wish to become too deeply embroiled in the Yemeni civil war, as the withdrawal of Russian pilots after their identity was exposed suggests. The prospects are that as the Yemeni civil war continues in a desultory fashion, Russian arms aid will continue at a level sufficient to prevent a defeat of the republican forces. The abandonment of the British role east of Suez opens the door for further Soviet arms aid penetration of the Persian Gulf states, as well as of other countries around the Indian Ocean basin. Unless the United States is willing to offer these states an alternative to Soviet arms aid, Moscow can be expected to exploit the opportunities presented by Britain's withdrawal.

At the western gate of the Mediterranean, the Soviet Union has become more firmly entrenched as arms aid supplier to Algeria and has even intruded into Morocco by arranging the purchase of Czech arms for that state. Because of its location along the vital access lane into the Mediterranean, Algeria is likely to remain a principal target of Soviet arms assistance efforts. To the extent that the USSR can reconcile military aid to Morocco with Algerian protests, the Soviet Union, or at its persuasion, one of the other Warsaw Pact members, will continue to try to lure Morocco away from the west with weapons aid.

At the center of the Middle East, in Egypt, Syria, and Iraq, Soviet influence seems assured as long as the Arab-Israeli conflict continues at its current level. The Soviet government will utilize its predominant position to exercise closer control over the use of its weapons in order to prevent the militant Arabs from launching another round of fighting with Israel. A key mechanism in exerting this influence lies in the control of the spare parts pipeline without which the Arabs cannot maintain combat readiness. The Soviet Union can hardly relish the prospects of a fourth war: Another Arab defeat would increase the pressure on the Russians to intervene with force. On the other hand, an Israeli defeat might cause the Americans to intervene. In either situation the chances of an armed encounter between Moscow and Washington would be measurably greater.

Thus the USSR faces a basic problem of trying to convert its newly won influence into more effective political control over the defense policies of its Arab clients. Since military aid remains the most important lever for the Soviet Union, its programs can be expected to continue. Soviet hints at some kind of multilateral arms control agreement for the Middle East, therefore, reflect more propaganda than serious intent. The chances of arriving at such an agreement appear extremely limited for the near future.

In South and Southeast Asia, the second most important area in Russian arms aid operations, the USSR experienced a major setback in Indonesia. The outpouring of military hardware to Djakarta did not bring Moscow any permanent degree of influence and left the Russians with a large claim on the Indonesian treasury without realistic prospects for recovery. The vehemently anti-communist outburst in Indonesia offers few immediate possibilities for the re-establishment of close Soviet-Indonesian ties. However, should Indonesian efforts fail to obtain desperately needed assistance in the west, there could conceivably be an opportunity for the Soviet Union to reassert some influence. It appears likely that any new Soviet initiative in Indonesia will take the form of economic aid and trade rather than a resumption of substantial military assistance. As long as the Suharto regime remains in power and manages to enlist western help, Soviet military aid to Indonesia is likely to remain quite modest and probably limited to the supply of spare parts and maintenance equipment.

Soviet arms aid diplomacy fared much better in the Asian subcontinent. The USSR had become India's largest supplier of military equipment by 1968. Because of its key position at the Indian Ocean rim, and because of the threat of Chinese influence in the subcontinent, India is rapidly becoming one of the most privileged arms aid recipients. The recent Russian military aid deliveries to Pakistan to offset Chinese penetration have understandably ruffled Indian feathers. Nevertheless, the USSR will in all likelihood continue its arms aid to Pakistan, even though it may limit Pakistan's selection of weapons. Washington's refusal to meet Pakistani defense requirements afforded Moscow as well as Peking the opportunity to create arms aid ties with Pakistan. To mitigate Indian concerns, the USSR will probably step up its arms aid offers to India, thereby accelerating the pace of its military aid shipments. Particularly if the discords between the Soviet Union and China deepen, the Russians are likely to intensify their arms aid efforts not only in South and Southeast Asia, but in other areas of the Indian Ocean littoral as well.

In sub-Saharan Africa the achievements of Soviet military aid diplomacy vary. The Soviet experience in Africa shows that relatively rudimentary nations pose as many obstacles to influencing national development and foreign policy as do more advanced societies. Most notable among these obstacles in Africa is the prevalence of tribalism and related centrifugal socio-economic forces which are inimical to national forms of political organization. In consequence, Soviet calculations as to whether a particular government merits arms aid are rendered more difficult. African distrust of the white man's colonial past is another impediment to the establishment of much more than ephemeral Soviet influence. Despite the absence of traditional overseas colonialism in Russian history, and notwithstanding Soviet attempts to identify its policies with anti-colonial activities, the USSR remains suspect in much of Africa.

Soviet endeavors to gain influence through military aid programs in western Africa have been disappointing. On the whole, the fluid politics of the newly independent states in western Africa argues against a marked increase in the level of the Russian military aid effort, although the Soviet leaders will undoubtedly remain alert to the possibility of exploiting new opportunities. For the near future Soviet attention seems likely to center on the geopolitically more important countries in the Horn of Africa and in east Africa, rather than on those of the west coast. To consolidate the Soviet position in the eastern Mediterranean and to protect Soviet supply lines from Europe to Asia when the Suez Canal is re-opened, the USSR can be expected to step up its aid diplomacy in the Somali Republic and in the Sudan. Britain's exodus from areas east of Suez presages Soviet probings in east African countries which may lead to new arms aid ties.

In Latin America, Soviet arms aid policies have won an often difficult ally in Cuba. Inasmuch as Cuba is located in America's own backyard, the establishment of a Soviet military aid presence there is a political success for the Russians, even though Cuba is of limited military value. More importantly, however, the missile gamble of 1962 turned into a resounding defeat for the Soviet Union. As a result, Moscow appears to have accepted the reality that the western hemisphere remains largely in the American sphere of influence.

The pragmatic and opportunistic nature of Soviet military aid diplomacy makes generalizations about its past difficult and projections of its future hazardous. Certain conclusions, however, are evident. In some instances Soviet arms aid programs developed in response to the challenge of American military aid to an emerging country, a response which took the form of similar aid to a neighboring state. More often, the refusal of the United States to provide arms aid to target countries led the USSR to move into such vacuums with its own military assistance program. The emergence of Communist China as a rival to the Soviet Union added another important dimension to Russian arms aid initiatives.

Within this broad framework certain regions and countries stand out as major and continuous recipients of Soviet arms aid. The militant Arab states of the Middle East, notably Egypt, and India of the South and Southeast Asia region, are clearly priority targets in Soviet military aid diplomacy. It can be anticipated that military assistance will become an instrument of growing foreign policy significance in these areas.

The Soviet government conducts its arms aid diplomacy on the basis of its perceived national interests. This need not prevent a limited degree of Soviet collaboration in international arms control arrangements. As before, the USSR will probably cooperate to some extent with arms control measures involving nuclear weapons, nuclear military technology, and outer space, since these are matters of the gravest importance to the security of the Soviet Union. It is highly improbable that Moscow will depart from its established practice of limiting its assistance to conventional weaponry. But otherwise, in the design and execution of its aid programs, the Soviet Union is, for the time being, unlikely to consider seriously proposals that impose restraints.

Thus, the next decade is likely to see an expansion of Soviet military aid in the Third World. Looking further into the future, however, the course and content of arms aid diplomacy will be largely determined by technological developments and the nature of the evolving international system.

Since World War II technology has advanced at such a fast pace that some of the weapons generations now last little more than five years. This means that many costly American and Soviet weapons systems are obsolete soon after they become operational. When the weapons are replaced, the old generation of arms could be scrapped. More likely, they will become part of an inventory which makes arms aid diplomacy a tempting way to gain influence in the emerging world. These weapons, while obsolete by American and Russian standards, will nevertheless become more and more technically sophisticated, costly, and destructive. Third World nations obtaining these systems will become more dependent than ever on the United States and the USSR. The increasingly destructive power of the arms, moreover, will heighten the dangers of escalation if a conflict erupts in the Third World.

At the same time, the nature of the international system will influence the use of military aid as a foreign policy tool of the superpowers. A number of developments suggest that U.S. and Russian decision-makers are beginning to perceive certain common problems. Their shared super-power position compels them into limited cooperation in such areas as retarding the spread of nuclear weapons, lessening the risk of surprise attack, and reducing the dangers of accidental war. Both superpowers, despite continued attempts to gain advantages in the Third World, find it vital to maintain sufficient stability in international politics to avoid nuclear confrontation.

At present the military power of either the Soviet Union or of the United States far overshadows that of any other nation or group of nations in the world. If the superpowers should widen further the gap between themselves and the rest of the world, the international system will become increasingly bipolar in nature. Under such circumstances, significant change in the distribution of influence in the Third World through arms aid would have the potential of seriously undermining the superpowers' mutual interests in avoiding confrontations. Both Moscow and Washington, therefore, would be likely to become increasingly cautious in their policies toward the Third World. Such caution might even extend, a decade or more hence, to the imposition of restrictions on their military aid to the developing nations which would go beyond the ban on providing nuclear weapons.

On the other hand, the future international system may witness not two superpowers, but five or six or more nations capable of waging nuclear war. Such a multipolar world would be more flexible than one dominated primarily by the United States and the Soviet Union. Alignments and alliances would continually shift; some neutrals would become identified with one or the other of the superpowers; some allies might become neutrals. Such a fluid international system could more easily absorb shifts in the balance of military power in the Third World occasioned by arms aid diplomacy. With the consolidation of numerous power centers, it is likely that arms diplomacy in the Third World by the advanced nations would assume an even greater role in the international arena of the future.

It is a sobering thought, however, that within a decade exploding populations may outstrip the capacity of many Third World governments to provide much more than the barest necessities of life for their peoples. It is tragic that such a large proportion of Soviet and American aid is in the form of weapons. In addition, arms diplomacy in the nuclear age is a dangerous form of competitive coexistence. Yet the Soviet Union shows no sign of abandoning arms diplomacy, and Washington cannot simply leave the field open to Moscow. Perhaps a solution would lie in a determined American effort to persuade the less developed countries to seek economic and social assistance rather than arms aid. Soviet-American competition might then contribute more positively to the welfare of the peoples of the Third World.

SELECTED BIBLIOGRAPHY

PUBLIC DOCUMENTS

Great Britain. *International Conference on the Settlement of the Laotian Question, Geneva, May 12, 1961 to July 23, 1962.* Laos No. 1, Cmnd. 1828. London: H. M. Stationery Office, 1962.
U.S. Arms Control and Disarmament Agency. *World-Wide Military Expenditures and Related Data.* Research Report 67-6. Washington: 1967.
U.S. Congress, Subcommittee on Foreign Economic Policy of the Joint Economic Committee. *New Directions in the Soviet Economy.* 89th Cong., 2nd sess., 1966.
U.S. Department of Defense. *Military Assistance Facts.* Volumes for 1966, 1967, and 1968. Washington: 1966, 1967, and 1968.
U.S. Department of State. *The Communist Economic Offensive through 1963.* Research Memorandum RSB-43. Washington: June 18, 1964.
————. *The Communist Economic Offensive through 1964.* Research Memorandum RSB-65. Washington: August 4, 1965.
————. *Communist Governments and Developing Nations: Aid and Trade in 1965.* Research Memorandum RSB-50. Washington: June 17, 1966.
————. *Communist Governments and Developing Nations: Aid and Trade in 1966.* Research Memorandum RSB-80. Washington: July 21, 1967.
————. *Communist Governments and Developing Nations: Aid and Trade in 1967.* Research Memorandum RSE-120. Washington: August 14, 1968.
————. *A Threat to the Peace: North Vietnam's Effort to Conquer South Vietnam.* Publication 7308. Washington: 1961.
————. *U.S. Participation in the United Nations: Report by the President to the Congress for the Year 1960.* Washington: 1962.

161

————. *Vietnam Information Notes: Wars of National Liberation.* No. 12. Washington: June 1968.

————. *World Strength of the Communist Party Organizations.* 18th Annual Report. Washington: 1966.

————. *Press Release No. 109.* Address by Joseph Palmer II, Assistant Secretary for American Affairs. May 9, 1967.

————. *Statement.* November 18, 1960.

U.S. Congress, House of Representatives, Subcommittee on Inter-American Affairs of the Committee on Foreign Affairs. *Castro-Communist Subversion in the Western Hemisphere. Hearings.* 88th Cong., 1st sess., 1963.

————. *Communism in Latin America. Hearings.* 89th Cong., 1st sess., 1965.

————. *Communist Activities in Latin America. Hearings.* 90th Cong., 1st sess., 1967.

————. *Communist Activities in Latin America, 1967. Report.* 90th Cong., 1st sess., July 3, 1967.

U.S. Congress, House of Representatives, Subcommittee on Foreign Operations of the Committee on Appropriations. *Hearings for FY 1962.* 87th Cong., 1st sess., 1961.

U.S. Congress, Senate, Committee on Foreign Relations. *Mutual Security Act of 1960.* 86th Cong., 2d sess., 1960.

NEWSPAPERS AND PERIODICALS

Africa Report. 1964-1968.
Africa Research Bulletin, Political, Social and Cultural Series. Vols. 2, 3, and 4, 1965-1967.
Al-Ahram. 1956, 1957, 1962.
Al-Akhbar. 1956-1957.
Asian Recorder. April 1-7, 1964.
Christian Science Monitor. 1959-1968.
El Comercio (Lima). October 5, 1967.
Daily Express (London). November 30, 1964.
Daily Telegraph (London). May 24, 1964.
East Africa Standard. January 1, 1967.
Financial Times (London). October 13, 1967.
Hindu Weekly Review. March 28, 1966.
Hindustan Times (New Delhi). 1961-1962.
Indian Express. September 7, 1965.
Indonesian Herald. 1965.
Marcha (Montevideo). September 1967.
Middle East Journal. 1957-1967.
Le Monde. 1966-1967.
Neue Zürcher Zeitung (Zurich). September 5, 1964.
New York Times. 1954-1968.
Nieuwe Rotterdamse Courant. January 6, 1961.
Observer (London). August 23, 1964.
Peruvian Times (Lima). 1967.
Pravda. 1962-1966.

La Prensa (Buenos Aires). February 1, 1968.
La Revue de Défense Nationale. January 1967.
Sun (Baltimore). 1967-1968.
Time. June 9, 1967.
The Times (London). 1965.
Times of India. 1960-1962.
Times of Indonesia. 1958.
Uganda Argus (Kampala). August 9, 1965.
Wall Street Journal. 1958-1967.
Washington Post. 1954-1968.
West Africa. November 2, 1966.
Za-Rubizhom. June 30, 1967.

ARTICLES

Beim, David. "The Communist Bloc and the Foreign Aid Game," *Western Political Quarterly*, Vol. 17, No. 4, December 1964.

Bulba, T. "International Significance of the Development of Communism in the USSR," *Kommunist Vooruzhennykh Sil* (Communist of the Armed Forces), No. 24, December 1964.

"Contemporary Stage of the National Liberation Movement," *Kommunist Vooruzhennykh Sil* (Communist of the Armed Forces), No. 6, March 1965.

Derkach, Nadia. "The Soviet Policy Towards Indonesia in the West Irian and the Malaysian Disputes," *Asian Survey*, Vol. 5, No. 11, November 1965.

Dolgopolov, E. "Armies of Liberated Africa," *Krasnaia Zvezda* (Red Star), September 25, 1965.

Eckov, G., and Prilepskii, Col. "World Socialist System: A Decisive Contemporary Factor," *Kommunist Vooruzhennykh Sil* (Communist of the Armed Forces), No. 22, November 1964.

Feith, Herbert, and Lev, Daniel S. "The End of the Indonesian Rebellion," *Pacific Affairs*, Vol. 36, No. 1, Spring 1963.

"Fifty Years of the Great October Socialist Revolution: Thesis of the Central Committee, CPSU," *Kommunist Vooruzhennykh Sil* (Communist of the Armed Forces), No. 14, July 1967.

Gibert, Stephen P. "Wars of Liberation and Soviet Military Aid Policy," *Orbis*, Vol. 10, No. 3, Fall 1966.

Gordon, Bernard K. "The Potential for Indonesian Expansionism," *Pacific Affairs*, Vol. 36, No. 4, Winter 1963-64.

Hangen, Welles. "Afghanistan," *Yale Review*, Vol. 56, No. 1, October 1966.

Hanna, Willard A. "The Indonesia Crisis—Mid-1964 Phase," *American Universities Field Staff, Southeast Asia Series*, Vol. 12, No. 7, August 1964.

Harrison, Selig S. "Troubled India and Her Neighbors," *Foreign Affairs*, Vol. 43, No. 2, January 1965.

Hindley, Donald. "Indonesia's Confrontation with Malaysia: A Search for Motives," *Asian Survey*, Vol. 4, No. 6, June 1964.

Hyder, Khurshid. "Recent Trends in the Foreign Policy of Pakistan," *The World Today*, Vol. 22, No. 11, November 1966.

Iman, Zafar. "Soviet Asian Policy Today," *Contemporary Review*, Vol. 209, No. 1, July 1966.

Kahin, George McT. "Malaysia and Indonesia," *Pacific Affairs*, Vol. 37, No. 3, Fall 1964.

Karpovich, Michael. "Russian Imperialism and Communist Aggression?" in Goldwin, Robert (ed.). *Readings in Russian Foreign Policy*. New York: Oxford University Press, 1959.

Kovner, Milton. "Soviet Trade and Aid," *Current History*, Vol. 49, No. 290, October 1965.

Kukonin, S. "The Character of our Epoch and the General Line of the World Communist Movement," *Kommunist Vooruzhennykh Sil* (Communist of the Armed Forces), No. 21, November 1964.

Laptev, L. "From Katanga to Biafra," *New Times* (Moscow), December 27, 1967.

Laquer, Walter. "The Hand of Russia," *Reporter*, June 29, 1967.

Lijphart, Arend. "An Analysis of Bloc Voting in the General Assembly: Critique and a Proposal," *American Political Science Review*, Vol. 57, No. 4, December 1963.

Pauker, Guy J. "Indonesia: Internal Development or External Expansion?" *Asian Survey*, Vol. 3, No. 2, February 1963.

Shwadran, Benjamin. "The Soviet Union in the Middle East," *Current History*, Vol. 52, No. 306, February 1967.

Simon, Sheldon W. "The Kashmir Dispute in Sino-Soviet Perspective," *Asian Survey*, Vol. 7, No. 3, March 1967.

Smith, Roger M. "Laos in Perspective," *Asian Survey*, Vol. 3, No. 1, January 1963.

Stein, Arthur. "India and the USSR: The Post-Nehru Period," *Asian Survey*, Vol. 7, No. 3, March 1967.

Vaidyanath, R. "Some Recent Trends in Soviet Policies toward India and Pakistan," *International Studies* (New Delhi), Vol. 7, No. 3, January 1966.

Weeks, George. "Wings of Change: A Report on the Progress of Civil Aviation in Africa," *Africa Report*, Vol. 10, No. 2, February 1965.

————. "The Armies of Africa," *Africa Report*, Vol. 9, No. 1, January 1964.

Wolfstone, Daniel. "Foreign Aid to Indonesia: From East and West," *Far Eastern Economic Review*, Vol. 26, No. 15, April 9, 1959.

BOOKS AND MONOGRAPHS

Alexander, H. T. *African Tightrope: My Two Years as Nkrumah's Chief of Staff*. New York: Praeger, 1965.

Bell, M. J. V. *Military Assistance to Independent African States*. London: Institute for Strategic Studies, 1964.

Black, Cyril E., and Thornton, Thomas P. (eds.). *Communism and Revolution*. Princeton, New Jersey: Princeton University Press, 1964.

Blackman, Raymond V. B. (ed.). *Jane's Fighting Ships: 1967–68*. Great Missenden, Bucks., England: Sampson Low, Marston and Co., Ltd., 1967.

Brzezinski, Zbigniew (ed.). *Africa and the Communist World*. Stanford: Stanford University Press, 1963.

Clubb, Jr., Oliver E. *The United States and the Sino-Soviet Bloc in Southeast Asia.* Washington: The Brookings Institution, 1962.

Cooley, John K. *East Wind Over Africa.* New York: Walker and Company, 1966.

Dinerstein, Herbert S. *Soviet Policy in Latin America.* Santa Monica, Cal.: Rand Corporation, 1966.

Dommen, Arthur. *Conflict in Laos: The Politics of Neutralization.* New York: Praeger, 1964.

Ganshof van der Meersch, W. J. *Fin de la Souveraineté Belge au Congo.* Brussels: Institut Royal des Relations Internationales, 1963.

Gehlen, Michael P. *The Politics of Coexistence.* Bloomington, Indiana: Indiana University Press, 1967.

Georgetown Research Project. *Africa and U.S. National Security.* Washington: 1966.

—————. *Castro-Communist Insurgency in Venezuela.* Washington: 1964.

Goldman, Marshall I. *Soviet Foreign Aid.* New York: Praeger, 1967.

Gordon, Bernard K. *The Dimensions of Conflict in Southeast Asia.* Englewood Cliffs, New Jersey: Prentice Hall, 1966.

Graham, Ian C. C. *The Indo-Soviet MiG Deal and Its International Repercussions.* Rand Corporation P-2842. Santa Monica, Cal.: Rand Corporation, 1964.

Green, William, and Punnett, Dennis. *MacDonald World Air Power Guide.* Garden City, New York: Doubleday & Co., 1963.

Griffith, William E. *Sino-Soviet Relations, 1964-1965.* Cambridge, Mass.: The M.I.T. Press, 1967.

—————. *The Sino-Soviet Rift.* Cambridge, Mass.: The M.I.T. Press, 1964.

Horelick, Arnold L. *The Cuban Missile Crisis: An Analysis of Soviet Calculations and Behavior.* Santa Monica, California: Rand Corporation, 1963.

Houart, Pierre. *La pénétration communiste au Congo.* Brussels: Centre de documentation internationale, 1960.

Howard, Michael, and Hunter, Robert. *Israel and the Arab World: The Crisis of 1967.* London: Institute for Strategic Studies, 1967.

Institute for Strategic Studies. *The Military Balance: 1967–1968.* London: 1967.

—————. *Strategic Survey, 1967.* London: 1968.

Kahin, George McT. (ed.). *Government and Politics of Southeast Asia.* Ithaca, New York: Cornell University Press, 1964.

Lancaster, Donald. *The Emancipation of French Indochina.* London: Oxford University Press, 1961.

Lefever, Ernest W., and Joshua, Wynfred. *United Nations Peacekeeping in the Congo: 1960-1964.* Vol. 2. Washington: The Brookings Institution, 1966.

Lieuwen, Edwin. *Arms and Politics in Latin America.* New York: Praeger, 1961.

Mackintosh, J. M. *Strategy and Tactics of Soviet Foreign Policy.* New York: Oxford University Press, 1963.

Marshall, Charles Burton (ed.). *Two Communist Manifestoes.* Washington: Washington Center of Foreign Policy Research, 1961.

McArdle, Catherine. *The Role of Military Assistance in the Problem of Arms Control.* Cambridge, Mass.: The M.I.T. Press, 1964.

Mecham, J. Lloyd. *The United States and Inter-American Security, 1889-1960.* Austin, Texas: University of Texas Press, 1961.

Morison, David. *The USSR and Africa.* London: Oxford University Press, 1964.

Müller, Kurt. *The Foreign Aid Programs of the Soviet Bloc and Communist China: An Analysis.* New York: Walker and Company, 1967.

Plank, John (ed.). *Cuba and the United States.* Washington: The Brookings Institution, 1967.

Ramazani, R. K. *The Northern Tier.* Princeton: D. Van Nostrand, 1966.

Russett, Bruce M. *Trends in World Politics.* New York: Macmillan Co., 1968.

Scalapino, Robert A. (ed.). *The Communist Revolution in Asia.* Englewood Cliffs, New Jersey: Prentice Hall, 1966.

Schneider, Ronald M. *Communism in Guatemala, 1944-1954.* New York: Praeger, 1959.

Sobel, Lester A. (ed.). *Cuba, the U.S., and Russia: 1960-1963.* New York: Facts on File, 1964.

Special Operations Research Office, American University. *Case Study in Insurgency and Revolutionary Warfare: Guatemala, 1944-54.* Washington: 1964.

Sutton, John L., and Kemp, Geoffrey. *Arms to Developing Countries: 1945-1965.* London: Institute for Strategic Studies, 1966.

Triska, Jan F., and Finley, David D. *Soviet Foreign Policy.* New York: Macmillan, 1968.

Wolfe, Thomas W. *Soviet Strategy at the Crossroads.* Cambridge: Harvard University Press, 1964.

Wood, David. *The Middle East and the Arab World: The Military Context.* London: Institute for Strategic Studies, 1965.

———. *The Armed Forces of African States.* London: Institute for Strategic Studies, 1966.

———. *Armed Forces in Central and South America.* London: Institute for Strategic Studies, 1967.

Zagoria, Donald S. *Vietnam Triangle.* New York: Pegasus, 1967.

INDEX

Afghanistan: Czech military aid to, 99; and Pushtunistan question, 56; Soviet economic aid to, 57, 97, 104n, 107, 108, 138; Soviet military aid to, 3–4, 54–55, 56–58, 73–75, 118, 136, 150
Afro-Asian Conference of 1955, 9
Afro-Asian Conference of 1965, 15, 63, 66
Afro-Asian Solidarity Conference of 1963, 33
Algeria: and re-export of arms, 18, 39, 47, 123; Soviet military aid to, 14–16, 23, 25, 26, 28, 114, 118, 119, 138, 155
Arab-Israeli war of June 1967, 1, 2, 16, 23, 25, 93, 105, 152, 153; aftermath of, 26–30, 43, 154
Arbenz Guzman, Jacob. *See* Guatemala
Argentina: Soviet economic aid to, 101
Armas, Carlos Castillo, 83

Baath Party of Iraq, 17
Baath Party of Syria, 16
Baghdad Pact, 9, 10–12, 13, 19, 56, 57, 101
Ben Bella, Ahmed, 14–15, 18, 19
Boumedienne, Houari, 15–16
Brazil: Soviet economic aid to, 101
Bulganin, Nikolai A., 3, 56
Burma: Soviet economic aid to, 102

Cambodia: Chinese economic and military aid to, 63; Soviet economic aid to, 63; Soviet military aid to, 62–64, 118, 138, 151
Castro, Fidel, 80–85 *passim*, 88–89, 93–94. *See also* Cuba
Castro, Raoul, 84
CENTO, 9, 19, 101, 134
Ceylon: Soviet economic aid to, 102

Communist China: and criticism of the Soviet Union, 15, 18, 26, 51, 60, 62, 64, 116, 128; and economic aid, 43, 47, 48, 63; and military aid, 33, 38, 39n, 41–42, 43, 48, 49, 63, 70, 110, 139, 156
Conference of Eighty-One Communist Parties in November 1960, 72
Congo-Brazzaville: Chinese military aid to, 43; Cuban military aid to, 43; Soviet military aid to, 42–43, 51, 137
Congo - Leopoldville (Congo - Kinshasa). *See* Lumumba, Patrice; Tshombe, Moise
Congolese rebels: Chinese military aid to, 38, 39n; Soviet military aid to, 18, 32, 38–39, 47, 50, 51, 118, 121
Cuba, 2, 4, 118, 120n, 132, 134, 135, 136; Czech military aid to, 84–85; and military aid in Africa, 41, 43, 47; and subversion in Latin America, 88–91; Soviet economic aid to, 87, 101; Soviet military aid to, 83–95, 101, 104, 153, 157
Cuban missile crisis, 2, 4, 32, 46–47, 68, 79, 84, 85–88, 150, 151
Cyprus: Czech military aid to, 22; Soviet military aid to, 14, 21–22, 118, 138, 141n
Czechoslovakia: military aid by, 3, 6, 10–12, 22, 24, 34, 43–44, 56, 57, 71, 82–83, 98–100

De Gaulle, Charles, 15
Dhani, Omar, 65n
Dulles, John Foster, 55

Eisenhower doctrine, 13
Egypt, 3, 104, 118, 121, 124, 138, 139, 149, 150, 157; Czech military aid to, 10–12,

THE JOHNS HOPKINS PRESS

*Composed in Linotype Times Roman text with Monotype Times New Roman display
by Baltimore Type and Composition Corporation*

*Printed on 60-lb. Perkins and Squier R
by Universal Lithographers, Inc.*

*Bound in Columbia Riverside Linen
by Moore & Co., Inc.*